THE  TIMES

IMPROVE YOUR BRIDGE GAME

Andrew Robson

First published in 2014 previously published in 2005 as
The Times Bridge Common Mistakes & How to Avoid Them

HarperCollins Publishers
Westerhill Road
Bishopbriggs
Glasgow
G64 2QT

www.harpercollins.co.uk

© 2005, 2014 Andrew Robson

10 9 8 7 6 5 4 3 2 1

The Times is a registered trademark of Times Newspapers Ltd

ISBN 978-0-00-755719-6

British Library Cataloguing in Publication Data
A catalogue record for this book is available from the British Library.

Collins uses papers that are natural, renewable and recyclable products made from wood
grown in sustainable forests. The manufacturing processes conform to the environmental
regulations of the country of origin.

Typeset in Great Britain by Davidson Publishing Solutions, Glasgow.

Printed and bound in Great Britain by Clays Ltd, St Ives plc.

MIX
Paper from
responsible sources
FSC
www.fsc.org   **FSC™ C007454**

CONTENTS

CONTENTS

INTRODUCTION

This is one of the few Bridge books aimed at the social or less experienced player, as opposed to the tournament player. If you long to improve, but find yourself repeating the same mistakes and perhaps not even knowing that they are mistakes, then this book is for you.

In the short opening section, 'The Game', I set out the keys to holding your head up high at the Bridge table. Incorporated into each of the three subsections – Bidding, Declarer Play, Defence – are all the tips. Each tip is numbered, enabling you to cross-reference it with the relevant deal in the main body of the book.

The pages that follow are based on my Friday column in *The Times*, entitled 'Common Mistakes for the Less Experienced'. Each page contains an instructive deal and a salutary lesson: what happened when the hand was played at the table, and what should have happened. The analysis ends with the numbered tip.

You can read 'The Game' first, in its entirety. Or you can flick back and forth from the numbered tip in 'The Game' to its deal in the main body of the book. Alternatively you can pick a deal at random, with the option of cross-referencing each tip in 'The Game'.

I hope you enjoy the book and find it instructive. If you are not a regular *Times* reader, you can access my daily column from *The Times* online **www.timesonline.co.uk**. For more information about myself and my Bridge School in South West London see **www.andrewrobson.co.uk**.

THE GAME

Bridge is the most widely played game in the world, and surely the best. It is endlessly fascinating at whatever level it is played, from complete beginner up to world champion. Even experts never truly conquer the game – a blessing, or Bridge would go the way of Noughts and Crosses. As if to emphasize this, Computer Bridge is lagging behind Computer Chess or Backgammon. The skills required to be a top Bridge player are so many and varied.

A microcosm of life, Bridge combines competition (against the opponents) and co-operation (with partner). Perhaps the single most important joy of the game is this partnership element. From the moment you pick up your 13 cards to form your 'hand', you try to convey messages to partner about it. This communication of information in the first phase of the game – the bidding (or auction) – leads to one partnership (the one making the final – higher – bid) contracting to make a designated number of tricks in their chosen trump suit. Then the play begins – will they prevail, or will they be prevented from achieving their trick target? A few minutes later, a totally new deal begins and with it a whole new set of challenges.

SECTION 1: *Bidding*

INTRODUCTION I will be teaching a simple version of English Standard Acol, incorporating a 12–14 'Weak' notrump and Four-Card Majors. I have focussed primarily on the first stages of an auction: if the first few bids are accurate, a sensible contract will normally be reached.

THE BASICS When first looking at your hand, count the high-card points (ace = four; king = three; queen = two; jack = one). An average hand will contain ten points (an ace, a king, a queen and a jack). Also look at your distribution. Are your suits of relatively similar length ('balanced'), or is there some disparity ('unbalanced')?

You must then try to describe your hand to partner during the first phase of Bridge: the bidding (or auction). There are two objectives of the bidding: you must ascertain (i) whether you have a mutually compatible trump suit, a 'fit' (eight or more cards in one suit between the partnership), and (ii) how many of the 13 tricks for which to aim with that suit as trumps. Bids must increase, starting from 1♣ then 1♦, 1♥, 1♠, 1 notrump (NT), 2♣, 2♦….7NT. Adding six to the number of the bid made tells you the number of tricks for which you have contracted. Thus 3♣ means that you must win nine tricks (or more) with clubs as trumps.

Clubs and diamonds are known collectively as the minor suits. They score 20 points each trick (over the six), so bidding and making 5♣ and 5♦ is required to score 'game' (100 points). Hearts and spades, the majors, score at 30 points each, so 4♥ and 4♠ win game. Notrumps – literally playing without a trump suit – score slightly more than the suits: 40 for the first trick (over six), reverting to 30. Thus 2NT scores 70 points and 3NT gives game. The three most attractive game contracts are 3NT, 4♥ and 4♠. Holding 25 high-card points between the partnership is a good guide for attempting one of those games. After winning the game, you become 'vulnerable': half way to rubber (the first side to two games). If you now fail in a contract, your opponents receive 100 per trick as opposed to 50. Playing Duplicate Bridge (or Chicago – four deal Bridge) a bonus is given for making a game: 300 (non-vulnerable) and 500 (vulnerable).

In Duplicate an extra 50 points is added to the score resulting from a making part-score. Thus Four Hearts bid and made (non-vulnerable) scores 300 (the non-vulnerable game bonus) + 120 (the tricks) = 420. Two Hearts making three (i.e. one overtrick) scores 50 (part-score bonus) + 90 (tricks made) = 140. Note that overtricks score at trick value (i.e. 30 a trick for notrumps and majors; 20 for minors).

OPENING THE BIDDING Dealer starts the bidding. If he has a bad hand, he does not open the bidding, instead saying 'No Bid' or 'Pass'. If he has a little above average or better, he opens. Typically he will open One of his Longest Suit.

Question: What is a little above average?

Answer: Always open the bidding with 12 or more points. You should also open when holding slightly less with a useful shape. Use The Rule of 20, which states that you should open when the number of cards in your two longest suits added to your high-card points totals 20 or more (Tip 1).

With a choice of two equal length suits, open the higher ranking (Tip 2), except with precisely four cards in both majors in which case prefer 1♥ (Tip 3).

NOTRUMPS That you can win game in notrumps with just nine tricks gives it a huge significance and arguably the most important opening bid (and perhaps the most common) is 1NT. This shows a balanced hand and 12, 13 or 14 points.

Question: What precisely is a balanced hand?

Answer: It is a hand with no void (a suit with no cards), no singleton (a suit with one card), and at most one doubleton (two cards). There are just three balanced distributions: 4432, 4333 and 5332.

With one of the above shapes and 12–14 points, you MUST open 1NT (Tip 4). It is a very precise bid, so don't open 1NT with more than 14 points, even if balanced (Tip 5), and do not open 1NT with an unbalanced hand, even if holding 12–14 points (Tip 6).

RESPONDING TO ONE NOTRUMP When responding to partner's 1NT opener, bear in mind that, because you know so much about partner's hand, you as responder are in charge. Partner will not bid again unless you make a strong bid. Although there will be occasions where responder needs more information, essentially the basic principle is:

1NT opener: 'This is what I've got'.

Responder: 'OK – I know so much about your hand that I can place the final contract right now.' (Tip 7).

Note that it is much better to have a go at the nine-trick game of 3NT rather than the 11-trick games of 5♣ and 5♦ (Tip 8). Also note that you should never bid to increase the size of the part-score: thus raising 1NT to 2NT invites 3NT, rather than trying for 70 points as opposed to just 40 (Tip 9).

RESPONDING TO ONE-OF-A-SUIT When partner opens One-of-a-Suit, he could have anything from 12 points (even less if he satisfied the Rule of 20) up to 19 (with 20 or more he would open at the two-level). Because he could have as many as 19 points, you as responder should keep the bidding open with at least six points (Tip 10).

The top priority response is support – always support partner with a known eight-card major-suit fit (Tip 11). And the stronger your hand, the more you should bid in support. Use the Responder Line (Tip 12), noting that no supporting bids, even jumps, force partner to keep bidding (Tip 13).

When you have less than four-card support for the suit opened, you should try to find a fit in another suit – the general principle being to bid your longest suit at the lowest level. Thus avoid precipitate leaps to 2NT (Tip 14) and 3NT (Tip 15). Also, to avoid a very common mistake, you should prefer a four-card suit at the one-level to the nebulous 1NT response (Tip 16). Note that with two four-card suits, you should prefer the cheaper (Tip 17).

The level of the response must be considered, however. Whereas a one-over-one response can be made with just six measly points, a two-over-one requires a modicum of extra strength. The partnership is already at the eight-trick level and has no guarantee of a fit. A useful guideline is The Rule of 14 (Tip 18): respond in a new suit at the two-level when your total high-card points added to the number of cards in the suit you are planning to bid gets to 14. Otherwise respond 1NT (Tip 19), the only occasion you should respond notrumps to a one-of-a-suit opener.

OVERCALLING If an opponent opens the bidding, you become the overcalling side. You do not need an opening hand to overcall, merely one chunky suit of at least FIVE cards (Tip 20). It is worth overcalling on relatively weak hands: even if you do not ultimately declare, you have disrupted the opposing auction and indicated a lead to partner. On the other hand, there will be some hands of opening strength that should not bid after an opponent's opening (Tip 21), especially with no five-card suit (Tip 22).

The knowledge that partner has at least a five-card suit for an overcall means that three cards are sufficient for support (Tip 23). And the more cards you have in support, the higher you should bid – straight away (Tip 24).

Bidding 1NT as an overcall over the opponents' one-of-suit opener, however, is more dangerous – you might be sandwiched between two strong hands. So a 1NT overcall shows a strong hand (15–19 points), more than a 1NT opener (Tip 25).

OPENER'S REBID Returning to the opening side, arguably the most pivotal bid in an uncontested auction is opener's rebid. It is this bid that gives much more specific information, both about shape (whether or not the hand is balanced) and strength.

A balanced opener should plan to bid/rebid notrumps (Tip 26), whereas an unbalanced opener should not (Tip 27). The three balanced distributions are 4432, 4333 and 5332 (Tip 28). With 12–14 balanced, you open 1NT; with 15–19 you open a suit and plan to rebid notrumps at the appropriate level (Tip 29), although you should in preference support with four cards in responder's major (Tip 30). The only time you cannot make your notrump rebid is if your right-hand opponent makes a higher bid. You should then pass (Tip 31).

An unbalanced opener has three choices of rebid after responder has changed the suit: supporting responder's suit, repeating his own suit, or trying a new suit. As usual, the top priority is support. You can use the Opener's Support Line (Tip 32), or, in certain situations, the Losing Trick Count (Tip 33). Without support, you should try to avoid repeating your first suit with fewer than six cards (Tip 34). The only time you may have to repeat a five-card suit is when it is cheaper to do so than introduce a new four-card suit. If introducing this second suit would force responder to the three-level in order to give preference back to the first suit, you have 'reversed'* and should have a decent 15 points or more (Tip 35).

When repeating a suit – implying six cards – you must remember to jump the bidding with 16+ points. Use the Opener's Repeat Line (Tip 36). Repeating a suit does normally show six cards, so you do not need to bid it a third time to confirm your sixth card (Tip 37). But note that just because you have six cards in a suit does not mean that you have to repeat it – it is better to bid a cheaper four-card suit than repeat an anaemic six-card suit (Tip 38).

Finally, let us consider the third option for an unbalanced opener with his rebid: introducing a new suit. Although it can create awkwardness for the (mercifully rare) 4441 shape, it is sensible to assume that bidding two suits shows (at least) a five-four shape. Put another way, you should not bid a second suit with just four cards in the suit you opened (Tip 39). Normally, you bid a new suit at the lowest level. But because responder is allowed to pass the new suit rebid with an unpromising six or seven points, if you want to force the bidding to game as soon as you hear partner respond, you must jump in your second suit (Tip 40).

RESPONDER'S REBID After opener has rebid, responder knows a huge amount. If opener has rebid notrumps (Tip 41), repeated his suit (Tip 42), or supported, responder knows the precise point-count and can act accordingly. Only when opener has bid a new suit does responder know less about his strength. When that happens (i.e. the first three bids are in different suits) it is responder's job to show his strength with his rebid (Tip 43), using the Responder Line (Tip 44).

Sometimes there is no good option for responder, and a return to opener's first suit should be regarded as preference (often on a doubleton) rather than genuine support (Tip 45). Sometimes there is more than one good option: with two fits, he should prefer the major to the minor at game level (Tip 46).

*NB: There is much to be said for not playing 'reverses'. Although you will occasionally bid too high, at least you KNOW that partner has six cards when he repeats his suit (provided he opens/rebids notrumps with a 5332 shape).

Two of the commonest mistakes here are responder forgetting to jump with 10+ points when repeating his suit (Tip 47), and forgetting that three cards in opener's first suit make a fit (Tip 48).

DOUBLE The literal meaning of double is to increase (by at least double) the size of penalty should the contract fail, but at the risk of increasing the opponents' reward should the contract succeed. However, until partner has bid, you cannot really judge whether or not their contract (if a suit bid) will fail; therefore such doubles are for 'take-out' (Tip 49).

Double – for take-out – is one of the most useful bids in Bridge, and one of the most underused. It is a popular bid with partner too, as it asks *him* to describe *his* hand: 'What do you think over there?' The double of a suit opening bid shows: Shortage in the suit opened, at least Opening values, and Support for all unbid suits (Tip 50). Assuming the next hand passes, partner *must* respond to the double (Tip 51). Until partner has made a positive bid, even later round doubles are for take-out (Tip 52); so if you don't want partner to bid (because you are happy defending), don't double (Tip 53).

If partner has made a positive bid, however, your double is for 'penalties'. All penalty doubles express the opinion that you think the opponents are going to fail in their contract, with the accompanying increase in score. Partner will therefore generally leave in a penalty double. Because it is nonsense to be short in the suit bid when it is notrumps, the double of a 1NT opener is for 'penalties' (Tip 54). This – by far the most common penalty double you will encounter – will only be removed by partner when holding a hand that is both very weak and very shapely (Tip 55).

Two of the commonest mistakes in respect of the take-out double are failing to double (for take-out) after the opponents have bid two suits with four or five cards in both unbid suits (Tip 56); and failing to jump in response to partner's take-out double with nine(+) points (Tip 57).

Perhaps the commonest mistake in the penalty double area is doubling the opponents too readily. They may then either retreat to safer havens or stay put and make the contract because you have revealed that you have good trumps (Tip 58). Better to keep quiet.

After the opponents double, you can redouble. This is an expression of confidence; but be wary of redoubling a contract you think you will make if you have reason to think the opponents might then wise up and bid on (Tip 59). Redouble is better restricted to those occasions in which an opponent has doubled partner's opening bid and you have 10+ points (Tip 60), but no good fit (Tip 61).

PRE-EMPTIVE BIDDING Bidding at a relatively high level with a weak hand and a long suit robs the opponents of bidding space on a deal where *you* do not need it (you have only one playable trump suit). The standard situation is a three-level opener, showing a seven-card suit and less than opening values (Tip 62). The suit must be good (Tip 63), but you should have as little outside the suit as possible and you certainly do not need an ace (Tip 64). With an eighth card in your suit (one more trick), open at the four-level (Tip 65).

To pre-empt after an opponent has opened, you need to make a double-jump (1♣ – 3♥) i.e. to miss out two lower levels of your suit (Tip 66). A single jump overcall (1♣ – 2♥) is a strong bid (Tip 67). Whether opening or overcalling pre-emptively, note that you have shown your hand so should not bid again (Tip 68).

Meanwhile, the partner of the pre-emptor should simply 'put up or shut up' (Tip 69). Because the pre-emptor will be profoundly short outside his suit, partner should value aces (especially) and kings, but attach little value to outside queens and jacks (Tip 70). Sometimes, partner may consider raising pre-emptively (with a poor defensive hand), and the more cards he has in the pre-emptor's suit, the more bold he should be, generally bidding to the 'level of the fit' (Tip 71).

Pre-empting is fun – although you will occasionally get caught for a big penalty. Defending against opposing pre-empts is less fun – you have to start at a high level and the splits are likely to be bad (Tip 72). However, do not be too frightened to enter the bidding – in spite of the high level; bear in mind that one opponent is very weak, so your partner rates to hold some values.

A reasonable rule of thumb is to double (for take-out) if you would have doubled a one-level opener in the suit (Tip 73); and overcall 3NT if you would have overcalled with 1NT over a one-level opener, bearing in mind that it is especially important to have a stopper in the pre-emptor's suit. There is a good chance of being able to shut the pre-emptor out of the play (Tip 74). But without a stopper (you cannot bid 3NT), or a good suit (you cannot overcall), or insufficient length in the other major(s) (you cannot double), you have little option but to go quietly (Tip 75).

TWO-LEVEL OPENERS Whereas the three-level is reserved for weak openers, the two-level is used for strong ones. 2NT is the only bid that can be passed by partner, and should be opened with a balanced hand (including a 5332 shape with a good five-card suit) and 20-22 points (Tip 76).

2♦/♥/♠ openers show unbalanced 20-22 point hands with good five/six card suits. But be prepared to upgrade a powerful-looking hand with just under 20 points if it has 'eight playing tricks' (Tip 77). You are sometimes stuck when you have 20-22 points with a good club suit, as 2♣ shows any 23+ point hand. In this case it is better to open 1♣ and hope the auction does not continue pass-pass-pass (Tip 78).

2♦/♥/♠ openers must be kept open a round by partner, even with nothing (Tip 79). With fewer than eight points, make the conventional negative reply of 2NT (Tip 80). The negative reply to 2♣ is 2♦ (0–7 points), on grounds of economy (Tip 81). These negative responses prioritise – such that all other bids (positives) show eight(+) points (Tip 82).

SLAMMING The ultimate goal in the bidding is to bid and make all 13 tricks on a deal – a grand slam. This is generally inadvisable – it's tough enough to make all 13 tricks, let alone to bid for them and risk losing everything if even one trick gets away.

More reasonable is to bid for 12 tricks – a small slam – which will be possible about one deal in fifteen. 33 partnership points is the guideline for contracting for a small slam – though less if there is a big fit and interesting distributions. A small slam is doomed, however, if the opponents have two aces (unless you have a void in one of those two suits).

Because of the importance of aces, the bid of 4NT 'Blackwood' is used to ask partner how many aces he possesses. But beware when clubs (and to a lesser extent diamonds) are trumps – the reply to Blackwood ($5\clubsuit = 0$ aces; $5\diamondsuit = 1$; $5\heartsuit = 2$; $5\spadesuit = 3$) may take you overboard (Tip 83). If the reply indicates that one ace is missing, go ahead and bid the small slam (Tip 84); to bail out in Five of the trump suit would be inconsistent with your decision to go slamming.

Blackwood is useful but, because it only solves the problem of how many aces partner has, only use the convention if that is the key piece of information about which you wish to know (Tip 85). If you are interested in a grand slam and the reply to Blackwood indicates that all the aces are present, you can follow with 5NT to ask for kings. But because grand slams are generally to be avoided, it will rarely be right to do so (Tip 86).

Note that the Blackwood bidder is in control – do not overrule him (Tip 87). Finally note that 4NT is not always asking for aces. If the immediately preceding bid was in notrumps, it is a quantitative invitation to 6NT, asking partner if his hand is minimum or maximum for his bidding to date (Tip 88).

Bidding to a sensible contract is one thing. Making it is quite another…

SECTION 2: *Declarer Play*

Planning

Your side has outbid the opponents and, since you introduced the trump suit (or notrumps) first, you are declarer. After your left-hand opponent has made the opening lead, dummy is tabled. You say 'thank you partner', and then control both the dummy (next to play) and your own hand.

Do not rush to play from dummy (Tip 89), or unthinkingly make the seemingly obvious play (Tip 90). Instead form a plan. This involves counting top tricks (Tip 91), seeing how many extra ones are needed for the contract, and focussing on where to get those extra tricks. In notrumps, the quest for those extra tricks should be attended to immediately, whereas in trump contracts there is the issue of when to get rid of the opponents' trumps.

Once the extra tricks have been garnered, the top tricks can be taken ('cashed'). Care needs to be taken to ensure that you do not get stranded from a winner in the other hand. If you are leading from the hand with the shorter length, lead the highest card; if you are leading from the hand with the longer length, lead the lowest card (Tip 92).

Notrump Play

MAKING EXTRA TRICKS Counting top tricks before embarking on the play is particularly important in notrumps; only by doing this will you know how many extra tricks are needed. The three basic methods of setting up those extra tricks are (a) by force (flushing out an opposing higher card), (b) by length (exhausting the opponents of all their cards in a suit in which you have greater length), and (c) by position (finessing – trying to promote a card even though the opponents hold a higher card in that same suit).

Because length and positional winners both require the split and location of missing cards to be favourable, force winners – if available – are usually to be preferred, even in a relatively short suit (Tip 93). But length *is* crucial in notrumps – overlook a long, weak suit at your peril (Tip 94). Many notrump contracts boil down to a race between both sides to set up their long suits and it is imperative that you (and for that matter the defence) lead your long suit each time you win the lead (Tip 95). Finessing, a technique equally useful in trumps and notrumps, involves assessing which card you are trying to promote, then leading from the opposite side. The hope is that the opposing higher card will be in the hand of the opponent playing second i.e. sitting ahead of your card (Tip 96).

DUCKING Deliberately not winning a trick is called ducking and plays a major role in notrump play. If the opponents lead a suit in which you have just one certain stopper (a stopper is a way of stopping the opponents running through a suit), you have a decision to make: when should you use the card (assume it's an ace – by far the most likely scenario)? By delaying winning with the ace, you can exhaust one opponent of all their cards of the suit (Tip 97). You should try to win your ace on that opponent's last card (Tip 98). The Rule of Seven (Tip 99), will often give you the right answer.

AVOIDANCE PLAY The danger of the opposition running off a long suit is an ever-present one in notrumps (in trumps you can simply trump). Often, just one opponent can create such problems for you – in which case he is the 'danger hand' and his partner is the 'safe hand' (Tip 100). Look for ways to prevent the danger hand from winning the lead (Tip 101). If you can choose which opponent to make the danger hand, choose the one who will not win a subsequent lead (Tip 102).

SETTING UP A SUIT If you need to set up a suit (usually five or more cards) in one hand, you must make sure that you have enough entries (ways of reaching that hand). Tricks will normally have to be lost in the establishment process and note that it is almost always better to lose the first round rather than a later round (Tip 103). This ensures that the high cards in the suit itself are meaningful entries (Tip 104), thereby retaining better communications (Tip 105). Counting your top tricks – and therefore how many extra tricks are needed from the long suit – can affect how you broach the suit (Tip 106).

ANALYSING THE OPENING LEAD AND THE RULE OF ELEVEN The standard opening lead against a notrump contract is fourth from the top of the longest suit. In those situations you can use the mathematically foolproof Rule of 11 (Tip 107). Taking the (fourth highest) opening lead from 11 tells you how many higher cards than the lead are in the other three hands (Tip 108). You can see your hand and dummy so can work out how many higher (although not which they are) are with the leader's partner. The Rule of 11 enables you to make strange-looking plays with later benefits (Tip 109). And in case you are wondering, after all this, why the opponents do lead fourth from the top and give you so much help, bear in mind that the opening leader's partner can also use the Rule of 11 (Tip 110).

Other inferences can be drawn from the 'fourth highest' opening lead. The lead of a two indicates that the leader holds precisely four cards in that suit (Tip 111). When the lead is a three, look out for the two: if the leader does not hold it, again he has just four cards in the suit led (Tip 112). If he has just four cards in the suit led, he will not have five cards in another suit – or he would have preferred to lead that suit (Tip 113). If he led from a very feeble four-card suit, he is unlikely to have another four-card suit (it would be stronger): thus his shape is probably 4333 (Tip 114).

SUMMARY Count up your top tricks and plan to establish your extra tricks early. Look out for the three basic methods of establishing tricks in notrumps – by force, length and position. And don't forget to analyze the opening lead – it can give you huge pointers.

Trump Play

DRAWING TRUMPS The key question is whether or not to get rid of ('draw') the opposing trumps at the beginning. If you need dummy's trumps, perhaps for trumping your losers (Tip 115), then you must delay. On the other hand drawing their trumps removes the risk of the opponents trumping your winners (Tip 116). Drawing trumps is particularly attractive, somewhat ironically, when you have weak trumps, because it gets rid of two of their (high) trumps together

(Tip 117). However, there is a middle route: you can draw all but one of their trumps. If the last remaining trump is higher than yours, leave it out. There is rarely any point in wasting two of your trumps to draw a trump that is going to win a trick anyway – The Rule of One (Tip 118).

TRUMPING IN THE DUMMY If you draw trumps, the trumps in your shorter trump length (typically, so let us assume, dummy) will not make tricks in their own right; they will fall under the longer trumps. Therefore if you can use dummy's trumps for 'ruffing' (trumping), the manoeuvre will create extra tricks. You will not generally be able to draw the opposing trumps first though, or dummy's trumps will be gone (Tip 119).

The process is to look for a suit that is shorter in dummy than in your hand, void it, trump your losers in dummy, and only then draw the opposing trumps (Tip 120). Trumping needlessly in your hand, however, shortens your trumps and risks losing control (Tip 121).

SETTING UP A SUIT Establishing a suit is often – mistakenly – associated only with notrumps. Yet it is even more profitable in a trump contract because you can set the suit up by trumping ('ruffing') and so avoid losers (Tip 122). It is usually correct to start setting up the suit as soon as possible – and that means before drawing trumps (Tip 123). As with notrumps, if you have to lose a trick, it is better (for entry-conserving reasons) to lose the first round (Tip 124). Even five small cards facing one small card can generate a trick (Tip 125), but there must be enough entries. The number of entries required is the number of times you need to trump, plus one to get back to the length winner at the end. In order to avoid squandering entries, lead to the lowest trump entry first (Tip 126).

THROWING AWAY LOSERS Whilst I recommend counting top tricks (i.e. winners) in both trump and notrump contracts, a quick tally of losers can help in trump contracts (Tip 127). When there are too many losers, look to see if there are any overlapping winners in dummy (Tip 128); if drawing trumps involves losing the lead, you must play out those winners first. Pay attention to the entry situation, perhaps overtaking a winner if the overlapping suit is blocked (Tip 129).

Spotting blockages early is important: provision may need to be made right away (Tip 130). The pressure to throw away losers is reduced when you can draw trumps without losing the lead; losers can then be discarded on overlapping winners *after* the opposing trumps have been drawn (Tip 131).

SUMMARY The three basic occasions when trump-drawing should be delayed are (a) when you must trump in dummy, (b) when you have a side-suit to set up and (c) when drawing trumps involves losing the lead and there is a suit with overlapping winners. Otherwise it will normally be safer to draw trumps early in the play.

Memory Aids

Here are a few practical tips for those of you who find it hard to remember what has happened when playing.

We have all wished we were in a different contract. But do not play in the contract you wish you were in, rather than the one you are really in (Tip 132). Tell partner not to put a plausible (but incorrect) trump suit on his right as he tables dummy.

When winning with an ace-king, choosing the ace may confuse the opposition slightly more (leaving the whereabouts of the king unknown). But if you are prone to forgetfulness, it is better to win with the king. At least you will know later that your ace is high (Tip 133).

When keeping count of a suit, just count the missing cards. Work out how many cards are missing, and reduce that number by one each time you see an opposing card. When you get to zero, the opposition have run out (Tip 134). It will help you to think of those missing cards in terms of their likely split (Tip 135).

The best tip for improving your Bridge memory, however, is to play more. Indeed playing Bridge is proven to improve your memory both at and away from the table.

SECTION 3: *Defence*

Though defence is often regarded as the toughest part of the game, it can be the most satisfying. Nothing rivals the pleasure at conducting a successful co-operative defence with partner.

The Opening Lead

INTRODUCTION The single most important card the defence play is the opening lead, starting the defence on a course that is often irreversible. It is the only card played without a sight of dummy, so there is little information on which to work. However, the opening leader has heard the auction – both his partnership's contribution and the opponents' – and he ignores it at his cost (Tip 136). The importance of the auction in determining the opening lead is such that a bid can be made to indicate an opening lead (Tip 137), with little intention of winning the auction. Note that when leading partner's suit, do not lead the old-fashioned top card unless you have a sequence or a doubleton (Tip 138).

VERSUS TRUMP CONTRACTS The natural temptation when defending is to try to take tricks quickly, cashing aces early. In general this is a mistake (Tip 139). However, ace from ace-king is the best lead of all (Tip 140). This is because you still hold the boss card of the suit and can decide whether to continue with it (the king), based on what you see in dummy and the signal partner gives you with his card. King from king-queen, queen from queen-jack and so forth are also long-term winners, combining safety with attack. Note that the top card of these sequences is led (Tip 141). Cashing an ace without a king, however, is usually unwise – and even worse is leading 'away from an ace' (Tip 142).

VERSUS NOTRUMP CONTRACTS Leading 'fourth from the top of your longest – and strongest – suit' against notrumps is the oldest maxim of all, dating back to the pre-Bridge days of whist. But do not be a slave to it. If your longest suit is headed by three touching high cards, or two then a gap of one card before a third, lead the top card (Tip 143). Similarly, lead top of an internal sequence

(Tip 144). When leading from a long weak suit, lead a high card ('lead high for hate') rather than the fourth from the top, to discourage a continuation from partner (Tip 145).

After the Lead

'TOP' DEFENCE Be a 'TOP' defender. The 'T' stands for Trick Target. Never lose sight of how many tricks you need to defeat the contract. If you only need one more trick and have an ace to lead, lead it (Tip 146). The 'O' of being a 'TOP' defender stands for Observe Dummy. When in doubt, look for dummy's weakest suit (Tip 147). It is almost never right to lead dummy's long, strong suit (Tip 148), even if you are leading through dummy rather than around to it. The 'P' of being a 'TOP' defender stands for Partner. Ask yourself what (on earth!) is he doing – and try to follow his defence (Tip 149).

SECOND AND THIRD HAND PLAYS On a low card, the defender playing second should generally play low (Tip 150). But he should usually cover an honour with an honour (Tip 151), because he is drawing out two opposing high cards for one of his. However, he should wait to cover the second of two touching honours (Tip 152).

When you are playing third to the trick, partner has already played a card (the lead). You need to play high, in order to prevent declarer from winning a cheap trick (Tip 153). With touching highest cards, you should play the lower (Tip 154). Partner (i.e. the leader) can draw valuable inferences from this (Tip 155). If dummy has an (unplayed) picture card, however, you should generally keep a higher card to beat that card (Tip 156). If dummy plays an honour on partner's lead, it will generally be correct for you to cover with a higher card, unless there is no hope of promoting a lower card (Tip 157).

SIGNALLING When you are *leading* (the first round of each suit), the motto (for spot cards i.e. nine and below) is 'Lead High for Hate, Lead Low for Like' (Tip 158). When *throwing*, however, either on partner's lead or when discarding, the motto is 'Throw High means Aye, Throw Low means No' (Tip 159).

Although the seven, eight and nine are usually high, and two, three and four usually low, you may have the wrong spot cards to convey the desired message; so partner must scrutinise the spot cards carefully before decoding your message (Tip 160). Also, avoid knee-jerk signals – such as playing top from two. First ask yourself whether you really want him to continue (Tip 161).

The signals we have been discussing are referred to as 'Attitude Signals' – giving your attitude to the suit partner led. Although they are by far the most important, giving 'count' on a suit declarer is leading can be crucial (Tip 162). The mnemonic for the Count Signal is HELO: High = Even; Low = Odd (Tip 163).

A final signal to add to your repertoire is the 'Suit Preference Signal', best limited (at least initially) to situations where you are leading a suit for partner to trump. The lead of a high spot card asks for the return of the higher-ranking suit; and the lead of a low spot card asks for the return of the lower-ranking suit (Tip 164). Forget it at your peril (Tip 165).

DISCARDING When you cannot follow suit (and cannot/do not wish to trump), you must discard. You have twin goals: (1) to keep the right cards in order to prevent declarer from scoring extra tricks which he should not be allowed to make (more important when declarer is on lead) and (2) to send the right message to partner (more important when partner is on lead).

Focussing on keeping the right cards, various principles will help, such as 'keep equal length with dummy' (Tip 166). Try to work out declarer's shape, so you can keep equal length with him too (Tip 167). If the defence need to keep two suits, then each defender should guard a different one (Tip 168). When declarer is running off a long suit, try not to void yourself of a suit or, when you reveal your absence of cards, the remainder will be marked with partner (Tip 169).

Moving to sending the right message to partner, you have a choice of throwing high in a suit you want him to lead (Throw High means Aye); or low in a suit you do not want him to lead (Throw Low means No). Particularly in notrumps, it will generally be right to preserve the suit you want led and to throw low in a suit you do not want (Tip 170). But make your discard count –

do not throw low from a suit partner was never going to lead (Tip 171); and discard the clearest card you can (Tip 172).

SUMMARY Defence is more than observing mottoes such as 'second hand low' and 'third hand high'. TOP defence involves focussing on the number of tricks needed to beat the contract, looking at dummy to see from where those tricks are coming, and, especially, co-operating with partner in the joint quest.

THE DEALS

Bidding

Deal 1

Dealer: South   **Vulnerability: Neither**

I am an advocate of the Rule of 20, which says that the bidding should be opened when the number of points in the hand added to the number of cards in the two longest suits gets to twenty or more.

```
                 ♠ 4 2
                 ♥ A Q 7 4
                 ♦ A 7 5 3 2
                 ♣ 6 3
  ♠ Q J 8 6                    ♠ 5 3
  ♥ 3 2            N           ♥ 8 6 5
  ♦ J 9 8 4    W     E         ♦ K Q 10
  ♣ A K 9          S           ♣ Q J 5 4 2
                 ♠ A K 10 9 7
                 ♥ K J 10 9
                 ♦ 6
                 ♣ 10 8 7
```

What happened

At the table our first deal was actually passed out. Would you have opened any of the four hands?

S	W	N	E
Pass(1)	Pass	Pass	Pass

(1) Mistake. South has a fabulous 11 point hand – and one that satisfies the Rule of 20.

Contract: Passed out
Opening Lead: –

S	W	N	E
1♠	Pass	2♦	Pass
2♥	Pass	4♥	End

Contract: 4♥
Opening Lead: ♣A

What should have happened

South was the guilty party. The Rule of 20 opens his hand (11 points and a five-four distribution). In fact South has a more promising hand than many twelve- or thirteen-point hands. He has both majors; he has a powerful 5431 shape with honours in his long suits; he has good intermediate cards; and he has no rebid problems.

Whichever way you look at it, South should have opened the bidding. North-South would have sped to 4♥.

West leads ♣A, follows with ♣K, then switches to ♦4. Declarer wins dummy's ♦A and seeks to establish his spades.

He cashes ♠AK and then trumps a third spade with dummy's ♥Q (East discarding). He returns to ♥9 and trumps a fourth spade with dummy's ♥A. He returns to his ♥10, draws East's last trump, cashes the established fifth spade, and merely concedes a club. 10 tricks and game made.

Tip 1   The Rule of 20: open the bidding when your high-card points added to the number of cards in your two longest suits gets to at least 20.

Deal 2

Dealer: South   **Vulnerability: Neither**

Our second deal addresses
the issue of which suit to
open. If one suit is longer,
then that suit must be
opened. Open 1♦ – even
with ♠AKQ9 and ♦97532.
The only way those small
diamonds are likely to win
tricks is if they are trumps.
If opener has two suits of
equal length, the rule is:
open the higher ranking
(the one exception will
be covered next deal).
By opening high,
opener has the option of
introducing his other suit more cheaply.

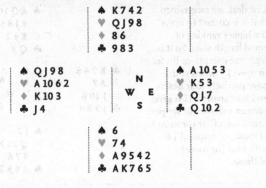

```
              ♠ K 7 4 2
              ♥ Q J 9 8
              ♦ 8 6
              ♣ 9 8 3
♠ Q J 9 8                   ♠ A 10 5 3
♥ A 10 6 2      N          ♥ K 5 3
♦ K 10 3    W     E        ♦ Q J 7
♣ J 4          S           ♣ Q 10 2
              ♠ 6
              ♥ 7 4
              ♦ A 9 5 4 2
              ♣ A K 7 6 5
```

What happened

West led the ♠Q (top of an honour sequence), covered
(questionably – East will have ♠A) by ♠K and East's
♠A. Declarer trumped East's ♠3 continuation and
correctly led ♦2. East won ♦J and led another spade
(best).

After trumping, declarer cashed ♦A and led a third
diamond, trumping in dummy (the opposing 3–3
split revealed). He crossed to ♣K, cashed ♣A, then,
correctly leaving the master ♣Q outstanding, he led
an established diamond winner. East trumped and led
a fourth spade (best). Declarer trumped with his last
trump, cashed the fifth diamond, and then gave up to
♥AK.

Eight tricks. Not bad...

What should have happened

...but how South wished he had opened the right suit
and thus finished a level lower.

S	W	N	E
1♣(1)	Pass	1♥	Pass
2♦	Pass	3♣(2)	End

(1) Mistake. Open the higher
ranking of two equal length
suits.

(2) Correctly returning to partner's first choice trump suit at
the cost of raising a level.

Contract: 3♣
Opening Lead: ♠Q

S	W	N	E
1♦	Pass	1♥	Pass
2♣	End		

Contract: 2♣
Opening Lead: ♠Q

Tip 2 Open the higher-ranking of two equal length suits.

Deal 3

Last deal, we ascertained
that it is correct to open
the higher ranking of
equal length suits. So it is...
with one exception. Prefer
to open 1♥ when you
have precisely four hearts
and four spades. This gives
partner a chance to support
hearts with four (or more)
of those, or respond 1♠
with four (or more)
of those.

```
              ♠ A Q 10 5
              ♥ K J 8 5
              ♦ K 4 2
              ♣ Q 3
  ♠ K 9 4 3                    ♠ 8 6 2
  ♥ A 7            N           ♥ 6 3 2
  ♦ J 10 8     W     E         ♦ A Q 5 3
  ♣ J 9 8 4        S           ♣ K 10 7
              ♠ J 7
              ♥ Q 10 9 4
              ♦ 9 7 6
              ♣ A 6 5 2
```

What happened

This deal taught North the error of his ways. The heart
suit got completely lost.

Against 1NT, West led the ♣4 to dummy's ♣Q,
East's ♣K and declarer's ♣2. East returned ♣10 and
declarer decided to win ♣A this time. He led ♥10 at
Trick Three, which held the trick, then followed with
♥4 to West's ♥A.

West cashed the ♣J9 (East discarding ♠2 and
dummy discarding the ♠105). West then found the
lethal switch to the ♦J.

Declarer ducked in dummy and ♦J scored, but
when West continued with ♦10, he tried dummy's
♦K. No good – East won ♦A, cashed ♦Q, and then his
remaining diamond. Declarer made the remainder but
was two down.

What should have happened

Correct bidding sees North-South alight comfortably in
2♥. Any lead from East is helpful for declarer (North).
At worst he should lose three diamonds, a club and the
ace of trumps. Contract made.

S	W	N	E
–	–	1♠(1)	Pass
1NT	End		

(1) Mistake – North should
open 1♥.

Contract: 1NT by S
Opening Lead: ♣4

S	W	N	E
–	–	1♥	Pass
2♥	End		

Contract: 2♥ by N
Opening Lead: ♠6

Tip 3 Open 1♥ with precisely four hearts and four spades (when not opening 1NT).

Deal 4

Auctions that begin with a 1NT opener are radically different from all other auctions. They are not conversations, rather: 'This is what I've got: now you choose!' A 1NT opener rarely bids again whereas a one-of-a-suit opener must bid again if his partner changes the suit. You must not forget/neglect to open 1NT when you are supposed to. You will never be able to correct

```
                ♠ 10 7 2
                ♥ A J 4
                ♦ J 9 4
                ♣ K J 9 4
    ♠ K J 8 5              ♠ A 9 6
    ♥ K 9 5          N     ♥ Q 8 7 2
    ♦ 6 3 2      W     E   ♦ 8 7 5
    ♣ 8 7 2          S     ♣ A 10 5
                ♠ Q 4 3
                ♥ 10 6 3
                ♦ A K Q 10
                ♣ Q 6 3
```

the mistake later. There is no bid that says 'Sorry partner, I forgot to open 1NT last time!' A 1NT opener shows 12–14 points and a balanced hand (no void, no singleton, and no more than one doubleton). There are just three balanced shapes – 4432, 4333 and 5332.

What happened

When South forgot (or was dazzled by his diamonds) to open 1NT, there was no recovery. His 2NT rebid theoretically showed a balanced hand with more than 14 points, so his partner went on to game (assuming there to be 25 partnership points).

West led ♠5 to East's ♠A. East returned the ♠9 to West's ♠J. West cashed ♠K felling ♠Q, then ♠8. He switched accurately to ♥5 and declarer played ♥4 from dummy, East winning ♥Q. East could do no more than cash ♣A at this point, but the contract was two down.

What should have happened

1NT making.

S	W	N	E
1♦(1)	Pass	2♣	Pass
2NT	Pass	3NT	End

(1) Mistake – should open 1NT.

Contract: 3NT
Opening Lead: ♠5

S	W	N	E
1NT	End		

Contract: 1NT
Opening Lead: ♠5

Tip 4 Never forget to open 1NT with a balanced hand and 12–14 points. You can't recover.

Deal 5

There are Bridge cultures – the USA and France amongst others – that prefer the Strong Notrump (15–17). In Britain the Weak Notrump (12–14) is more commonly played. The pluses and minuses of the Weak Notrump versus the Strong Notrump can be argued ad nauseam. What matters more is that you and partner know which notrump you play, and

	♠ K 3 2	
	♥ Q 10 3 2	
	♦ K 4 3	
	♣ J 6 3	

♠ J 9 7 5		♠ 10 8 6
♥ 9 6 4	**N**	♥ A 7 5
♦ 10 7 5 2	**W E**	♦ J 9 6
♣ A 5	**S**	♣ K Q 9 8

	♠ A Q 4	
	♥ K J 8	
	♦ A Q 8	
	♣ 10 7 4 2	

that you stick to it. Throughout this book I will assume a Weak Notrump. Indeed that is my preference. I like to open 1NT with those oh-so-common flat minimums, describing my hand so well in one go. However, do not open 1NT merely because your hand 'looks notrumpy' and you can't think of an alternative.

What happened

When South opened 1NT, his partner passed, 'knowing' that the partnership could not have the 25 points required for game. Declarer won ♠5 lead with ♠Q and led ♥K at Trick Two. He quickly established three heart tricks to go with three in spades and three in diamonds.

Nine tricks made – underbid.

What should have happened

3NT – game bid and made.

S	W	N	E
1NT(1)	End		

(1) Mistake – too many points (playing Weak Notrump).

Contract: 1NT
Opening Lead: ♠5

S	W	N	E
1♣	Pass	1♥	Pass
1NT(1)	Pass	2NT(2)	Pass
3NT	End		

(1) By rebidding notrumps, South shows a balanced hand with more than 14 points.
(2) North can then invite game.

Contract: 3NT
Opening Lead: ♠5

Tip 5   Do not open 1NT with more than 14 points (assuming you play the Weak Notrump).

Deal 6

Dealer: South   **Vulnerability: Neither**

Last deal we observed that
you must stick to your
notrump point range
(assumed to be 12–14).
This deal we stress that
your hand must also be
balanced. *Question*: What is
a balanced hand?
Answer: The word
'balanced' refers not to the
location of the honours but
to the number of cards in
each suit. There are three
balanced distributions –
4432, 4333 and 5332. Do not
open 1NT unless you have
one of these three distributions.
Or you may suffer South's fate...

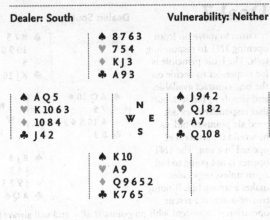

```
              ♠ 8 7 6 3
              ♥ 7 5 4
              ♦ K J 3
              ♣ A 9 3
 ♠ A Q 5              N        ♠ J 9 4 2
 ♥ K 10 6 3                    ♥ Q J 8 2
 ♦ 10 8 4         W       E    ♦ A 7
 ♣ J 4 2              S        ♣ Q 10 8
              ♠ K 10
              ♥ A 9
              ♦ Q 9 6 5 2
              ♣ K 7 6 5
```

What happened

Against 1NT, West led the ♥3 to East's ♥J and
declarer's ♥A. At Trick Two declarer led a diamond
to dummy's ♦K and East won the ♦A. East returned
♥2 to West's ♥10 and West cashed the ♥K, then led
back ♥6 to East's ♥Q (declarer and dummy discarding
clubs). East then switched to the ♠2. Declarer tried
the ♠K but West won the ♠A, cashed ♠Q, then led to
East's ♠J9. The defence took four spades, three hearts
and a diamond. Down two.

What should have happened

Declaring 2♦, South wins the likely ♥3 lead (the unbid
suit) with ♥A and plays to ♣A, back to ♣K, and leads
a third club (establishing his fourth club). On retaining
the lead he forces out ♦A and emerges with eight tricks:
a heart, four trumps and three clubs. Contract made.

S	W	N	E
1NT(1)	End		

(1) Mistake – South has two
doubletons so is unbalanced.

Contract: 1NT
Opening Lead: ♥3

S	W	N	E
1♦	Pass	1♠	Pass
2♣(1)	Pass	2♦	End

(1) Giving partner a second
choice of trump suit.

Contract: 2♦
Opening Lead: ♥3

Tip 6 Do not open 1NT with an unbalanced hand.

Deal 7

It's time to move on from opening 1NT to responding to it. The basic principle is for responder to decide on the best contract available, and simply to bid it! Note that responder does not need six points to bid, as he would if partner had opened in a suit. The 1NT opener is not going to bid again unless responder makes a strong bid. Bidding two-of-a-suit is a rescue

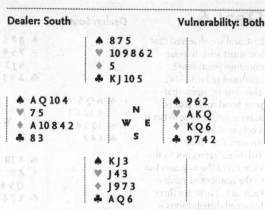

```
            ♠ 875
            ♥ 109862
            ♦ 5
            ♣ KJ105
♠ AQ104                 ♠ 962
♥ 75           N        ♥ AKQ
♦ A10842    W     E     ♦ KQ6
♣ 83              S     ♣ 9742
            ♠ KJ3
            ♥ J43
            ♦ J973
            ♣ AQ6
```

operation – consistent with no points at all – and will always be passed. Are you listening North? Incorrectly leaving South to stew in 1NT, he saw the following carnage take place:

What happened

West led ♦4 to East's ♦Q, East cashed ♦K, then led ♦6. Declarer played ♦9, but West won ♦10, cashed ♦A (East discarding ♠2) and then led ♦8 (East discarding ♣2).

Discarding a low card in a suit is a signal of disinterest so at Trick Six West switched to ♥7. East won the ♥Q and, rather than cash his ♥AK, astutely switched to ♠9. Declarer tried ♠J, but West won ♠Q and led ♥5. East won ♥K, cashed ♥A (West discarding ♣3) then led ♠6. West beat declarer's ♠K with ♠A, cashed ♠10, then ♠4. Declarer finally won a trick, the very last, with a club, but the contract was six down!

What should have happened

North should remove 1NT to 2♥. His partner would read it as a terminal bid, a so-called 'Weakness Take-out'. Declarer would probably end up scoring two trump tricks and four clubs – that's five more tricks than in a notrump contract!

S	W	N	E
1NT	Pass	Pass(1)	Pass

(1) Mistake – North should rescue into 2♥.

Contract: 1NT
Opening Lead: ♦4

S	W	N	E
1NT	Pass	2♥	End

Contract: 2♥
Opening Lead: ♦K

Tip 7 The responder to a 1NT opener can usually place the final contract immediately.

Deal 8

Dealer: South　　　　　　**Vulnerability: Neither**

Last deal we noted that the responder to a 1NT opener can generally place the final contract immediately. Bids which invite or force the 1NT opener to speak again are 2NT (invitational) or jumps to three of a suit (forcing). Other bids are terminal.

The 2NT response is an invitation for the 1NT opener to bid 3NT with a maximum. Jumps to 3♥/3♠ show game-going hands with five cards in the major, the 1NT opener raising to 4♥/♠ with three(+) cards and bidding 3NT with just two. What about jumps to 3♣/♦? Because five-of-a-minor is such a hard game to make, responder should only jump to 3♣/♦ when he is very distributional and is genuinely interested in playing five (or six) of that minor. There is no point in jumping to 3♣/♦ if he is merely hoping his partner will bid 3NT. He should simply bid 3NT himself!

```
              ♠ K 7 4
              ♥ 7 4
              ♦ A K Q J 9
              ♣ 8 4 2
♠ 10 8 6 2              ♠ A J 9 5
♥ Q 10 8 5 2      N      ♥ K J 9
♦ 3            W   E      ♦ 7 5
♣ J 9 7            S      ♣ Q 10 6 5
              ♠ Q 3
              ♥ A 6 3
              ♦ 10 8 6 4 2
              ♣ A K 3
```

What happened

5♦ (by North) stood little chance. The defence were bound to score a spade, a heart and a club. Down one.

S	W	N	E
1NT	Pass	3♦(1)	Pass
5♦	End		

(1) Mistake – what will mentioning diamonds achieve when you know you wish to table your hand in 3NT?

Contract: 5♦ by N
Opening Lead: ♣5

What should have happened

How would 3NT have fared? With eight top tricks, declarer needs to establish a spade trick. West leads ♥5 and declarer ducks East's ♥K and ducks his ♥J continuation (key play). He wins his ace on the third round, runs five diamond tricks, then leads a spade towards his queen. East cannot gain by playing the ace – he has no hearts left to lead because declarer delayed winning his ace. The ♠Q and ♣AK bring his total to nine. Game made.

S	W	N	E
1NT	Pass	3NT	End

Contract: 3NT by S
Opening Lead: ♥5

Tip 8 Do not respond 3♣/♦ to partner's 1NT opener without extreme shape (or strength).

Deal 9

This deal we look at the understandable temptation to raise a 1NT opener to 2NT with a flat hand and a smattering of points, say, eight, nine or ten. The key point here is that you do not bid to improve the size of the part-score in any form of Bridge. All raises of partner show genuine game-interest. Take a raise of 1NT to 2NT: this should be a genuine invitation to game; given that he is facing 12–14 points, responder must have 11–12 points for this bid (with more he simply jumps to 3NT).

```
                ♠ A K 9
                ♥ Q 8 2
                ♦ 9 8 3
                ♣ J 8 4 2

  ♠ J 8 6 5 3          N          ♠ 10 4 2
  ♥ A 6 4                          ♥ 10 9 7 3
  ♦ K J 10 5     W         E       ♦ Q 6
  ♣ Q                  S          ♣ K 10 9 6

                ♠ Q 7
                ♥ K J 5
                ♦ A 7 4 2
                ♣ A 7 5 3
```

What happened

Declarer had no hope. He won ♠5 lead with ♠Q and played ace and another club in the vain hope that an opponent held king-queen doubleton. West discarded on the second club so he ducked in dummy. East won the nine and played a second spade. Declarer won dummy's king and, abandoning clubs, led a heart to his king. West won the ace and led a third spade. Winning in dummy, declarer could make no more than two more hearts and the ace of diamonds. Three spades, two hearts and the minor-suit aces made seven tricks. Down two.

S	W	N	E
1NT	Pass	2NT(1)	Pass
3NT(2)	End		

(1) Mistake – there cannot be the 25 points required for game.
(2) Theoretically correct – with a maximum point-count.

Contract: 3NT
Opening Lead: ♠5

What should have happened

Left to declare a peaceful 1NT declarer would not even bother to broach clubs. With five top tricks, flushing out the ♥A is certain to give him two extra. Again, seven tricks, but this time contract made.

S	W	N	E
1NT	End		

Contract: 1NT
Opening Lead: ♠5

Tip 9 Do not bid to increase the size of the part-score.

Deal 10

We now turn to responding to a one-of-a-suit opener. The golden rule is that you must respond with six or more points. This is because opener could have up to 19 points, and 19 + 6 = 25 (25 points for game). Pass partner's opener with six points and you risk missing game.

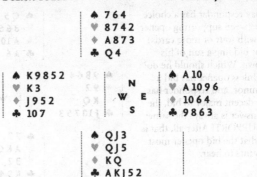

```
              ♠ 7 6 4
              ♥ 8 7 4 2
              ♦ A 8 7 3
              ♣ Q 4
  ♠ K 9 8 5 2           ♠ A 10
  ♥ K 3         N       ♥ A 10 9 6
  ♦ J 9 5 2   W   E     ♦ 10 6 4
  ♣ 10 7        S       ♣ 9 8 6 3
              ♠ Q J 3
              ♥ Q J 5
              ♦ K Q
              ♣ A K J 5 2
```

What happened

North's hand was unmemorable. But he had too much to pass the 1♣ bid. Actually the lowly contract only just made.

East won West's ♠5 lead with the ♠A and returned his ♠10. West beat declarer's ♠J with ♠K and led a third spade for East to trump. East led back a low heart. West beat declarer's jack with the king, returned the ♥3 to East's ace, and East led a third heart for West to trump. The defence had taken the first six tricks but that was the end of the road. Declarer won West's diamond switch with the queen, crossed to the queen of trumps, returned to the jack, cashed the ace (drawing the opposing trumps), led his ♦K and tabled his last two trumps. Seven tricks.

S	W	N	E
1♣	Pass	Pass(1)	Pass

(1) Mistake – North has six points so must respond.

Contract: 1♣
Opening Lead: ♠5

What should have happened

Against 3NT, West leads the ♠5 to East's ace, wins East's ♠10 return with the king, and leads a third spade to declarer's queen. Declarer carefully unblocks the ♦KQ before crossing to dummy's ♣Q. He cashes the ♦A (discarding a heart), then leads dummy's second club. He wins ♣AKJ, and tables ♣5 (a winner by virtue of its length). Nine tricks and game made.

S	W	N	E
1♣	Pass	1♦ (1)	Pass
3NT(2)	End		

(1) Correctly bids the cheaper of his four-card suits.
(2) Can jump straight to game – 19 + 6 = 25.

Contract: 3NT
Opening Lead: ♠5

Tip 10   Respond to a one-of-a-suit opener with six(+) points.

Deal 11

Say responder has a choice between supporting opener (with four or more cards) or bidding a suit of his own. Which should he do? Unless opener has bid a minor, and responder has a decent major to bid, the answer is always the same: SUPPORT! After all, that is what the bid opener most wants to hear.

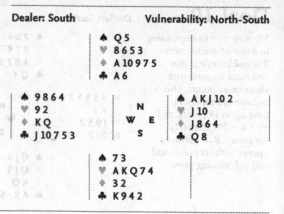

```
            ♠ Q 5
            ♥ 8 6 5 3
            ♦ A 10 9 7 5
            ♣ A 6
  ♠ 9 8 6 4              ♠ A K J 10 2
  ♥ 9 2          N       ♥ J 10
  ♦ K Q       W   E      ♦ J 8 6 4
  ♣ J 10 7 5 3    S      ♣ Q 8
            ♠ 7 3
            ♥ A K Q 7 4
            ♦ 3 2
            ♣ K 9 4 2
```

What happened

North might have recovered from his failure to support if the opponents hadn't entered the bidding. But suddenly he was faced with the decision of whether to bid 4♥ over 3♠ (with a hand that hardly justified it) or to go quietly. He should probably have bid 4♥, but it was less of an error to pass at this point than to have bid 2♦ last time.

Defending East's 3♠, South cashed ♥AK then switched to ♦3. North won ♦A, cashed ♣A, led ♣6 to ♣K, but declarer won South's ♦2 exit in dummy. He led to his ♠AK, felling North's ♠Q, and claimed eight tricks. Down one but N–S had better available...

S	W	N	E
1♥	Pass	2♦(1)	2♠
Pass	3♠	End	

(1) Mistake – known major-suit fit so must support.

Contract: 3♠ by E
Opening Lead: ♥A

What should have happened

If North had supported immediately, jumping to 3♥ to show fair strength, East would have been silenced (the three-level being just too high) and South would have carried on to game (just!).

West leads ♦K and the simplest route to success is to win ♦A, cross to ♥AK (noting the 2–2 trump split), then lead to ♣A, back to ♣K, trump ♣4, and concede ♦10 to West's ♦Q. West switches to ♠9, and East takes his ♠AK, but declarer has the remainder, able to trump ♣9 in dummy. Ten tricks and game made.

S	W	N	E
1♥	Pass	3♥	Pass
4♥	End		

Contract: 4♥ by S
Opening Lead: ♦K

Tip 11 Always support partner when you know there is an eight-card major fit. Think: 'Fit First'.

Deal 12

Dealer: South **Vulnerability: East-West**

As responder, you must immediately support a Major when you have four(+) cards. The more you bid, the better your hand. Say partner opened 1♠ and you have four-card support. Use the Responder Line (see below) to determine how many to bid based on your point-count. Note that you should be prepared to upgrade with an interesting shape. For example a singleton is worth about as much as an extra king.

Pts:	0----5	6-----9	10---12	13----
Bid:	Pass	Two	Three	Four

```
              ♠ Q 6 4 3
              ♥ 4
              ♦ K Q 6 5 2
              ♣ A 5 3
♠ 7                       ♠ J 9 8 5
♥ A 10 6 5 2     N        ♥ K J 9 3
♦ 10 8 3      W     E     ♦ 9 7
♣ Q 10 9 8       S        ♣ K 7 4
              ♠ A K 10 2
              ♥ Q 8 7
              ♦ A J 4
              ♣ J 6 2
```

What happened

West led ♣10 against 2♠, and declarer played low in dummy, East winning ♣K and returning ♣7 to ♣J, ♣Q and ♣A. There was no need to trump hearts in the dummy, as dummy's diamonds would provide plenty of winners after trumps were drawn.

Declarer crossed to ♠K and then led ♠2 to ♠Q, noting West discard. Because he had had the foresight to keep his ♠A10 finessing position in case of a bad split, he was able to play ♠4 to ♠9 and ♠10, cash ♠A (felling ♠J), then begin on diamonds. He cashed ♦A, then ♦J, then ♦4 to ♦Q. He followed with ♦K6, bringing his total to ten tricks. Sadly he was languishing in a part-score.

What should have happened

Though a 3♠ bid expresses his point-count, North should have upgraded his hand in the light of his singleton heart and gone straight to 4♠. 10 tricks and game made.

S	W	N	E
1♠	Pass	2♠(1)	Pass
Pass(2)	Pass		

(1) Underbid – theoretically showing 6–9 points.
(2) Facing at most nine points (thus no game), South passes.

Contract: 2♠
Opening Lead: ♣10

S	W	N	E
1♠	Pass	4♠(1)	End

(1) 11 points and a singleton is easily enough to bid 4♠.

Contract: 4♠
Opening Lead: ♣10

Tip 12

When supporting as responder, use the Responder Line:

Pts:	0----5	6-----9	10---12	13----
Bid:	Pass	Two	Three	Four

Deal 13

'How could you pass?
I jumped the bidding', said
a surprised North. 'If you
had wanted me to go on to
game, you should have bid
it yourself!' replied South
coolly. South was right.
All supporting bids are
'Limit Bids', showing hands
of defined strength. Partner
is always allowed to pass.
Quite simply, the higher
the supporting bid, the
better the hand.

```
              ♠ 8 5
              ♥ K Q 6 4
              ♦ A 7 6 3
              ♣ K J 3
  ♠ A Q 10 7              ♠ K 9 6 4
  ♥ 10 8 7         N      ♥ 9
  ♦ Q J 10 8    W   E     ♦ K 9 5 4
  ♣ 9 7            S      ♣ 10 8 4 2
              ♠ J 3 2
              ♥ A J 5 3 2
              ♦ 2
              ♣ A Q 6 5
```

What happened

North's 3♥ bid actually showed 10–12 points and
invited partner to go on to game with an above-
minimum hand (which South did not have). South then
proceeded (cruelly but impressively) to show the folly
of his partner's ways by making the absolute maximum
number of tricks.

He won ♦Q lead with ♦A and immediately trumped
♦3. He cashed ♥A, led ♥3 to ♥Q (East discarding),
then trumped ♦6. He crossed to ♣J, trumped ♦7
(with ♥J), crossed to ♣K, then cashed ♥K (drawing
West's last trump and discarding ♠2 from hand). Next
he led ♣3 to ♣Q and cashed ♣A discarding ♠5. He
conceded one spade trick, but dummy's remaining
trump took the last trick. 12 tricks!

Usually it is pointless to trump in the hand with the
longer trump length (generally declarer's). But if you
can trump enough times to make it into the shorter
length (as here) then it becomes worthwhile. It is a
technique known as 'Dummy Reversal'.

What should have happened

4♥ plus two.

S	W	N	E
1♥	Pass	3♥(1)	End

(1) Mistake – North knows
the values for game are present (with 13 points facing an
opener) so must jump to 4♥,
not bid a non-forcing 3♥.

Contract: 3♥
Opening Lead: ♦Q

S	W	N	E
1♥	Pass	4♥	End

Contract: 4♥
Opening Lead: ♦Q

Tip 13 All supporting bids – even jumps – are non-forcing, so if you know the values
for game are present, bid it!

Deal 14

Dealer: North **Vulnerability: Neither**

When making your initial response to a one-of-a-suit opener, avoid notrumps where possible. Opener has his rebid planned over a suit response, but not necessarily notrumps.

```
                    ♠ A Q 6 5 3
                    ♥ A J 6 3
                    ♦ 9 6 4
                    ♣ 6
   ♠ J 9 4 2                      ♠ 10 8
   ♥ 9 8              N           ♥ 10 5 4
   ♦ A 3          W     E         ♦ K J 8 7 2
   ♣ A Q 9 7 3       S           ♣ K 10 5
                    ♠ K 7
                    ♥ K Q 7 2
                    ♦ Q 10 5
                    ♣ J 8 4 2
```

What happened

As soon as South responded 2NT, it was impossible for North-South to reach their optimum contract: a heart part-score. For a 3♥ bid by North over 2NT would be forcing.

Against 2NT, West led the ♣7 to East's ♣K and East's ♣10 return was covered by declarer's ♣J and won by West's ♣Q. West cashed the ♣A, ♣9, then ♣3, and switched to the ♦A and ♦3 to East's ♦K. The defence had taken the first seven tricks. Down two.

S	W	N	E
–	–	1♠(1)	Pass
2NT(2)	Pass	Pass(3)	Pass

(1) Using the Rule of 20 – see Deal One.
(2) This does show 10–12 balanced, but it is unwieldy and should be avoided.
(3) Would like to bid 3♥. But (i) does not have the values for game (3♥ would be a forcing bid) plus (ii) does not know whether partner has four hearts (or three spades).

Contract: 2NT by S
Opening Lead: ♣7

What should have happened

Against 3♥, East leads the ♦7 to West's ♦A. West returns the ♦3 to East's ♦K and East leads a third diamond for West to trump. West cashes the ♣A and leads a second club.

Declarer trumps and plays carefully. He cashes the ace of trumps, crosses to the queen (West discarding a club), cashes the ♠K, crosses to the ♠A, then trumps a low spade with the king of trumps. He crosses back to his jack of trumps (drawing East's ten), then tables the ♠Q (felling West's ♠J) and the ♠6, a length winner. Nine tricks and contract made.

S	W	N	E
–	–	1♠	Pass
2♣(1)	Pass	2♥	Pass
3♥	End		

(1) Bids the cheaper four-card suit and allows partner to make his natural rebid.

Contract: 3♥ by N
Opening Lead: ♦7

Tip 14 Bid a suit to a suit. Avoid jumping to 2NT over a one-of-a-suit opener.

Deal 15

Think of bidding as a conversation. A stratospheric leap in notrumps by responder at his first turn is premature and often causes headaches for opener.

```
              ♠ A 8 6 5 3
              ♥ A Q 6 4
              ♦ 8 7
              ♣ J 4
♠ Q J 9                        ♠ 10 4
♥ J 8              N           ♥ 10 9 3 2
♦ K 10 6 4 2   W     E         ♦ Q J 9
♣ Q 9 7           S            ♣ K 10 8 5
              ♠ K 7 2
              ♥ K 7 5
              ♦ A 5 3
              ♣ A 6 3 2
```

What happened

Against 3NT West led the ♦4 to East's ♦J, and declarer correctly delayed winning his ♦A until the third round, exhausting East of diamonds. With seven top tricks, he needed to establish the long spades without West winning the lead.

He crossed to dummy's ♥Q and led a low spade to his king, and a second spade to the jack and ace. He led a third spade and hoped that it would be East who held the queen. No good: West won and cashed his two long diamonds. One down, unavoidably.

What should have happened

If South responds 2♣, North rebids 2♥. This shows that he has at least five spades (with 4–4 in the majors he would open 1♥, and in any event 4–4 hands would open or rebid in notrumps). Knowing the partnership holds an eight-card spade fit, South jumps to 4♠.

On the ♦Q lead, declarer wins the ♦A, cashes the ace-king of trumps, then, leaving the master trump outstanding, plays out his hearts. It does not matter that West can trump the third heart. Dummy's remaining trump takes care of the fourth heart and ten tricks are made.

S	W	N	E
–	–	1♠(1)	Pass
3NT(2)	Pass	Pass(3)	Pass

(1) Using the Rule of 20.
(2) Descriptive (13–15 balanced). But unwieldy and should be avoided.
(3) Stymied – not knowing whether partner has three spades or four hearts.

Contract: 3NT
Opening Lead: ♦4

S	W	N	E
–	–	1♠	Pass
2♣	Pass	2♥(1)	Pass
4♠(2)	End		

(1) Showing (at least) five spades and four hearts.
(2) Knows there is a spade fit and the values for game.

Contract: 4♠ by N
Opening Lead: ♦Q

Tip 15 Wherever possible, bid a suit to a suit as responder. Do not leap to 3NT in response to a one-of-a-suit opener. It will probably give partner a problem.

Deal 16

Dealer: North　　　　**Vulnerability: East-West**

Responder to a one-of-a-
suit opener should bid a
suit to a suit wherever
possible, in order to locate
a fit. A 'one-over-one'
response (e.g. 1♦ – 1♠)
does NOT show more than
four cards or more than six
points. If you have enough
to respond, then you have
enough to change the suit
at the one-level. There is
a common misconception
that a 1NT response is

```
              ♠ J 5
              ♥ A K 7 5
              ♦ A K 9 8 6
              ♣ 10 5
♠ A K 9 8 3 2        N        ♠ 10 6
♥ 10 8                        ♥ 6 3
♦ 10 5         W   E          ♦ J 7 3 2
♣ K Q 9            S          ♣ A J 7 6 4
              ♠ Q 7 4
              ♥ Q J 9 4 2
              ♦ Q 4
              ♣ 8 3 2
```

weaker than a one-of-a-suit response. Nonsense! The confusion arises because whereas
there is no maximum point count for a one-over-one suit response, there is a maximum
of nine points for a 1NT response. The 1NT response should only be made when you
have a weak hand with no higher ranking four-card suit.

What happened

It is doubtful whether North would have bid even 2♥
if West had not been able to overcall 2♠. It was out of
the question for him to bid 3♥ in search of the fit
(that theoretically he could not have in the light of
South's failure to respond 1♥). Against West's 2♠
contract, North cashed ♦AK and ♥AK, before switching
to ♣10. Declarer won ♣Q, cashed ♠AK and simply
played on clubs, later conceding ♠Q. Eight tricks and
contract made.

S	W	N	E
–	–	1♦	Pass
1NT(1)	2♠	End	

(1) Mistake – the 1NT
response denies a four (five)
card suit that can be bid at
the one-level.

Contract: 2♠ by W
Opening Lead: ♦A

What should have happened

Against 3♥ West leads ♠AK and switches to ♣K,
winning. He continues with ♣Q and then a third
spade. But declarer carefully trumps with dummy's ♥K,
to avoid East overtrumping. He cashes ♥A, crosses to
♥J, then plays his top diamonds. Nine tricks and
contract made.

S	W	N	E
–	–	1♦	Pass
1♥(1)	1♠	3♥(2)	End

(1) Correct. Simply shows 6+
points and 4+ hearts.
(2) Showing the fit and some
extra values.

Contract: 3♥ by S
Opening Lead: ♠A

Tip 16 Respond a suit (four(+) cards) at the one-level in preference to 1NT.

Deal 17

Unless he can support – top priority – the basic principle for responder is to bid a suit to a suit. He does this in order to locate a fit. To this end, with two four-card suits, he should bid the cheaper, that is to say the one he reaches first as he works up the bidding ladder. If responder bids four-card suits 'up the line', no fit can be missed.

```
                ♠ 8 6
                ♥ 3
                ♦ A Q 7 5
                ♣ A K 8 7 4 2

    ♠ Q 5 3                    ♠ K J 10 9
    ♥ A K 10 9 7 4    N        ♥ Q J 8
    ♦ J 9          W     E     ♦ 10 6 3
    ♣ J 5             S        ♣ Q 10 6

                ♠ A 7 4 2
                ♥ 6 5 2
                ♦ K 8 4 2
                ♣ 9 3
```

What happened

South made the mistake of responding 1♠. 'I was worried about missing a spade fit', was his excuse. The point is that if opener has four spades, HE will rebid 1♠ and the fit will be found. At least South did not respond 1NT – a worse mistake (see last deal).

South's failure to respond 1♦, the cheaper of his four-card suits, resulted in the suit never being mentioned. It was normal for North to compete to 3♣ over West's 2♥ overcall and then give in.

Defending 3♥, North led ♣AK and continued with ♣2 which was trumped by South and overtrumped. Declarer drew trumps and led ♠Q. South won ♠A and switched to ♦2. North won ♦AQ. Down one but better was available...

S	W	N	E
–	–	1♣	Pass
1♠(1)	2♥	3♣	3♥
End			

(1) Mistake – no reason to bypass diamonds.

Contract: 3♥ by W
Opening Lead: ♣A

What should have happened

Against 5♦, West leads ♥A and switches to ♠3. Declarer wins ♠A, crosses to ♣K, back to ♦K, up to ♣A, then cashes ♦AQ, trumps ♣2, trumps ♥5, then cashes the established ♣874. Eleven tricks and game made.

S	W	N	E
–	–	1♣	Pass
1♦(1)	1♥	4♦(2)	Pass
5♦(3)	End		

(1) Correctly bids the cheaper suit.
(2) Very powerful hand in support of diamonds.
(3) ♦K and ♠A are two huge cards.

Contract: 5♦ by S
Opening Lead: ♥A

Tip 17   Bid the cheaper of four-card suits as responder.

Deal 18

Dealer: North   **Vulnerability: Game All**

You may be wondering
if it is EVER appropriate
for responder to reply
notrumps to a suit bid?
The answer is yes, but
only with a weak hand
that has no higher-ranking
four-card suit (which can
be bid at the one-level).
A two-over-one response
(e.g. 1♥ – 2♦) should not
be made with six measly
points. Some schools think
10 points must be held;

```
                 ♠ A K 5 3 2
                 ♥ 5
                 ♦ J 9 7 6
                 ♣ A K 9
    ♠ J 10 7 4              ♠ 9 8
    ♥ Q J 9         N       ♥ K 10 8 6 4
    ♦ A Q 2     W     E     ♦ K 10 8 5
    ♣ 5 4 2         S       ♣ 6 3
                 ♠ Q 6
                 ♥ A 7 3 2
                 ♦ 4 3
                 ♣ Q J 10 8 7
```

some a good eight. The reality is that the criteria should be a combination of the overall
strength of your hand combined with the length of the suit in which you wish to respond.
I offer you The Rule of 14: Respond in a new suit at the two-level if the number of
high-card points in your hand added to the number of cards in your suit reaches 14.
If not, respond 1NT.

What happened

East led the ♥6 against North's 2♠. Declarer won with
dummy's ♥A; he cashed ♠Q, led ♠6 to ♠K, and cashed
♠A (East discarding ♥4). He next (questionably) gave
West his ♠J. West defended well, cashing ♦A, following
with ♦Q and then leading ♦2 to ♦9 and East's ♦10
then ♦K. Declarer trumped ♥K and claimed (only)
eight tricks.

What should have happened

Defending 5♣, West leads ♥Q and declarer wins ♥A.
He cashes ♠Q and crosses to ♠K. He now scores all
his eight trumps separately: he trumps ♠3, trumps ♥2,
trumps ♠5, trumps ♥3, trumps ♠A(!), trumps ♥7, and
later scores ♣QJ. All eight trumps, ♠AK and ♥A make
eleven tricks. Game made.

N	E	S	W
1♠	Pass	1NT(1)	Pass
2♦	Pass	2♠	End

(1) Mistake – South passes
the Rule of 14 (five clubs
and nine points), so should
respond 2♣.

Contract: 2♠ by N
Opening Lead: ♥6

N	E	S	W
1♠	Pass	2♣	Pass
2♦	Pass	2♠	Pass
3♣(1)	Pass	5♣(2)	End

(1) Showing the delayed
support for partner's clubs.
(2) Facing the likely
5♠1♥4♦3♣ shape, South's
♥Axxx looks huge.

Contract: 5♣ by S
Opening Lead: ♥Q

Tip 18   The Rule of 14. Make a two-over-one response only if your high-card points
added to the number of cards in your suit reaches 14.

Deal 19

Dealer: North   **Vulnerability: Game All**

The Rule of 14 tells the
responder to a one-of-a-
suit opener whether he
has enough to make a
two-over-one response
(e.g. 1♠ – 2♣). The crux is
this: only respond in a new
suit at the two-level if the
number of high-card points
in your hand added to the
number of cards in your
suit reaches 14. Otherwise,
assuming you have no
higher-ranking four-card

```
              ♠ A 5 3
              ♥ A J 7 5 4
              ♦ 4
              ♣ A K 7 4
♠ J 10 9 8              ♠ K 7 2
♥ 9 2          N        ♥ K Q 10 8
♦ A 10 9 6   W   E      ♦ Q 8
♣ Q 10 5       S        ♣ J 8 3 2
              ♠ Q 6 4
              ♥ 6 3
              ♦ K J 7 5 3 2
              ♣ 9 6
```

suit which can be bid at the one-level, a responding hand that fails the Rule of 14 bids
1NT (or a single raise with three-card support). The 1NT response is not a genuine
notrump bid – the hand may easily be unbalanced; rather it is an expression of weakness,
a slowing-down manoeuvre. In practice, you will have six, seven, eight or occasionally
nine points.

What happened

East led ♠2, the unbid suit, against North's 3NT.
Declarer played low from dummy and won ♠A. At
Trick Two, he led ♦4 to ♦J and ♦A. West led ♠9 to ♠K
and dummy won East's ♠7 return with ♠Q. Declarer
cashed ♦K (discarding ♣4), and led ♦3 to ♦J and ♥Q.
East switched to ♣2 to ♣Q and ♣K. Declarer cashed
♥A and led ♣4 to East's ♥10. East led ♣3 to ♣10 and
♣A. Declarer led ♥5 but East won the last three tricks
with ♥K and ♣J8. Down three.

S	W	N	E
–	–	1♥	Pass
2♦(1)	Pass	3♣	Pass
3♦	Pass	3NT(2)	End

(1) Mistake – insufficient
(failing the Rule of 14)
to make a two-over-one
response.

(2) Expecting more for the
two-over-one response.

Contract: 3NT by N
Opening Lead: ♠2

What should have happened

Against 2♦, West leads ♠J to ♠3 and East's ♠K. East
switches to ♥K to dummy's ♥A, (anyone for a duck?),
and ♦4 is led to ♦J and ♦A. West leads ♥9 to ♥J and
♥Q and ♥10 is trumped with ♦7 and overtrumped
with ♦9. West leads ♠10 to ♠Q and declarer cashes
♦K. He ends up with two spades, a heart, three
trumps and two clubs. Eight tricks and contract made.
Big difference!

S	W	N	E
–	–	1♥	Pass
1NT	Pass	2♣	Pass
2♦	End		

Contract: 2♦
Opening Lead: ♠J

Tip 19 Do not make a two-over-one response when you fail the Rule of 14.

Deal 20

Dealer: North　　　　　　　　**Vulnerability: Neither**

Imagine an opponent has opened the bidding. Do you now need opening points to enter? NO! There is only one opening bid in Bridge and it has already been made. If you bid, you do not promise opening points. But you do promise a good suit. What do I mean by 'good'? I mean at least five cards headed by a couple of honours (remember the ten is an honour). With a

```
                ♠ J 6 3
                ♥ K 3
                ♦ A Q 8 7 4 2
                ♣ K 9
   ♠ 8 2                      ♠ K Q 10 9 5
   ♥ Q 10 5 4 2      N        ♥ 9 8 6
   ♦ 9 6          W     E     ♦ K 5
   ♣ Q 10 5 2        S        ♣ 8 6 4
                ♠ A 7 4
                ♥ A J 7
                ♦ J 10 3
                ♣ A J 7 3
```

lovely five-card suit, I encourage you to enter the bidding (at the one-level) with as little as six or seven points. If you have a five-card suit you would like partner to lead – one that can be introduced at the one-level – then bid it. Partner is not clairvoyant.

What happened

North-South sailed unopposed to 3NT and West naturally led ♥4. Declarer won ♥J in hand and ran ♦J, losing to ♦K. East continued with ♥9. Winning in dummy with ♥K, declarer was able to cash five diamonds, ♣AK, and the two major suit aces. 11 tricks.

S	W	N	E
–	–	1♦	Pass(1)
2♣	Pass	2♦	Pass
3NT	End		

(1) Mistake – a fine suit like East's spades is easily worth a one-level overcall.

Contract: 3NT
Opening Lead: ♥4

What should have happened

If East overcalls 1♠ over 1♦, West leads ♠8 (top from two) vs 3NT. Dummy plays ♠3, East ♠9 and declarer ♠4. East continues with ♠K, again ducked. Winning the third spade with ♠A, declarer leads ♦3 to ♦A. Note this play: he does not mind losing the lead to West should he hold the guarded ♦K (West has no more spades). He leads to ♦A in case East has a singleton ♦K. Not this time!

Declarer next leads ♦2 but East wins ♦K and tables two winning spades. Down one.

S	W	N	E
–	–	1♦	1♠
2♣	Pass	2♦	Pass
3NT	End		

Contract: 3NT
Opening Lead: ♠8

Tip 20 An overcall does not promise opening bid values.

Deal 21

Focussing on overcalling, let us say that you have an opening hand without a decent suit. Is it good tactics to overcall? NO! Just because you were going to open the bidding does not mean you should bid after an opponent has opened. If your suit is poor, and the hand looks like it will 'blow up in your face' should partner have a lousy hand, PASS!

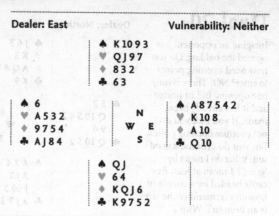

```
              ♠ K 10 9 3
              ♥ Q J 9 7
              ♦ 8 3 2
              ♣ 6 3
   ♠ 6                      ♠ A 8 7 5 4 2
   ♥ A 5 3 2        N       ♥ K 10 8
   ♦ 9 7 5 4    W       E   ♦ A 10
   ♣ A J 8 4        S       ♣ Q 10
              ♠ Q J
              ♥ 6 4
              ♦ K Q J 6
              ♣ K 9 7 5 2
```

What happened

How South wished he had kept quiet. West's double of his 2♣ overcall showed a confident expectation of defeating the contract. How right he was!

West led his singleton spade and East won ♠A. At Trick Two East switched to ♦A (dummy's weakness) and followed with ♦10. Declarer won with ♦J and led a heart (a trump would work better). West rose sharply with ♥A and led a third diamond which East trumped with ♣10. East then cashed ♥K and led a second spade. West trumped with ♣4 and led his fourth diamond. East overtrumped dummy's ♣6 with ♣Q and led a third spade.

Declarer, down to just his five trumps, tried ♣7, but West overtrumped with ♣8. West exited with a heart and declarer trumped perforce and led another trump. West won ♣J and ♣A. The defence had scored an unbelievable ten tricks, which included all six trumps. Five down and 1100 points to East-West.

What should have happened

Without the overcall, East-West would alight in an uninspiring 2♠ contract. It would probably make an overtrick.

N	E	S	W
–	1♠	2♣(1)	Dble
End			

(1) Mistake – the suit is far too emaciated. Just because South would have opened does not mean he should overcall.

Contract: 2♣ (Doubled) by S
Opening Lead: ♠6

N	E	S	W
–	1♠	Pass	1NT
Pass	2♠	End	

Contract: 2♠ by E
Opening Lead: ♦K

Tip 21 Just because you would have opened the bidding does not mean you should bid after an opponent has opened.

Deal 22

There is one aspect of overcalling that cannot be stressed enough. An overcall must contain at least FIVE cards. One or two tournament players experiment with the odd four-card overcall. But (1) their success is at best mixed and (2) they are tournament players and more experienced in handling the 4–3 fits that frequently result. My advice is: Don't overcall on four-card suits.

```
              ♠ 8 7 5
              ♥ Q 9 4
              ♦ 10 8 5
              ♣ K Q J 9

  ♠ Q 10 6 4         N        ♠ 9 2
  ♥ 8 6                       ♥ A K J 10 2
  ♦ A Q J 6     W       E     ♦ 9 3
  ♣ 6 5 2            S        ♣ A 7 4 3

              ♠ A K J 3
              ♥ 7 5 3
              ♦ K 7 4 2
              ♣ 10 8
```

What happened

South's four-card spade suit was so chunky that he decided to risk the overcall. Not a good idea! North naturally supported him to 2♠, expecting his three cards to give a fit of eight. West chanced a penalty double and led ♥8, to ♥9, ♥10 and ♥3.

At Tricks Two and Three, East cashed ♥AK, West discarding ♣2, then switched to ♦9 (dummy's weakness). Declarer played ♦2 and West won ♦J. West returned ♣6 to East's ♣A and East led ♦3, to ♦4, ♦Q and ♦8. West cashed ♦A and correctly continued with ♦6. East overtrumped dummy's ♠8 with ♠9 and led a fourth heart. Declarer discarded ♣10 and West trumped with ♠10. He exited with ♣5 and declarer trumped with ♠3 and led out ♠AKJ, losing Trick 13 to West's ♠Q. He was down five. +1100 to East-West on a part-score deal!

What should have happened

Left to their own devices, East-West would have an awkward auction. East's 2♣ rebid implies five hearts, so West's 'false preference' bid of 2♥ is the best he can do.

A 2♥ contract would make easily enough. Big deal – compared to an 1100 penalty.

S	W	N	E
–	Pass	Pass	1♥
1♠(1)	1NT	2♠	Pass
Pass	Dble	End	

(1) Mistake – you must have 5+ cards to overcall.

Contract: 2♠ (Doubled) by S
Opening Lead: ♥8

S	W	N	E
–	Pass	Pass	1♥
Pass	1♠	Pass	2♣
Pass	2♥	End	

Contract: 2♥ by E
Opening Lead: ♠A

Tip 22 An overcall should contain at least FIVE cards.

Deal 23

The whole essence of an overcall is the suit, not the hand – a measly six or seven points are OK if the suit is good. The corollary is that the partner of an overcaller should be very keen to support but very cautious about bidding a different suit. And – note – only three cards are required to support an overcall (remember – partner must have at least five cards).

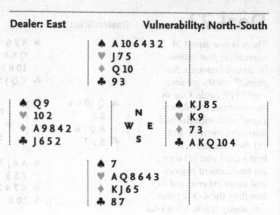

```
              ♠ A 10 6 4 3 2
              ♥ J 7 5
              ◆ Q 10
              ♣ 9 3
  ♠ Q 9                    ♠ K J 8 5
  ♥ 10 2         N         ♥ K 9
  ◆ A 9 8 4 2  W   E       ◆ 7 3
  ♣ J 6 5 2       S        ♣ A K Q 10 4
              ♠ 7
              ♥ A Q 8 6 4 3
              ◆ K J 6 5
              ♣ 8 7
```

What happened

North tried 2♠ rather than 2♥, and neither South (fearing a misfit) or North (the three-level being rather high) saw fit to bid over 3♣.

South led ♠7 to ♠A and North returned ♥5, to ♥9, ♥Q and ♥2. South cashed ♥A, then switched to ◆5. Declarer rose with dummy's ◆A, drew trumps and just conceded a diamond. Contract made by East-West.

If only North had supported hearts immediately and left the rest to partner...

What should have happened

South has a very powerful hand once he hears support. A jump to game is in order. West leads ♣2 against the 4♥ contract, and East wins ♣Q and cashes ♣A. He switches to ◆7 and West wins ◆A and leads back ◆4. Declarer wins dummy's ◆Q and leads ♥5. When East plays low he finesses ♥Q (key play). He cashes ♥A and sees ♥10 and ♥K fall. He now claims the rest. Game made by North-South.

S	W	N	E
–	–	–	1♣
1♥	2♣	2♠(1)	3♣
End			

(1) Known eight-card heart fit, so North should support partner, rather than wading into unknown territory.

Contract: 3♣ by E
Opening Lead: ♠7

S	W	N	E
–	–	–	1♣
1♥	2♣	2♥	2♠
4♥	End		

Contract: 4♥ by S
Opening Lead: ♣2

Tip 23   Support an overcall with three cards.

Deal 24

Dealer: North **Vulnerability: Both**

When supporting an
overall, it is imperative
to be bold with a good fit
for partner. Put simply,
the more trumps held,
the higher the supporting
bid should be.

```
                    ♠ 7 5
                    ♥ K J 7 6
                    ♦ 6 3
                    ♣ A K J 4 2
  ♠ Q J 10 6 2                      ♠ A K 9 4 3
  ♥ Q 5              N              ♥ 8
  ♦ J 10 8 5 4    W     E           ♦ A Q 2
  ♣ 5                S              ♣ 9 7 6 3
                    ♠ 8
                    ♥ A 10 9 4 3 2
                    ♦ K 9 7
                    ♣ Q 10 8
```

What happened

By bidding just 3♠, West gave North the chance to get
his heart support across at an acceptable level. This in
turn enabled South to bid on to 5♥ over East's 4♠.

Against 5♥, West led the ♠Q then switched to
♣5. Declarer won with ♣10, cashed ♥A, crossed to
dummy's ♥K (drawing West's ♥Q), then reverted to
clubs. He led ♣4 to ♣Q, ♣8 back to ♣J, then cashed
♣AK, discarding ♦97. He was forced to concede to
East's ♦A but 11 tricks were his. Game made for
North-South.

What should have happened

If West had made the recommended 4♠ bid, the
auction would have been too high for North to have
safely revealed his heart support. With no knowledge
of the fit, South would probably have (reluctantly)
passed too.

South leads ♣8 against East's 4♠ contract, won by
North's ♣K. North switches to ♥6 to South's ♥A and
South returns ♥4 to North's ♥K, trumped by declarer.
Declarer cashes ♠A, crosses to ♠J (drawing the three
opposing trumps) then runs ♦J. The finesse loses to
South's ♦K, but that is the last trick for the defence.
10 tricks and game made for East-West.

S	W	N	E
–	–	1♣	1♠
2♥	3♠(1)	4♥	4♠
5♥	End		

(1) Mistake – West has a
shapely hand with a known
ten card fit. He should jump
to 4♠ and really put the
pressure on.

Contract: 5♥ by S
Opening Lead: ♠Q

S	W	N	E
–	–	1♣	1♠
2♥	4♠	End	

Contract: 4♠ by E
Opening Lead: ♣8

Tip 24 Be bold – very – when supporting an overall with a big fit and some shape.

Deal 25

Dealer: East　　　　　　　　　　**Vulnerability: Both**

There is a huge difference between a suit opening (four(+) cards, 12+ points), and a suit overcall (five(+) cards, maybe as few as six or seven points). What about a 1NT overcall? Does it show the same 12–14 points as a 1NT opener? NO! If you were going to open 1NT, you must not overcall 1NT. Because it is more dangerous to try for notrumps once an opponent has revealed opening points, a 1NT overcall shows a balanced hand with 15–18 points (even a bad 19).

```
              ♠ Q 7 6
              ♥ K J 6
              ♦ A 3 2
              ♣ 6 5 3 2
  ♠ 8 4                      ♠ K 10 9 5 2
  ♥ 8 5 3         N          ♥ A Q 10 4
  ♦ Q 10 9 5    W   E        ♦ 8 6
  ♣ Q J 9 4        S         ♣ K 10
              ♠ A J 3
              ♥ 9 7 2
              ♦ K J 7 4
              ♣ A 8 7
```

What happened

South made the mistake of overcalling 1NT on the grounds that he was going to open 1NT. Presuming him for 15–19 points, North was theoretically correct to raise to 3NT. The play was not pretty.

West led ♠8, and the first trick continued ♠6, ♠5, ♠J. Declarer led ♦4 to ♦A and returned ♦2 to ♦J. The diamond finesse failed and West, after winning ♦Q, led ♠4 to ♠7, ♠9 and ♠A. Declarer cashed ♦K next, hoping for a 3–3 split. No luck – East discarded ♥4.

Declarer's next shot was to lead ♥2 to ♥J. East won ♥Q, cashed ♠K102, then exited with ♣K. South won ♣A and led ♥7 to dummy's ♥K. East won ♥A, cashed ♥10, then, at Trick 13, led to his partner's ♣Q. Oh dear: down four and -400.

S	W	N	E
–	–	–	1♠
1NT(1)	Pass	3NT	End

(1) Mistake – a 1NT overcall shows more than a 1NT opener (15–19).

Contract: 3NT by S
Opening Lead: ♠8

What should have happened

South quietly passes, and 1♠ becomes the final contract. It might make, especially if South (reasonably) leads ♥7. It might fail by one trick. Either way, South's silence is rewarded.

S	W	N	E
–	–	–	1♠
End			

Contract: 1♠ by E
Opening Lead: ♦4/♥7

Tip 25　Do not bid 1NT as an overcall with a 1NT opener. Bidding 1NT as an overcall shows 15–19.

Deal 26

Returning to opener, it is vital for him to tell partner whether or not his hand is balanced (4432, 4333 or 5332). This he does by either opening 1NT (12–14), opening a suit and rebidding notrumps (15–19), or opening 2NT (20–22).

```
                    ♠ K J 5 3
                    ♥ Q 6 4
                    ♦ J 4 3
                    ♣ A Q 4
      ♠ Q 10 8 4              ♠ 9 7 2
      ♥ 8 5          N        ♥ J 10 9 7
      ♦ A K 7     W     E     ♦ Q 9 8 6
      ♣ 10 8 6 3     S        ♣ 9 7
                    ♠ A 6
                    ♥ A K 3 2
                    ♦ 10 5 2
                    ♣ K J 5 2
```

What happened

South held a balanced hand (4432), but by mistakenly bidding two suits he implied an unbalanced hand with five cards in his first suit and four in his second.

West led ♦A against the seven-card fit 4♥ contract. He continued with ♦K and a third diamond to East's ♦Q. East knew the contract was failing – his trump holding had to win a trick. But seeking to garner the second undertrick, at Trick Four East found the fine play of leading his fourth diamond. Declarer discarded a club, West trumped with ♥8 and dummy overtrumped with ♥Q. Declarer led to his ♥AK, but West discarded on the second round and East had to score two trump tricks. Down two.

What should have happened

If South had rebid 1NT, North would have had an easy raise to 3NT. West would probably have led from his longest suit, ♣3. Declarer would win ♣A and cash a total of two spades, three hearts and four clubs. Game made.

Declarer would have had a slightly more worrying time if West had begun with ♦A. But with the suit splitting 4–3 the contract would still have made, the only difference being that the defence would take the first four tricks as opposed to the last four tricks.

S	W	N	E
1♥	Pass	1♠	Pass
2♣(1)	Pass	4♥	End

(1) Mistake – implies an unbalanced hand with (at least) five hearts and four clubs.

Contract: 4♥
Opening Lead: ♦A

S	W	N	E
1♥	Pass	1♠	Pass
1NT(1)	Pass	3NT	End

(1) The correct rebid, showing 15–16 balanced.

Contract: 3NT
Opening Lead: ♣3

Tip 26 A balanced opener should plan to bid notrumps with either his first or second bid, as opposed to bidding two suits.

Deal 27

Opener clarifies many things with his first rebid, particularly whether or not his hand is balanced (4432, 4333, 5332). He rebids notrumps with one of those three distributions, but not with, say, a 5431 shape.

```
              ♠ 10 8 6 5
              ♥ K J 4
              ♦ K J 3
              ♣ A J 4
♠ J 4 3 2              N        ♠ A K 9 7
♥ 9 5             W       E     ♥ 10 8 3
♦ 10 8 7 2            S         ♦ A 6 4
♣ 9 7 5                         ♣ 10 3 2
              ♠ Q
              ♥ A Q 7 6 2
              ♦ Q 9 5
              ♣ K Q 8 6
```

What happened

After opening 1♥ and hearing his partner respond 1♠, South should have rebid his second suit, clubs, implying an unbalanced hand with a five-four distribution. Instead he could not resist rebidding notrumps, arguing that 'Partner has the spades, I have the other suits; let's try notrumps'. But this painted a false picture of his hand to his partner and the inferior game contract was reached.

West led ♦2 against the 3NT contract, and East won dummy's ♦3 with ♦A. There was clearly no future in diamonds, looking at dummy's ♦KJ. So East tried a switch to ♠A, felling declarer's ♠Q. He next led ♠7 (key play) to West's ♠J, declarer discarding ♥2. West returned a third spade and East held ♠K9 over dummy's ♠108. Declarer tried ♠8 but East took ♠9 and cashed ♠K. Down one.

What should have happened

Had South made the natural rebid of 2♣, implying his five-four shape, North, knowing of the eight-card heart fit, would have leapt straight to 4♥. West would probably again have led ♦2 to East's ♦A and East would have switched to ♠A then ♠K. Declarer would have trumped, drawn the trumps in three rounds, then cashed all his minor suit winners. 11 easy tricks.

S	W	N	E
1♥	Pass	1♠(1)	Pass
1NT(2)	Pass	3NT	End

(1) Theoretically correct – longest suit at lowest level.
(2) The fatal error, theoretically showing a balanced hand with 15–16 points.

Contract: 3NT
Opening Lead: ♦2

S	W	N	E
1♥	Pass	1♠	Pass
2♣(1)	Pass	4♥	End

(1) The correct rebid, showing an unbalanced hand with (at least) five hearts and four clubs.

Contract: 4♥
Opening Lead: ♦2

Tip 27 Do not rush into notrumps with an unbalanced opener.

Deal 28

A 5332 shape is balanced. Though contentious because it is out of line with traditional thinking, most modern experts (including your author) prefer to open 1NT with a 5332 shape and 12–14 points, even when the five-card suit is a major. Less contentious is the correct strategy with 15–16 points and a 5332 shape with a five-card major. After opening One-of-the Major, it is most certainly correct to rebid in notrumps rather than repeat the suit. Motto: avoid repeating a five-card suit wherever possible.

```
                    ♠ K J 5 2
                    ♥ 2
                    ♦ 8 6 4 2
                    ♣ A 8 6 2
   ♠ 10 9 7 6                      ♠ A 4 3
   ♥ J 8 5            N            ♥ Q 10 9 3
   ♦ K Q          W     E         ♦ A 10 7 3
   ♣ J 9 5 3          S            ♣ 10 7
                    ♠ Q 8
                    ♥ A K 7 6 4
                    ♦ J 9 5
                    ♣ K Q 4
```

What happened

South regretted his (inadvisable) choice of rebid when he saw dummy. West led ♦K against the 2♥ contract. When it held the trick he continued with ♦Q. He then switched to ♠10 and East won ♠A. East cashed ♦A and then led ♦10. Declarer trumped with ♥6, but West overtrumped with ♥8 and switched to ♣3. Declarer won ♣Q and cashed ♥AK, but East had to score ♥Q10 and the contract was down two.

S	W	N	E
1♥	Pass	1♠	Pass
2♥(1)	End		

(1) Remember the motto: avoid rebidding five-card suits wherever possible.

Contract: 2♥
Opening Lead: ♦K

What should have happened

South would have registered a plus score had he found the correct rebid of 1NT, accurately expressing his point count, and pinpointing his shape as either 5332, 4432 or 4333. North would pass and West would lead ♣3. Declarer would beat East's ♣10 with ♣Q and lead ♠Q at Trick Two, in order to flush out ♠A. East would win ♠A and lead his second club. Declarer would win ♣K, and cash ♠KJ, ♥AK and ♣A. Seven tricks and contract made.

S	W	N	E
1♥	Pass	1♠	Pass
1NT(1)	End		

(1) The recommended rebid, showing a balanced hand with 15–16 points.

Contract: 1NT
Opening Lead: ♣3

Tip 28 An opener with a 5332 shape should plan to open or rebid notrumps.

Deal 29

Arguably the most pivotal bid in an uncontested auction is opener's first rebid. At this stage opener tells his partner whether or not his hand is balanced (5332, 4432 or 4333), and, if so, how strong his hand is. Opener is Balanced:

12–14: Open 1NT.

15–16: Open One of Longest Suit. Rebid notrumps at the lowest level over partner's new suit bid.

```
              ♠ K Q J 4
              ♥ Q 7 6 3
              ♦ 4 2
              ♣ 9 8 3
  ♠ 8 6                    ♠ 10 7 5 2
  ♥ A 10 5         N       ♥ K J 9
  ♦ 10 7 5    W        E   ♦ K 9 8 6
  ♣ A J 6 4 2      S       ♣ 10 7
              ♠ A 9 3
              ♥ 8 4 2
              ♦ A Q J 3
              ♣ K Q 5
```

17–18: Open One of Longest Suit. Rebid notrumps with a jump over partner's new suit bid.

19: Open One of Longest Suit. Rebid 3NT over partner's new suit bid.

20–22: Open 2NT.

What happened

South overstated his values, his jump to 2NT, theoretically showing 17–18, rather than the 16 he actually held. Holding eight points, North expected the partnership to have the 25 points needed for game, so naturally raised the 2NT to 3NT.

West led ♣4 to East's ♣10. Declarer won ♣Q, crossed to ♠J and led to ♦J. The finesse succeeded so he cashed ♠A, crossed to dummy's ♠KQ, (West discarding ♥5 and ♦7) and played to ♦Q. He cashed ♦A and had eight tricks in the bag. Searching vainly for a ninth, he led ♥2. West played ♥10, and East beat dummy's ♥Q with ♥K, cashed ♦K (West discarding ♣2) and led ♣7. Declarer tried ♣K, but West won ♣A and cashed ♣J6 and ♥A. Down one.

What should have happened

1NT plus one with the play proceeding identically.

S	W	N	E
1♦	Pass	1♥	Pass
2NT(1)	Pass	3NT(2)	End

(1) This jump showed 17–18 points balanced, an overstatement of his actual values.

(2) 17 + 8 = 25 so North goes on to game.

Contract: 3NT
Opening Lead: ♣4

S	W	N	E
1♦	Pass	1♥	Pass
1NT(1)	Pass	Pass(2)	Pass

(1) The correct rebid of 1NT shows 15–16 points.

(2) The partnership cannot have 25 points, so North passes.

Contract: 1NT
Opening Lead: ♣4

Tip 29   A 1NT rebid shows 15–16 balanced.

Deal 30

Dealer: South **Vulnerability: Neither**

I have been emphasising in the importance of opener revealing whether or not his hand is balanced (5332, 4432, 4333). He does this with his first bid when holding 12–14 (opening 1NT) or 20–22 (opening 2NT). With 15–19 he opens a suit but rebids notrumps. The only time a balanced opener should *not* bid notrumps with either his first or second bid (in response to a new suit bid by responder) is when he has support for his partner's major (not minor) suit response.

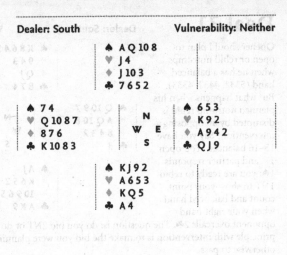

What happened

South was so ingrained into rebidding notrumps with 15–19 balanced (jumping where appropriate) that he forgot to support his partner's 1♠ response. And so it was that he ended up declaring a hopeless 3NT contract with 4♠ very playable.

In 3NT, West's ♣3 lead went to East's ♣J and declarer withheld his ♣A. He won ♣Q continuation with ♣A and cashed his four spade winners. He then led ♦K. East won ♦A, led ♣9 to West's ♣K10, and West exited with ♥7 to ♥J, ♥K and ♥A. Declarer cashed ♦Q and led to ♦J, but West won the last trick with ♥Q. Down one.

S	W	N	E
1♥	Pass	1♠	Pass
2NT(1)	Pass	3NT	End

(1) 2NT does show 17–18 balanced, but supporting his partner's spades is a higher priority.

Contract: 3NT by S
Opening Lead: ♣3

What should have happened

In 4♠ by North, East leads ♣Q. South's ♣A wins and ♣4 is led straight back. The defence win and switch to a trump (best), but declarer wins ♠8, trumps ♣6 with ♠9, overtakes ♠J with ♠Q, trumps ♣7 with ♠K then leads ♦K. East wins ♦A and leads back ♦2. Declarer wins ♦J, cashes ♠A, crosses to ♦Q, cashes ♥A, concedes a heart, and wins the last trick with ♠10. Game made.

S	W	N	E
1♥	Pass	1♠	Pass
3♠(1)	Pass	4♠	End

(1) Correct. South's jump support shows around 16–18 points with four spades.

Contract: 4♠ by N
Opening Lead: ♣Q

Tip 30 Support responder's major with four cards in preference to rebidding notrumps.

Deal 31

Opener should plan to open or rebid notrumps when he has a balanced hand (5332, 4432, 4333). But what happens when his planned notrump rebid is disrupted by an opposing intervention? Say you have 15–16 balanced. You open 1♥ and partner responds 1♠; you are ready to rebid 1NT to show your point count and balanced hand when your right hand opponent overcalls 2♣. The question is: do you bid 2NT or do you shut up? The basic principle with intervention is to make the bid you were planning to make if you are able; otherwise to pass.

```
                    ♠ K 8 6 4 3
                    ♥ 9 4 3
                    ♦ Q J
                    ♣ 8 7 4
  ♠ Q 10 9 7              N          ♠ 5 2
  ♥ A Q 10 8                         ♥ J 7
  ♦ 8 4 3 2        W         E       ♦ A K 7
  ♣ 3                    S           ♣ Q J 10 6 5 2
                    ♠ A J
                    ♥ K 6 5 2
                    ♦ 10 9 6 5
                    ♣ A K 9
```

What happened

South did not follow the principle. He paid the penalty. Declaring 2NT, he received ♣3 lead to ♣10. Winning ♣K, he led ♦5 to ♦J (best). East won ♦K and led ♣Q. Declarer won ♣A and led to ♦Q. East won ♦A and cashed ♣J652. Declarer discarded ♥52 and ♦9; West kept all his hearts.

At Trick Nine East advanced ♥J. Declarer forlornly tried ♥K but West won ♥A and cashed ♥Q108. Declarer took the last trick (with ♠A) but was down five! He lost 500 points, and would have lost 1400 if doubled!

S	W	N	E
1♥	Pass	1♠	2♣
2NT(1)	End		

(1) South cannot make his planned rebid (1NT to show 15–16). A 2NT bid, being a jump over partner's new suit response, indicates 17–18 points.

Contract: 2NT by S
Opening Lead: ♣3

What should have happened

Defending 2♣, South leads ♠A, then ♠J to North's ♠K. When North leads ♠3 and declarer ruffs with ♣10, South discards to promote his ♣9. East loses three trump tricks (to ♣AK9) and makes 2♣ (exactly); rather better for North-South than 2NT down five!

S	W	N	E
1♥	Pass	1♠	2♣
Pass(1)	Pass	Pass	

(1) South cannot bid 1NT, so makes a disciplined pass.

Contract: 2♣ by E
Opening Lead: ♠A

Tip 31 If you cannot make your planned bid (when limiting your strength) in the light of opposing intervention, pass.

Deal 32

Dealer: North **Vulnerability: East-West**

Moving on to the rebid
strategies of an *unbalanced*
opener after responder
has changed suit, his three
options are:
(a) Support responder.
(b) Repeat his first suit.
(c) Introduce his second suit.
The top priority is Option
(a): supporting. Four (or
more) cards should be held
and it is important that the
right level be selected.
Here is the Opener's

```
              ♠ K J 10 4
              ♥ A K 7 5 4
              ♦ 6
              ♣ A J 5
♠ 9 5 3                      ♠ 8 2
♥ Q 10 8 3          N        ♥ J 6
♦ A Q 10 5      W     E      ♦ J 9 7 2
♣ 9 2              S         ♣ K Q 8 6 4
              ♠ A Q 7 6
              ♥ 9 2
              ♦ K 8 4 3
              ♣ 10 7 3
```

Support Line. Bear in mind that hands with interesting distribution can be upgraded (*or use
The Losing Trick Count – see next deal*):

```
        12-----------15   16-----------18   19------ points
Support:  at lowest level   with a jump      to game
```

What happened

Opener forgot to jump in support when extra values
were held. Defending 2♠, West led ♣9 (top from two)
and declarer played low in dummy. East won ♣Q and
switched to ♦2. Declarer tried ♦K, but West won ♦A and
led ♣2. Rising with the ♣A, declarer set about establishing
dummy's hearts before drawing all the missing trumps
(key strategy). He cashed ♥AK, trumped ♥4 with ♠6
(East discarding ♣6), cashed ♠A, led ♠7 to dummy's
♠10, trumped ♥5 with ♠Q, trumped ♦3, cashed ♠K
(drawing West's last trump), then cashed the established
♥7. He conceded the last trick, ♣J, to East's ♣K.

Despite the unfavourable layout in every suit apart
from trumps, declarer had made 10 tricks.

What should have happened

How he wished he had been in 4♠ (making game), not
merely 2♠!

S	W	N	E
–	–	1♥	Pass
1♠	Pass	2♠(1)	End

(1) Not enough. Quite apart
from holding 16 high-card
points, the 5431 shape is very
powerful.

Contract: 2♠
Opening Lead: ♣9

S	W	N	E
–	–	1♥	Pass
1♠	Pass	3♠(1)	Pass
4♠(2)	End		

(1) With 16 points and a
singleton diamond North is
actually almost worth 4♠.
But his 3♠ bid gives partner
the chance to pass with six or
so points.
(2) Nine points and good
trumps is ample to bid 4♠.

Contract: 4♠
Opening Lead: ♣9

Tip 32 The Opener's Support Line.

Deal 33

Dealer: North **Vulnerability: Neither**

When an unbalanced opener is supporting responder with his rebid (e.g. 1♥ – 1♠ – 3♠), he can use high-card points as a guide (the Opener's Support Line). But unless he upgrades his hand when he has an interesting shape (as he is almost bound to have, given that he is unbalanced), such a method is less accurate than the Losing Trick

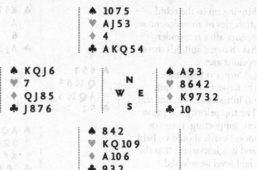

```
            ♠ 10 7 5
            ♥ A J 5 3
            ♦ 4
            ♣ A K Q 5 4
♠ K Q J 6              ♠ A 9 3
♥ 7          N        ♥ 8 6 4 2
♦ Q J 8 5   W   E     ♦ K 9 7 3 2
♣ J 8 7 6      S      ♣ 10
            ♠ 8 4 2
            ♥ K Q 10 9
            ♦ A 10 6
            ♣ 9 3 2
```

Count (LTC). Here is how Opener uses the LTC:

(a) Opener adds up his Losing Tricks. (Think of the ace as taking the first round of each suit; the king the second; and the queen the third). The number of these he does not have – up to the number of cards held – represents the number of losing tricks.

(b) He adds this number to his partner's presumed number of Losing Tricks (nine for a one-over-one response and eight for a two-over-one response).

(c) He subtracts the total of those two numbers from 18 and bids the answer.

What happened

Defending 2♥, West led ♠K, continued with ♠Q, then led ♠6 to East's ♠A. East switched to ♦3 (anyone for a trump?), declarer winning ♦A. Unless both clubs and trumps were splitting four-one, declarer could make the rest by simply drawing all the opposing trumps, then playing out the clubs (trumping the fourth round if trumps were three-two and clubs four-one).

Declarer saw an even better line. After winning ♦A at Trick Four, he trumped ♦6 with ♥J. He then led ♥3 to ♥9 and trumped ♦10 with ♥A. He led ♥5 to ♥KQ10 and took the last three tricks with dummy's ♣AKQ.

10 tricks made but – oh dear – the contract was just 2♥.

S	W	N	E
–	–	1♣	Pass
1♥	Pass	2♥(1)	End

(1) North has six Losing Tricks. Three spades, (♠A, ♠K, ♠Q); two hearts (♥K, ♥Q); one diamond (♦A) and no clubs. Assuming partner for nine (one-over-one response), he subtracts 15 (nine + six) from 18. So he should have bid 3♥.

Contract: 2♥
Opening Lead: ♠K

What should have happened

Same – but in 4♥.

S	W	N	E
–	–	1♣	Pass
1♥	Pass	3♥	Pass
4♥(1)	End		

(1) Clear to go on to game over the jump rebid, with chunky trumps and an outside ace.

Contract: 4♥
Opening Lead: ♠K

Tip 33 When unbalanced with four(+) card support, you can use The Losing Trick Count.

Deal 34

Dealer: South　　　　　　**Vulnerability: East-West**

Opener has three choices of rebid when he is unbalanced (i.e. not 5332, 4432, 4333):
(a) Support responder's change of suit.
(b) Repeat his first suit.
(c) Bid a second suit.
In general, repeating what you have already said is not particularly attractive unless the suit is really worth stressing. Better to support partner if possible,

```
                    ♠ Q 4 3
                    ♥ A 9 3 2
                    ♦ 7 4
                    ♣ A 8 6 3
  ♠ K J 10 6                      ♠ A 9 5 2
  ♥ J 7 5            N            ♥ Q 10 8 4
  ♦ Q 10 9 3      W     E         ♦ J 8
  ♣ K 9             S            ♣ Q 10 7
                    ♠ 8 7
                    ♥ K 6
                    ♦ A K 6 5 2
                    ♣ J 5 4 2
```

or to introduce a new suit in the hope of finding a fit in that third suit. Except in rare circumstances, six(+) cards should be present to repeat a suit – opener will generally have a better choice than to repeat a five-card suit. Either he will be 5332 (balanced) in which case he can open/rebid notrumps; or he will have a four-card suit as well (in which case he can bid it).

What happened

Declarer could not avoid losing two spades, two trumps and two clubs in his inferior 2♦ contract. Down one.

S	W	N	E
1♦(1)	Pass	1♥	Pass
2♦(2)	End		

(1) Using the Rule of 20.
(2) Mistake. Introducing a second suit – when cheaper to do so – should always be preferred to repeating a five-card suit.

Contract: 2♦
Opening Lead: ♠J

What should have happened

3♣ would make on careful play. West leads ♠J and wins the trick with it. He continues with ♠6 to East's ♠A and declarer trumps ♠9. Declarer then leads ♣4 and ducks West's ♣9 (key play). He wins West's ♥5 switch with ♥A, cashes ♣A, crosses to ♦AK, trumps ♦2 with ♣6, overtrumped by East's ♣Q. He wins East's ♥8 with ♥K, trumps ♦5 with ♣8, trumps ♥3 with ♣J and cashes the established ♦6. Contract made.

S	W	N	E
1♦	Pass	1♥	Pass
2♣	Pass	3♣(1)	End

(1) Note that North would have returned to 2♦ with a weak hand and the same length in both minors.

Contract: 3♣
Opening Lead: ♠J

Tip 34 Always mention a cheaper four-card suit ahead of repeating a five-card suit.

Deal 35

Dealer: South   **Vulnerability: Both**

I have stressed that
repeating a suit should
(90%) imply SIX cards.
Take the auction 1♥ – 1♠
– 2♥. There is no shape for
opener that should bid that
way with just five hearts.
Here is a list of all shapes
with a longest suit of five
cards: 5530, 5521, 5440,
5431, 5422, 5332. If he has
a second suit of four/five
cards, he should bid that
suit. The only remaining
shape, 5332, is balanced; it should therefore either open or rebid in notrumps.

```
              ♠ 9 5
              ♥ J 9 6 4 2
              ♦ A 4
              ♣ A 8 7 5
   ♠ K 7 4              ♠ 6 3 2
   ♥ 10 7 3      N       ♥ K Q 8
   ♦ Q 9 7 6   W   E    ♦ K 10 5
   ♣ K Q 10      S       ♣ J 9 4 2
              ♠ A Q J 10 8
              ♥ A 5
              ♦ J 8 3 2
              ♣ 6 3
```

The only occasion in which opener should repeat a five-card suit in reply to partner's
new suit response is when he has a four-card suit that is inconvenient to introduce. Say
he has five spades, four diamonds and a minimum opener. If, after opening 1♠, he hears
partner respond 2♣, all is well: he can rebid 2♦ conveniently. But if partner responds
2♥, rebidding 2♠ is wiser than bidding 3♦. The 3♦ bid in the auction 1♠ – 2♥ – 3♦ is
called a 'Reverse' (meaning that it forces responder to give preference to opener's first
suit – should he wish to – at the *three*-level). 1♦ – 1♠ – 2♥ and 1♥ – 2♦ – 2♠ are further
examples. Ideally, at least a good 15 points should be held, although it is a mistake to
become obsessed with the reverse (such that this deal will be its only mention in the book).

What happened

3NT drifted two down, declarer scoring four spades and
three aces.

S	W	N	E
1♠	Pass	2♥(1)	Pass
3♦(2)	Pass	3NT	End

(1) Just worth 2♥ in
preference to 1NT.
(2) Though this bid shows
South's shape, it lifts the
bidding to an uncomfortably
high level.

Contract: 3NT by N
Opening Lead: ♣2

What should have happened

2♠ makes. Win ♣K lead with ♣A, cash ♦A and lead
♦4. East wins ♦K and switches to ♠2 (best). Rise with
♠A and trump ♦8 in dummy. Five trumps and three
aces make eight tricks.

S	W	N	E
1♠	Pass	2♥	Pass
2♠(1)	End		

(1) Opener should try to have
six cards to repeat a suit. But,
occasionally, repeating a five-
card suit is the only sensible
course of action.

Contract: 2♠
Opening Lead: ♣K

Tip 35   A 'reverse' is a second suit bid that forces
responder to the three-level to give preference
back to the first suit. Ideally a good 15+ points
should be held.

Deal 36

Dealer: South **Vulnerability: North-South**

Except in rare
circumstances, opener
should hold *six* cards in
order to repeat a suit. And
when doing so, he must
remember to *jump* when he
has extra values – about 16
or more points – using the
Opener's Repeat Line.

```
              ♠ K964
              ♥ 865
              ♦ J53
              ♣ AJ3
  ♠ AJ7                      ♠ Q1083
  ♥ K9            N          ♥ 107
  ♦ 10987      W   E         ♦ KQ62
  ♣ 9764          S          ♣ 852
              ♠ 52
              ♥ AQJ432
              ♦ A4
              ♣ KQ10
```

Opener's Six-card Repeat Line.

12----------15	16----------19	20----------22
Repeat suit at lowest level	Repeat suit with a jump	Open Two of suit

---

What happened

South forgot to jump to show his additional strength
and a game contract was missed. In the 2♥ contract,
West led ♦10 (top of a sequence). Declarer won ♦A
and sought to avoid a trump loser by finessing. He led
♣10 to dummy's ♣J and returned ♥5 to ♥7 and his ♥J.
Had East held the missing ♥K, his ♥J would have won.
He would then have repeated the finesse by leading ♣Q
to ♣A and finessing ♥Q.

But West held ♥K and took ♥J with the card.
He then led ♦9 to East's ♦Q and East tried to cash
♦K. Declarer trumped, cashed ♥A drawing the two
remaining trumps, then turned his attention to spades,
needing to promote dummy's ♠K to score his tenth
trick (to go with five trumps, ♦A and three clubs).

At Trick Seven declarer led ♠2 and West played ♠7.
He tried dummy's ♠K, in the even money hope that
West held ♠A (another finesse). Success – ♠K held the
trick and he made two overtricks (cashing his trumps
and clubs and conceding a spade at the end).

What should have happened

A game needing one out of two finesses to work is an
excellent proposition (a three to one on chance). South
should have jumped to 3♥ (and thus bid and make
4♥) by playing the hand as above.

S	W	N	E
1♥	Pass	1♠	Pass
2♥(1)	Pass	Pass(2)	Pass

(1) South forgets to jump,
showing fewer than
16 points...
(2) ...so North thinks game is
not there.

Contract: 2♥
Opening Lead: ♦10

S	W	N	E
1♥	Pass	1♠	Pass
3♥(1)	Pass	4♥(2)	End

(1) Correct, showing six cards
and 16+ points.
(2) With North-South holding
25+ points, North bids game.

Contract: 4♥
Opening Lead: ♦10

Tip 36 When repeating your suit as opener, use the
Opener's Repeat Line, jumping the bidding
with 16 or more points.

Deal 37

Dealer: North   **Vulnerability: North-South**

It is a sound principle of bidding that you should try to tell partner something new with each bid. And that if you have already revealed your hand, you should respect partner's choice of contract. We have observed that the sequence 1♥ – 1♠ – 2♥ shows SIX hearts. So if partner chooses, say, 3NT as the contract, you should not overrule him merely because you have the six hearts you have already shown.

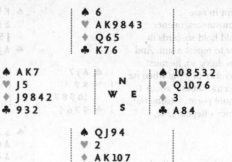

```
              ♠ 6
              ♥ A K 9 8 4 3
              ♦ Q 6 5
              ♣ K 7 6
♠ A K 7                      ♠ 10 8 5 3 2
♥ J 5               N        ♥ Q 10 7 6
♦ J 9 8 4 2    W       E     ♦ 3
♣ 9 3 2            S         ♣ A 8 4
              ♠ Q J 9 4
              ♥ 2
              ♦ A K 10 7
              ♣ Q J 10 5
```

What happened

North was blinded by 'Six Appeal' – the overstatement of his six-card suit. Instead of reasoning (correctly) that, 'I have already shown my six hearts, now it's up to my partner', North thought, 'What a lovely suit – I must play in hearts'.

4♥ stood no chance on the four-two trump split (the most likely split missing six cards). Declarer had to lose a spade, two trumps and ♣A. He won ♦3 lead with ♦Q, cashed ♥AK and tried a third round (hoping for an even split). East won ♥10, cashed ♥Q, cashed ♣A, then tried ♠8. West won ♠K and, though declarer trumped ♠A and claimed the rest, he had lost four tricks. Down one.

S	W	N	E
–	–	1♥	Pass
1♠	Pass	2♥	Pass
3NT	Pass	4♥(1)	End

(1) Having shown his six hearts already, North has no reason not to respect his partner's choice of contract.

Contract: 4♥ by N
Opening Lead: ♦3

What should have happened

3NT would have fared altogether better, as you would expect when good stoppers are held in all suits and there is no eight-card fit. West's ♦4 lead would run to declarer's ♦10. Declarer would not bother with dummy's hearts, the safe route to success being to flush out ♣A. His ♣5 lead would go to ♣K and East's ♣A. There is nothing the defence can do to prevent declarer from scoring ♥AK, four diamonds and ♣QJ10. Nine tricks and game made.

S	W	N	E
–	–	1♥	Pass
1♠	Pass	2♥	Pass
3NT	Pass	Pass(1)	Pass

(1) Correctly resists the 'Six Appeal'.

Contract: 3NT
Opening Lead: ♦4

Tip 37   If you have shown your hand, respect partner's choice of final contract.

Deal 38

Dealer: South **Vulnerability: Neither**

Let us remind ourselves of opener's three choices of rebid when he is unbalanced (i.e. not 5332, 4432, 4333):

(a) Support responder's change of suit.
(b) Repeat his first suit.
(c) Bid a second suit.

In general, introducing a new suit in an auction – exploring all possible trump suits – is good Bridge. *Question*: What should opener do when he

```
              ♠ 5
              ♥ A Q 4
              ♦ J 10 9 8
              ♣ K 10 6 5 2

♠ A Q 10 8              N        ♠ K 9
♥ 10 9 5          W         E    ♥ K 8 7 6 3
♦ 7 6 4                S         ♦ 3 2
♣ A 8 4                          ♣ Q 9 7 3

              ♠ J 7 6 4 3 2
              ♥ J 2
              ♦ A K Q 5
              ♣ J
```

has a six-card suit and a four-card suit? Should he repeat the six, or try the four?

Answer: Assuming the suits are of similar quality, he should do what is cheapest. Say he has: ♠5

♥AQ8642
♦74
♣AQ95

He opens 1♥. If his partner responds 2♦, it is cheaper (thus better) to rebid 2♥ rather than 3♣. But if partner responds 1♠ it is preferable to rebid 2♣ than 2♥.

What happened

Defending 2♠, West led ♥10 to dummy's ♥4 and East's ♥K. A club switch (East doing well – a diamond does look tempting) to West's ♣A ensured – with the defence holding no fewer than four trump tricks – that 2♠ failed.

S	W	N	E
1♠	Pass	2♣	Pass
2♠(1)	End		

(1) Mistake. It is cheaper – thus better – to introduce the strong four-card diamond suit.

Contract: 2♠
Opening Lead: ♥10

What should have happened

3♦ would almost certainly have succeeded, declarer scoring two hearts, a club and six trumps (not drawing trumps and trumping twice in one hand).

S	W	N	E
1♠	Pass	2♣	Pass
2♦(1)	Pass	3♦	End

(1) Bidding two suits shows more of his cards (nine – see next deal) than repeating his first suit.

Contract: 3♦
Opening Lead: ♥10

Tip 38 Introduce a decent four-card suit – if cheaper – rather than repeating an anaemic six-card suit.

Deal 39

Question: Say the bidding goes 1♥ – 1♠ – 2♣. What is opener saying about his hand? Clearly he has four clubs, but has he shown more than four hearts or might he be just four-four in his two suits?

Answer: He has shown (at least) five hearts. With a four-four hand he would open/rebid notrumps (the awkward – and mercifully rare – 4441 shape is perhaps best handled by rebidding notrumps when partner has responded in the singleton). His

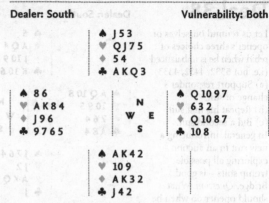

```
              ♠ J 5 3
              ♥ Q J 7 5
              ♦ 5 4
              ♣ A K Q 3
♠ 8 6                        ♠ Q 10 9 7
♥ A K 8 4          N         ♥ 6 3 2
♦ J 9 6        W     E       ♦ Q 10 8 7
♣ 9 7 6 5          S         ♣ 10 8
              ♠ A K 4 2
              ♥ 10 9
              ♦ A K 3 2
              ♣ J 4 2
```

failure to bid notrumps therefore indicates an unbalanced hand with at least a five-four shape. *General Rule*: A player who bids two suits shows (at least) a five-four shape. The corollary to this – and our common mistake – is that a player should not bid a second suit of four cards unless he has (at least) five cards in his first suit.

What happened

Declaring the inferior 4♠ contract, South received ♥AK lead and a third heart. He won with ♥Q, crossed to ♦K and led to ♠J. But when East won ♠Q and the suit split four-two, he could not avoid defeat.

S	W	N	E
1♠	Pass	2♣	Pass
2♦(1)	Pass	4♠(2)	End

(1) South implies 5+ spades by this bid...
(2) ...so North, with the values for game, simply jumps to 4♠.

Contract: 4♠
Opening Lead: ♥A

What should have happened

3NT is easy. Declarer wins ♥4 lead with ♥9 in hand and has nine top tricks – two spades, a heart, two diamonds and four clubs. By forcing out ♥AK, he can even make a risk-free overtrick.

S	W	N	E
1♠	Pass	2♣	Pass
2NT(1)	Pass	3♠(2)	Pass
3NT	End		

(1) Correct rebid, showing a balanced 15–16 points.
(2) North carefully shows his delayed support, giving South the option of a 4♠ contract should he hold a 5332 shape with five spades.

Contract: 3NT
Opening Lead: ♥4

Tip 39 Do not bid a second suit unless you have five(+) cards in your first suit.

Deal 40

Dealer: North

Vulnerability: North-South

Let us remind ourselves of an unbalanced opener's three types of rebid:
(a) Support responder's change of suit.
(b) Repeat his first suit.
(c) Bid a second suit.
With 16+ points, opener jumps when either
(a) supporting responder or (b) repeating his own suit. Focussing on option (c): *Question:* Should opener jump in a new suit every time he holds 16+ points?

```
              ♠ 6 4
              ♥ A 7 5 3 2
              ♦ K 5
              ♣ A K Q 3
  ♠ K 10 8 5              ♠ A 9 3
  ♥ K 10 4      N         ♥ Q J 9 6
  ♦ Q J 10 9  W   E       ♦ 6 4
  ♣ 9 4          S        ♣ J 10 6 5
              ♠ Q J 7 2
              ♥ 8
              ♦ A 8 7 3 2
              ♣ 8 7 2
```

Answer: No. If opener jumps in a new suit, he is forcing the bidding to game. Given that responder is only showing six points (for a one-over-one response), opener needs a very good 18 or 19 points (not merely 16) before he jumps.

What happened

North jumped in his second suit with insufficient values. He met a predictable fate. Declaring 3NT, his partner received ♦Q lead. He won ♦K and, for want of anything better, led ♠4 to ♠J. West won ♠K and continued with ♦9. Declarer won ♦A, crossed to ♣Q, then led ♠6. East won ♠A and led ♣J. Declarer won dummy's ♣K, cashed ♣A but, when West discarded (a spade), cashed ♥A and resigned. Down three.

S	W	N	E
–	–	1♥	Pass
1♠	Pass	3♣(1)	Pass
3NT	End		

(1) Not worth the game-forcing jump. North would need a good 18 or 19 points.

Contract: 3NT by S
Opening Lead: ♦Q

What should have happened

In the correct contract of 2♣ (by North), declarer wins ♦6 lead with ♦A, crosses to ♥A, trumps ♥2, crosses to ♦K, trumps ♥3, and later comes to ♣AKQ. Contract made.

S	W	N	E
–	–	1♥	Pass
1♠	Pass	2♣	Pass
Pass(1)	Pass		

(1) North's change of suit is not quite forcing, so South is delighted to drop the bidding.

Contract: 2♣ by N
Opening Lead: ♦6

Tip 40 A jump rebid in a new suit by opener is forcing to game, thus should only be done with a very good 18 or 19 points.

Deal 41

We move on to responder's rebid, the fourth bid of an uncontested auction. As we have seen, opener's rebid defines his hand accurately. So responder is in a strong position to judge whether game should be played and in which denomination. Say opener has rebid notrumps – to show a balanced hand with 15–19 points (with less he opened NT; with more he opened 2NT):

```
              ♠ A 7 5 4
              ♥ 6 3
              ♦ K 10 9 3
              ♣ Q 10 4
 ♠ Q 10              N        ♠ J 9 6 3
 ♥ Q 10 9 4                   ♥ J 7
 ♦ 7 4 2        W     E       ♦ A 8 6 5
 ♣ A J 8 2          S         ♣ 7 5 3
              ♠ K 8 2
              ♥ A K 8 5 2
              ♦ Q J
              ♣ K 9 6
```

15–16: He rebid notrumps at the lowest level over responder's new suit.

17–18: He rebid notrumps with a jump over responder's new suit.

19: He rebid 3NT over responder's new suit.

What happened

North made a faulty calculation. Reasoning that, with a below-average hand, he was not strong enough to try for game facing a 1NT rebid, he stopped the auction prematurely.

In just 1NT, declarer (South) received ♣2 lead, which went round to his ♣9. He correctly realized that the suit with the most promising source of extra tricks was *diamonds* (not the longer hearts or spades).

At Trick Two declarer led ♦Q, which East ducked (best). Declarer next led ♦J and overtook with dummy's ♦K (key play) so that he would be in dummy to continue the suit if ♦A was withheld again. In fact East won ♦A and led a second club. West won ♣A and led a third club to declarer's ♣K. Declarer crossed to ♠A, cashed ♦109, then returned to ♥AK and ♠K. Nine tricks made.

What should have happened

As above but in 3NT – game made.

S	W	N	E
1♥	Pass	1♠	Pass
1NT(1)	Pass	Pass(2)	Pass

(1) 15–16 points and a balanced hand.
(2) Incorrect. If South has 16 points, there are 25 (enough to try for game). North should invite game.

Contract: 1NT
Opening Lead: ♣2

S	W	N	E
1♥	Pass	1♠	Pass
1NT	Pass	2NT(1)	Pass
3NT(2)	End		

(1) Invitational. Are you minimum or maximum for your point range?
(2) Accepts the invitation with 16 points.

Contract: 3NT
Opening Lead: ♣2

Tip 41   Think of the combined partnership assets, not merely of your own collection.

Deal 42

Dealer: South   **Vulnerability: Both**

After opener has made two
bids, responder knows
much. If opener is
balanced, he has rebid (or
opened) notrumps to show
his precise point-count. If
opener is unbalanced then
he has three rebid options:
(a) Support responder's
suit with four cards.
(b) Repeat his own suit
with six cards.
(c) Try a new suit.
In (a) and (b) opener is

```
              ♠ K 5 3
              ♥ Q 5 2
              ♦ J 4
              ♣ Q J 10 5 3
  ♠ J 10 8               ♠ 7
  ♥ 10 9 8 4      N      ♥ A K 7 6
  ♦ A 10 3 2   W   E     ♦ 9 7 6 5
  ♣ A 7           S      ♣ K 8 4 2
              ♠ A Q 9 6 4 2
              ♥ J 3
              ♦ K Q 8
              ♣ 9 6
```

able to limit his strength to within narrow bounds. With up to 15 points, he will rebid at
the lowest possible level. With more he will jump.

What happened

Responder, North, did not appreciate that opener had
limited his hand to a minimum by rebidding at the
lowest level. The partnership went overboard and the
defence was merciless.

West led ♥10 and East won ♥K, cashed ♥A, and
switched to ♦9 (the lead of a high spot card denying an
interest in the suit). West won ♦A and sensibly laid
down ♣A (the fourth defensive trick). East played ♣8
('throw high means aye') so West then led his second
club. East won ♣K and, even though he knew declarer
had run out, led a third club.

What could declarer do? If he trumped with ♠9,
West would overtrump. In fact he trumped with ♠Q,
and West discarded. He crossed to ♠K, returned to ♠A,
but West had the third round master. The defence had
organized a perfect trump promotion to extract the
maximum – down three.

What should have happened

2♠ down one if the defence is as hot.

S	W	N	E
1♠	Pass	2♣	Pass
2♠(1)	Pass	4♠(2)	End

(1) Up to 15 points. No more
(or South would rebid 3♠).
(2) Incorrect. North is not
even worth 3♠. He knows
game values are not present.

Contract: 4♠
Opening Lead: ♥10

S	W	N	E
1♠	Pass	2♣	Pass
2♠	Pass	Pass(1)	Pass

(1) Correct. Apart from the
lack of points needed to
try for game, North should
remember the motto: 'Beware
the aceless hand'.

Contract: 2♠
Opening Lead: ♥10

Tip 42 It takes more than a good fit to make game.
It takes high cards: 25 points should be held
without compensating shapely distribution.

Deal 43

Because opener has generally shown his shape and his point count with his first two bids, responder's second bid is usually a simple placement of the final contract. The only time the strength of opener's hand is unlimited is if his rebid is in a new suit. Take the (uncontested) auction 1♥ – 1♠ – 2♣.

Opener has shown an unbalanced hand with

♠	Q J 10 2
♥	A 9 6 4
♦	A 6 5
♣	K 7

♠ 6		♠	7 5 4 3
♥ J 8 5 3	N	♥	K Q 10
♦ K Q 10 7	W E	♦	9 4 3 2
♣ Q 10 9 4	S	♣	J 6

♠	A K 9 8
♥	7 2
♦	J 8
♣	A 8 5 3 2

five(+) hearts and four(+) clubs. Responder's options are (in approximate order of preference and omitting a bid of the fourth suit – a special convention): (i) Support Opener's Major. (ii) Support Opener's Minor. (iii) Repeat his own suit. (iv) Bid notrumps. And here is the crux: he must make these bids at the correct level to show his strength (the auction will be very hit and miss if neither opener nor responder shows his strength at any point). We must revisit –

The Responder Line

Points:	0------5	6---------9	10----------12	13----------
Bid:	Pass	Two	Three	Four

NB: Two includes 1NT; Three includes 2NT; Four includes 3NT.

What happened

North neglected to use The Line. Declaring just 3♠, declarer won ♦K lead with ♦A and correctly set about establishing his clubs. He cashed ♣K, crossed to ♣A, trumped ♣3 with ♠Q (East discarding), led ♠2 to ♠8, trumped ♣5 with ♠J, overtook ♠10 with ♠K (West discarding), and cashed ♠A9 drawing East's last trumps. He tabled the established ♣8 and crossed to ♥A. In spite of the four-one trump split and the four-two club split, declarer made 11 tricks.

What should have happened

The same – but in game. 4♠ plus one.

S	W	N	E
1♣	Pass	1♥	Pass
1♠	Pass	3♠(1)	Pass
Pass(2)	Pass		

(1) Incorrect. This bid shows 10–12 points ...

(2) ...so South is correct to pass.

Contract: 3♠
Opening Lead: ♦K

S	W	N	E
1♣	Pass	1♥	Pass
1♠	Pass	4♠(1)	End

(1) Correct. North knows – with 14 points – that he has enough for game. See The Responder Line.

Contract: 4♠
Opening Lead: ♦K

Tip 43

The only bids that force partner to bid again are bids in new suits. Bids of old suits – even jumps – limit the hand and are non-forcing.

Deal 44

Dealer: South **Vulnerability: Neither**

Say the (uncontested) auction has started with three different suits (e.g. 1♥ – 1♠ – 2♣). Responder's options (in approximate order of preference and omitting a bid of the fourth suit – a special convention) are:

(i) Support opener's major.
(ii) Support opener's minor.
(iii) Repeat his own suit.
(iv) Bid notrumps.

```
              ♠ K J 8 7 4
              ♥ A Q 7
              ♦ J 9 5
              ♣ 10 2
  ♠ 10 5                      ♠ A 9 6 3 2
  ♥ 6 5 2          N          ♥ 8 4
  ♦ A 8 7 2     W     E       ♦ 6 4
  ♣ K Q 7 4        S          ♣ A 8 6 5
              ♠ Q
              ♥ K J 10 9 3
              ♦ K Q 10 3
              ♣ J 9 3
```

Responder must use the following Line in order to limit the strength of his hand:

The Responder Line

Points:	0------5	6---------9	10----------12	13----------
Bid:	Pass	Two	Three	Four

NB: Two includes 1NT; Three includes 2NT; Four includes 3NT.

Say the auction has started 1♥ – 1♠ – 2♦. What should responder bid next with?

♠AQ85	♠KJ742	♠Q9832
♥Q73	♥432	♥KJ6
♦A42	♦752	♦A3
♣Q53	♣Q4	♣J96
4♥	2♥	3♥

Note that just three cards are sufficient to give the delayed support for opener's first suit (known to contain five(+) cards).

What happened

North was correct to give delayed support for hearts, but did not use The Responder Line correctly. In 4♥ declarer, South received ♣K lead from West, then ♣4 to ♣A. East switched to ♦6 to West's ♦A. West returned ♦2 to declarer's ♦Q. Declarer trumped ♣J (with ♥Q) then tried ♠4. But East rose sharply with ♠A to fell declarer's singleton ♠Q. Down one.

What should have happened

Declarer loses the same four tricks in 3♥ – ♠A, ♦A and two clubs. Part score made.

Tip 44 Use The Responder Line unless bidding a new suit.

S	W	N	E
1♥	Pass	1♠	Pass
2♦	Pass	4♥(1)	End

(1) Too much.

Contract: 4♥
Opening Lead: ♣K

S	W	N	E
1♥	Pass	1♠	Pass
2♦	Pass	3♥(1)	Pass
Pass(2)	Pass		

(1) Correct. 10–12 points and three card support.
(2) 12 aceless points facing 10–12.

Contract: 4♥
Opening Lead: ♣K

Deal 45

Dealer: South   **Vulnerability: Both**

Question: Take the uncontested auction:
1♥ – 1♠ – 2♦ – 2♥. Has responder shown genuine support (i.e. three cards) for opener's hearts?

Answer: No. He may have support, but, equally, he may merely be giving preference. There will be many responder hands in the 6–9 point range that have no better alternative.

E.g. 1♥ – 1♠ – 2♦ – ?

All these hands must bid 2♥:

```
(a)♠A8532   (b)♠J9842   (c)♠Q753
   ♥Q3         ♥97          ♥J7
   ♦J4         ♦4           ♦853
   ♣9764       ♣AJ742       ♣A742
```

```
                    ♠ A J 5 3 2
                    ♥ 9 7
                    ♦ 7 2
                    ♣ Q 7 5 3
  ♠ K 8 3                        ♠ Q 10 7
  ♥ K 8 3            N           ♥ A 4 2
  ♦ A 9 8 4      W       E       ♦ J 10 6
  ♣ 10 9 2           S           ♣ K J 8 4
                    ♠ 9 6
                    ♥ Q J 10 6 5
                    ♦ K Q 5 3
                    ♣ A 6
```

None of the three example hands is strong enough to bid at the three level (or 2NT), so it is clear to put partner back to his first choice trump suit – even with hand (c) where responder actually prefers diamonds (a 5–2 fit generally plays better than a 4–3 fit).

What happened

Playing 2NT, North received the inspired ♦J opening lead from East. Leading through dummy's second suit, when strength in all suits has been shown (clubs inferentially by the 2NT bid), is often a good bet. West beat dummy's ♦Q with ♦A and led back ♦4 to ♦10 and ♦K. Seeking to set up hearts, ♥5 was led to ♥9 and ♥A. East led to West's ♥98 and then came a switch to ♣10. This ran to ♣A and ♥Q was led to West's ♥K. West pushed through ♣9 and North covered with ♣Q. East took ♣KJ8 and switched to ♠7 to West's ♠K. North won ♠A but had to lead away from ♠J5 to East's ♠Q10. North had garnered just three tricks! Down five!

S	W	N	E
1♥	Pass	1♠	Pass
2♦	Pass	2NT(1)	End

(1) Too much. This bid shows 10–12 points.

Contract: 2NT by N
Opening Lead: ♦J

What should have happened

In a 2♥ contract on ♣10 lead, declarer could not make fewer than one spade, three trumps, one diamond and one club. At worst down two.

S	W	N	E
1♥	Pass	1♠	Pass
2♦	Pass	2♥(1)	End

(1) Correct. Going back to opener's first suit at the lowest level is often mere preference, rather than actual support. It shows 6–9 points.

Contract: 2♥ by S
Opening Lead: ♣10

Tip 45 Going back to opener's first suit is often mere preference (on a doubleton) rather than genuine support.

Deal 46

Dealer: South   **Vulnerability: East-West**

If partner (opener) and you (responder) have started the auction with three different suits (e.g. 1♥ – 1♠ – 2♦), you have the following options with your rebid:
(i) Support opener's major.
(ii) Support opener's minor.
(iii) Repeat your own suit.
(iv) Bid notrumps.
(v) Bid the fourth suit.
When selecting your option, you do not simply bid at the lowest level (unless using option (v)). You must follow...

```
              ♠ 9 6
              ♥ J 6 4
              ♦ A J 5 3
              ♣ A J 7 4
♠ A K 10 3              ♠ J 8 7 4 2
♥ 8 3           N       ♥ A 9 2
♦ 9 7 2      W     E    ♦ 8 4
♣ 10 9 8 2      S       ♣ 6 5 3
              ♠ Q 5
              ♥ K Q 10 7 5
              ♦ K Q 10 6
              ♣ K Q
```

The Responder Line

Points:	0------5	6---------9	10----------12	13----------
Bid:	Pass	Two	Three	Four

NB: Two includes 1NT; Three includes 2NT; Four includes 3NT.

What happened

North, responder, had two attractive options at his second turn. Opener's 1♥ then 2♦ route showed a five-four shape so he had guarantees of fits in two suits. But he forgot that opener had promised a fifth heart and so the 10-trick game was missed in favour of the 11-trick game.

Defending 5♦, West led ♠A – ace from ace-king is a very powerful lead – and continued with ♠K. At trick three he switched to ♣10 round to declarer's ♣Q, but declarer's task was hopeless. After drawing trumps in three rounds he had to knock out ♥A. Down one.

S	W	N	E
1♥	Pass	2♣	Pass
2♦	Pass	3♦(1)	Pass
5♦	End		

(1) Supporting a major suit is preferable to supporting a minor suit: game requires fewer tricks.

Contract: 5♦
Opening Lead: ♠A

What should have happened

4♥ would have lost the same three tricks, declarer drawing trumps as soon as possible. But losing three tricks in 4♥ means chalking up game! Quite a difference!

S	W	N	E
1♥	Pass	2♣	Pass
2♦	Pass	3♥(1)	Pass
4♥	End		

(1) Correct. His 3♥ bid shows three-card support and 10–12 points.

Contract: 4♥
Opening Lead: ♠A

Tip 46 In the game zone, prefer a major-suit fit to a minor-suit fit.

Deal 47

Modern bidding is so efficient that, barring a very awkward mesh or a slam deal, the first four bids of the partnership should be sufficient to enable a sensible contract to be reached. We are currently focussing on the last of those four bids, responder's rebid. If the first three bids are in different suits (opener thus revealing a five-four shape), responder has the following choices:

(i) Support opener's major.
(ii) Support opener's minor.
(iii) Repeat his own suit.
(iv) Bid notrumps.
(v) Bid the fourth suit.

```
              ♠ A 7 6 3
              ♥ Q 7
              ♦ 8 7
              ♣ A K J 6 5

♠ Q J 4            N            ♠ K 10 5
♥ J 10 6 5                      ♥ 4
♦ A K 9       W        E        ♦ J 10 6 5 3 2
♣ 10 7 2           S            ♣ 9 8 4

              ♠ 9 8 2
              ♥ A K 9 8 3 2
              ♦ Q 4
              ♣ Q 3
```

Options (i) and (ii) are a priority – a known fit. In this deal we look at Option (iii). Responder should have SIX cards to repeat his suit (opener has at most four cards outside his two suits). And he must show his strength using The Responder Line:

Points:	0------5	6---------9	10----------12	13----------
Bid:	Pass	Two	Three	Four

What happened

South (responder) failed to show his strength correctly and a game was missed. In (only) 2♥, West cashed ♦AK and switched to ♠Q (best). Declarer won dummy's ♠A, cashed ♥Q then led to ♥K, East discarding on this trick to reveal the 4–1 trump split. Declarer cashed ♥A then (leaving ♥J out) turned his attention to clubs. He cashed ♣Q, then led to ♣J. He cashed ♣A, both opponents following to reveal the 3–3 split, discarding ♠8 from hand, then led ♣K, discarding ♠9 as West trumped. 10 tricks were made in spite of the bad trump split.

What should have happened

Same tricks, but in 4♥. Game made.

Tip 47

When repeating your six-card suit as responder, jump the bidding when holding 10+ points.

S	W	N	E
–	–	1♣	Pass
1♥	Pass	1♠	Pass
2♥(1)	Pass	Pass(2)	Pass

(1) South is too strong to bid 2♥. Using the Responder Line, this bid shows just 6–9 points.
(2) North has good cards (e.g. ♥Q). But, believing that 25 points are not held, he bows out.

Contract: 2♥
Opening Lead: ♦A

S	W	N	E
–	–	1♣	Pass
1♥	Pass	1♠	Pass
3♥(1)	Pass	4♥	End

(1) Correct. 3♥ shows six cards and 10–12 points.

Contract: 4♥
Opening Lead: ♦A

Deal 48

Dealer: South　　　　　　**Vulnerability: Neither**

Responder should not rush to bid notrumps. It is better for him to bid a suit to a suit, and let opener introduce notrumps. Why? Firstly, subsequent bidding will be smoother; secondly, it pays to have the stronger hand (usually opener) declare a notrump contract. With his first bid, responder should almost never reply 2NT or 3NT to a one-of-a-suit opener.

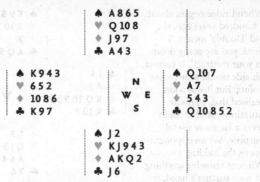

```
              ♠ A 8 6 5
              ♥ Q 10 8
              ♦ J 9 7
              ♣ A 4 3
♠ K 9 4 3              ♠ Q 10 7
♥ 6 5 2        N      ♥ A 7
♦ 10 8 6    W   E    ♦ 5 4 3
♣ K 9 7        S      ♣ Q 10 8 5 2
              ♠ J 2
              ♥ K J 9 4 3
              ♦ A K Q 2
              ♣ J 6
```

Instead he should prefer a simple change-of-suit. There will be some occasions, however, where he will be forced to respond 1NT with 6–9 points, lacking the strength to bid a new suit at the two-level. With his second bid (after three partnership bids in new suits), responder is in a better position to assess when it is likely to be right for him to bid notrumps. But it will still be relatively rare: typically when he has good stoppers in the two suits opener has not bid; when he has no fit for either of opener's suits; and when he has no six-card suit to repeat. He will show his strength as follows:

6----------9	10----------12	13----------
1NT	2NT	3NT

What happened

North preferred to rebid notrumps than show his support for opener's known-to-be five-card major. Unwise! Against 3NT by North, East led ♣5. Dummy's ♣J was covered by West's ♣K, and declarer withheld ♣A. He ducked ♣9 too, but won the third club with ♣A. Needing heart tricks he next led ♥Q, but East grabbed ♥A and cashed ♣Q10. Down one.

S	W	N	E
1♥	Pass	1♠	Pass
2♥	Pass	2NT(1)	Pass
3NT	End		

(1) With a known heart fit – and just one 'stopper' in both partner's unbid suits – this is a misguided rebid.

Contract: 3NT by N
Opening Lead: ♣5

What should have happened

In 4♥, declarer would have just lost three tricks – the second round of both black suits and ♥A. Opportunity wasted!

S	W	N	E
1♥	Pass	1♠	Pass
2♦	Pass	3♥(1)	Pass
4♥	End		

(1) Correct. 3♥ shows three-card support and 10–12 points.

Contract: 4♥ by S
Opening Lead: ♣7

Tip 48　When opener has bid two suits (showing a five-four shape), three cards in his first suit make a fit.

Deal 49

When bridge began, about a hundred years ago, the bid 'Double' meant, 'I think you are going down in your contract'. If correct, his side would score more points. But it was soon realised that, in many situations, double could serve a far more useful purpose. Say an opponent opens the bidding 1♦. Without knowing anything of your partner's hand, it

```
              ♠ K 9 8 6
              ♥ K 10 7 2
              ♦ 7
              ♣ A Q 5 2

♠ J 4                        ♠ A Q 10 7 2
♥ A 3            N           ♥ 5 4
♦ K Q 10 9 5 2  W   E        ♦ J 8
♣ K 10 3            S        ♣ J 9 8 4

              ♠ 5 3
              ♥ Q J 9 8 6
              ♦ A 6 4 3
              ♣ 7 6
```

would be most unlikely that you could be confident enough of defeating the contract to double. Thus doubles of suit bids before partner has spoken are not statements that the contract will fail (so-called 'Penalty, or Business, Doubles'). Rather they are so-called 'Take-out Doubles' asking partner to take out the double into their best suit.

What happened

North forgot to make a take-out double with a hand perfect for the role. He sold out to 2♦. His ♥2 lead went to ♥J and ♥A. Declarer (West) led to ♦J. South won ♦A and switched to ♣7. Declarer played low and North won ♣Q, cashed ♣A and led ♣5 for South to trump. South led ♥6 to North's ♥10 and North led ♣3, South trumping and declarer overtrumping. Declarer cashed ♦K, then led ♠J, running it successfully when North played low. Eight tricks – contract made.

S	W	N	E
–	1♦	Pass(1)	1♠
Pass	2♦	End	

(1) North knew he could not overcall a suit – such a bid would guarantee five cards. But he forgot to say 'Double' for take-out.

Contract: 2♦ by W
Opening Lead: ♥2

What should have happened

If North doubles the 1♦ opener (for take-out), South declares 2♥. West leads ♦K to ♦A and declarer leads ♣6 to ♣Q (the finesse succeeding), cashes ♣A, trumps ♣2, then leads to ♠K. East wins ♠A and leads ♥4 (best). West takes ♥A and leads ♥3. Declarer wins and cross-trumps four more tricks. Contract made with an overtrick.

S	W	N	E
–	1♦	Dble(1)	1♠
2♥(2)	End		

(1) The perfect take-out double: opening points with shortage in the suit opened and support for every other suit.
(2) South knows his partner has a suitable hand.

Contract: 2♥ by S
Opening Lead: ♦K

Tip 49 Doubling a suit opening bid is for take-out.

Deal 50

Dealer: West **Vulnerability: Both**

Until partner has made a positive bid, the double of a suit bid is for take-out. It shows:

Shortage (0, 1, 2 cards) in the suit opened.

Opening points or more.

Support (three(+) cards) in all unbid suits.

Note that all the 'SOS' criteria must be satisfied. It is a common mistake to double an opening bid merely to show opening points, without shortage in the opposing suit and/or support for all unbid suits.

```
                ♠ Q 5
                ♥ J 9 3
                ♦ Q J 10 5
                ♣ A K 8 5
   ♠ A K J                      ♠ 10 4 2
   ♥ 8 4               N        ♥ A K 7 6
   ♦ A K 6 4 2    W       E     ♦ 9 3
   ♣ 7 6 2            S         ♣ 10 9 4 3
                ♠ 9 8 7 6 3
                ♥ Q 10 5 2
                ♦ 8 7
                ♣ Q J
```

What happened

North's inadvisable double of 1♦ met its deserved fate. West cashed ♦AK against South's inelegant 2♠ contract. He continued at Trick Three with ♦4, East astutely trumping it with ♠10 and South frustratedly discarding ♥2. East cashed ♥AK and led ♥6 for West to trump with ♠J. West's ♠AK meant the part-score drifted three down. East-West +300.

S	W	N	E
–	1♦	Dble(1)	1♥
1♠	1NT	Pass	Pass
2♠(2)	End		

(1) An error. North has too many diamonds and not enough spades. Pass is indicated.

(2) Perfectly justified facing a proper double.

Contract: 2♠
Opening Lead: ♦A

What should have happened

If North keeps quiet, West declares 1NT. North leads ♣5 to South's ♣J, winning the trick. South cashes ♣Q and switches to a spade. Declarer rises with ♠K and leads ♦AK and ♦2. North wins ♦J, South discarding a spade, and cashes ♣AK. Declarer has no good discard on the fourth club. To throw either major leaves him potentially vulnerable to a lead of that suit, so he probably discards ♦4. North cashes ♦Q and exits with ♥3. Declarer wins dummy's ♥K and finesses ♠J (not knowing ♠Q is now singleton). North grabs his lone honour – one down and North-South +100.

A 400 point swing on a part-score deal, almost entirely due to North's take-out double.

S	W	N	E
–	1♦	Pass(1)	1♥
Pass	1NT	End	

(1) Just because you have an opening hand does not mean you have to bid after an opponent has opened. Note that a 1NT overcall would show 15–19.

Contract: 1NT by W
Opening Lead: ♣5

Tip 50 You must satisfy all the 'SOS' criteria in order to double an opening bid, not merely have an opening hand.

Deal 51

Dealer: West **Vulnerability: Neither**

The double of an opening bid is for 'take-out', asking partner to bid his best suit. And when I say *asking* what I really mean is *commanding*. For unless the double is cancelled by the next hand bidding, the partner of the doubler MUST bid. Say the bidding proceeds 1♣ – double – pass – ? If the partner of the doubler fails to bid, then the final contract

		♠ A K 6 4	
		♥ A K 7 5	
		♦ Q J 10 4	
		♣ 2	
♠ Q 5		**N**	♠ J 10 8 3 2
♥ Q 3			♥ J 10 8
♦ A K 6	**W**	**E**	♦ 9 7 3
♣ A Q J 10 6 3		**S**	♣ K 9
		♠ 9 7	
		♥ 9 6 4 2	
		♦ 8 5 2	
		♣ 8 7 5 4	

(assuming opener is content) will be 1♣ doubled. And, bearing in mind that the doubler is short in clubs, that contract will probably make easily. Disaster.

What happened

South made the common mistake of not responding to partner's double. Instead of thinking, 'I have no points at all, so how can I bid?', South should have thought, 'I have been commanded to bid whatever the strength of my hand'.

1♣ doubled was never in doubt, with declarer holding six trumps and ♦AK. In fact he made a ninth trick when North simply cashed his ♠AK and ♥AK, enabling declarer to discard his diamond loser on dummy's ♥J. Two doubled overtricks for East-West.

S	W	N	E
–	1♣	Dble	Pass
Pass(1)	Pass		

(1) An error. South must respond!

Contract: 1♣ (Doubled) by W
Opening Lead: ♠A

What should have happened

If South dutifully responds to the double by bidding his best suit (outside clubs), he declares 3♥. West cashes ♦A and switches (say) to ♥3. Declarer rises with ♥K and leads ♦Q (best). West takes ♦K and leads ♥Q. Winning ♥A, declarer cashes ♠AK, trumps ♠4, crosses to ♦10, trumps ♠6, and the defence only subsequently come to a club and ♥J. Contract made for North-South. What a difference!

S	W	N	E
–	1♣	Dble	Pass
1♥(1)	2♣	3♥(2)	End

(1) Because he is forced to speak, South's bid does not imply any strength.
(2) Though he has a powerful hand, North is aware that his partner might have nothing. He therefore cannot go all the way to game.

Contract: 3♥ by S
Opening Lead: ♦A

Tip 51 When partner doubles an opening bid in a suit and the next hand passes, you must respond. Even with nothing.

Deal 52

Dealer: North **Vulnerability: North-South**

There are two basic types of double.

(1) *Take-out.* You are asking partner to take out your double and to bid his best of the unbid suits. The 'SOS' requirements are:
Shortage (0, 1, 2 – occasionally 3 – cards) in suits bid by the opposition.
Opening points or more.
Support (three(+) cards) in unbid suits.

(2) *Penalty.*

```
              ♠ A J 6 4
              ♥ K J 10 6 3
              ♦ 8 5
              ♣ A 3
♠ 9 7 5                      ♠ 8
♥ 9 8 4          N           ♥ A Q 2
♦ A J 10 6   W     E         ♦ K Q 7 4
♣ Q 6 5          S           ♣ K 8 7 4 2
              ♠ K Q 10 3 2
              ♥ 7 5
              ♦ 9 3 2
              ♣ J 10 9
```

You are expressing a confidence that the opposing contract will fail, and expecting your partner to pass and defend. It is vital that partner knows which type of double you are making (of a suit bid). Here is the crux: *If the doubler's partner has not yet bid (pass not counting), double is take-out. If the doubler's partner has bid, double is penalty.*

What happened

West misinterpreted his partner's double, with disastrous consequences.

In 2♠ doubled, declarer (South) won ♣5 led with ♣A, led ♠4 to ♠10, then led ♥5 to ♥10. East won ♥Q, cashed ♣K, then switched to ♦K and ♦4 to ♦10. West led ♥9 to ♥J and ♥A but that was it. Declarer drew trumps and claimed his contract, doubled into game.

S	W	N	E
–	–	1♥	Pass
1♠	Pass	2♠	Dble(1)
Pass	Pass(2)	Pass	

(1) Because West has not yet bid positively, this double is for take-out.
(2) Oops! West misinterprets East's double.

Contract: 2♠ (Doubled) by S
Opening Lead: ♣5

What should have happened

It did not matter that East's double was on the second round of bidding. Because West had not bid, the double requested a bid. In 3♦ (East-West's correct contract), declarer (West) would lose North's (questionable) ♠A lead, win ♥J switch with ♥Q, cross to ♦10, lead ♣5 to ♣K, then lead ♣2 to ♣6, North's ♣A 'beating air'. He wins ♥K return with ♥A, draws two more trumps, cashes ♣Q, trumps ♠7, then follows with ♣87. 11 tricks.

S	W	N	E
–	–	1♥	Pass
1♠	Pass	2♠	Dble(1)
Pass	3♦	End	

(1) A perfect take-out double, asking partner to pick an unbid suit (clubs or diamonds).

Contract: 3♦ by W
Opening Lead: ♠A

Tip 52 If the doubler's partner has not yet bid (pass not counting), double (of a suit bid) is take-out. If the doubler's partner has bid, double is for penalty.

Deal 53

We are focussing on when a double (of a suit bid) is take-out and when it is penalty. Here is the crux: *If the doubler's partner has not yet bid (pass not counting), double is take-out. If the doubler's partner has bid, double is penalty.*

```
              ♠ A
              ♥ J 5 2
              ♦ K 5 2
              ♣ A Q 10 8 4 2
♠ J 8 6              N          ♠ Q 10 9 7
♥ Q                            ♥ A K 9 8 6 3
♦ Q J 10 9     W       E       ♦ A 8
♣ K J 9 7 5         S          ♣ 6
              ♠ K 5 4 3 2
              ♥ 10 7 4
              ♦ 7 6 4 3
              ♣ 3
```

What happened

North was so tempted to express his opinion about clubs that he forgot that his double of the 2♣ bid was for take-out (partner having not bid). The result was unfortunate to say the least...

West led ♥Q against the resulting 2♠ doubled contract. When this held the trick, he switched to ♦Q. Declarer played low from dummy (best), expecting East to hold ♦A, and West continued with ♦J. Again playing low from dummy, East won his bare ♦A. He cashed ♥AK, West discarding clubs, then led a fourth heart (best). Declarer trumped with ♠2, West overtrumped with ♠6, and dummy's bare ♠A took the trick.

Dummy's ♣A was cashed and a second club led. East trumped with ♠9 and declarer discarded ♦6 (overtrumping with ♠K works no better). East led a fifth heart and declarer trumped with ♠3, West overtrumping with ♠8. West led ♦10, East trumping dummy's ♦K with ♠7, then led a sixth heart. Declarer trumped with ♠4 but West overtrumped with ♠J and East held ♠Q10 to declarer's ♠K5. Declarer could only score his ♠K and had garnered just three tricks: ♠AK and ♣A. Down five and 1400 points to East-West!

What should have happened

Had North passed 2♣, East-West would have done rather less well, merely making a quiet 2♥ part score.

S	W	N	E
–	–	–	1♥
Pass	2♣	Dble(1)	2♥
2♠(2)	Pass	Pass	Dble(3)
End			

(1) Mistake. This is a take-out double situation.

(2) South expects to find spade support opposite.

(3) No one is in any doubt this double is for penalty.

Contract: 2♠ (Doubled) by S
Opening Lead: ♥Q

S	W	N	E
–	–	–	1♥
Pass	2♣	Pass(1)	2♥
End			

(1) Double would be take-out, so North passes.

Contract: 2♥ by E
Opening Lead: ♣3

Tip 53

If partner hasn't bid, double of a suit bid asks – commands – him to bid. So don't double if you don't want him to speak!

Deal 54

Dealer: South **Vulnerability: North-South**

We are focussing on when a double is take-out and when it is penalty. If the doubler's partner has not yet bid (pass not counting), double is take-out. If the doubler's partner has bid, double is penalty. But there is a very important exception – *Doubles of notrump bids are for penalty*. This makes logical sense. If a player doubles a 1NT opener, it cannot

```
              ♠ K 10 4 2
              ♥ K 10 9 6
              ♦ 9 8
              ♣ Q 10 6
  ♠ 9 6                      ♠ J 5 3
  ♥ Q 4            N         ♥ 8 7 3 2
  ♦ A K Q J 7 5 3  W   E     ♦ 6 2
  ♣ A 3              S       ♣ J 7 4 2
              ♠ A Q 8 7
              ♥ A J 5
              ♦ 10 4
              ♣ K 9 8 5
```

really be for take-out. In which suit is he short? How can he have adequate support for all four suits? No: the double of a 1NT opener can only be for penalty. It shows a better hand than the opener: 16+ points. His hand does not have to be balanced – many of the biggest penalties come when the doubler has a long suit. The partner of the doubler should tend to pass, as in all penalty double situations. Only if he has a very weak hand with a very long suit should he remove the double.

What happened

Though West was left to play in 2♦ (when North-South could have made a spade contract) and he made his contract (scoring seven trump tricks and ♣A), this was hardly a victory. Can you see what would have happened if East had passed the double?

S	W	N	E
1NT	Dble(1)	Pass	2♣(2)
Pass	2♦	End	

(1) More points to gain by penalizing the opponents than by making a diamond part-score...

(2) ...but East, mistakenly, has other ideas.

Contract: 2♦ by W
Opening Lead: ♦8

What should have happened

East-West would have been defending 1NT doubled. And no prizes for guessing which suit West would lead! He would cash the first seven tricks in his diamond suit and then table ♣A. Down two and 500 points to East-West.

S	W	N	E
1NT	Dble	Pass	Pass(1)
Pass			

(1) East correctly passes. Only weak hands with long suits should remove the double.

Contract: 1NT (Doubled) by S
Opening Lead: ♦A

Tip 54 The double of a 1NT opener is for penalty.

Deal 55

The double of a 1NT opener shows any hand with 16+ points. The partner of the doubler should only remove the double with a weak hand and a long suit. He should leave in the double with a weak hand and no long suit (last deal's common mistake) or with a goodish hand (say six(+) points) and a long suit (this deal's common mistake).

```
              ♠ Q 8 6
              ♥ 9 6 5 2
              ♦ 8 5
              ♣ 8 6 4 3
  ♠ 10 9                    ♠ A K J 5 3
  ♥ A K Q 10 3      N       ♥ 4
  ♦ J 6 4        W     E    ♦ 9 7 3 2
  ♣ A K 9           S       ♣ 7 5 2
              ♠ 7 4 2
              ♥ J 8 7
              ♦ A K Q 10
              ♣ Q J 10
```

What happened

It would have been reasonable for East to have bid 2♠ if ♠AK were ♠42. But not with his actual hand. Expecting less, West passed 2♠ and South led ♦A, continued with ♦KQ, and then ♦10. North overruffed dummy's ♠9 with ♠Q and, though declarer was now in a position to draw trumps and make the remainder, he had only chalked up a part-score with one overtrick.

What should have happened

If East leaves in the double, carnage results. West leads ♥A, then follows with ♥KQ (felling declarer's ♥J), and continues with ♥103. East discards two low clubs and two low diamonds, denying interest in those suits, so West switches to ♠10. Declarer covers with dummy's ♠Q, but East wins ♠K, cashes ♠AJ, and follows with ♠53.

As East cashes his last spade winner, declarer has to discard from ♦A and ♣QJ10. West, discarding after declarer, holds ♦J and ♣AK9. If declarer discards ♦A, West discards ♣9 and wins the last three tricks with ♦J and ♣AK; but if declarer discards ♣10, West discards ♦J and wins the last three tricks with ♣AK9. Either way declarer scores not one single trick, losing 2000 points!

S	W	N	E
1NT	Dble(1)	Pass	2♠(2)
End			

(1) For penalty, showing 16+ points.
(2) Wrong. East is too strong to remove the double.

Contract: 2♠ by E
Opening Lead: ♦A

S	W	N	E
1NT	Dble	Pass	Pass(1)
Pass			

(1) Correct. East should expect a bigger score by defending 1NT doubled.

Contract: 1NT (Doubled) by S
Opening Lead: ♥A

Tip 55 Pass partner's double of 1NT unless you are very weak and shapely.

Deal 56

Dealer: West **Vulnerability: Neither**

Double is the most
underused bid in bridge.
If you play with bidding
boxes in your local club,
look at the red double card.
It's brand new!

```
              ♠ K J 9 7 2
              ♥ J 9 2
              ♦ 10 8 5 3
              ♣ 4
   ♠ 10                      ♠ 8 5 4
   ♥ Q 7 4          N        ♥ A K 8 6 5
   ♦ A K Q 7 4   W     E     ♦ 9 6
   ♣ J 9 8 6         S        ♣ 10 7 3
              ♠ A Q 6 3
              ♥ 10 3
              ♦ J 2
              ♣ A K Q 5 2
```

What happened

South failed to remember to double (showing both the
unbid suits in one go). Instead he bid one of the suits
and hoped to be able to introduce the other later. He's
still waiting.

The defence to 2♣ was perfect. West cashed ♦A and
switched immediately to ♥4. East won ♥K, cashed ♥A,
then, knowing declarer was now out of the suit (West
would have led ♥7 from ♥74), switched back to his
remaining diamond. West won ♦Q and now made
the key play of returning ♦4. East trumped with ♣10
and declarer (unwisely) overtrumped with ♣Q. He
cashed ♣AK and could have settled for down one by
abandoning trumps and running spades. But playing to
make his contract – hoping the two remaining trumps
were one-one – he led a low trump.

Oh dear! West took his ♣9, cashed ♣J (drawing
declarer's last trump), then cashed ♦K7 and ♥Q.
Declarer was down four.

S	W	N	E
–	1♦	Pass	1♥
2♣(1)	End		

(1) Why show just one of your
suits when you can show both
by doubling?

Contract: 2♣ by S
Opening Lead: ♦A

What should have happened

Had South made a take-out double of 1♥, showing both
black suits, North would have declared a spade part-
score and made nine easy tricks, losing just two tricks in
each red suit.

S	W	N	E
–	1♦	Pass	1♥
Dble	2♦	2♠(1)	3♥
3♠	End		

(1) South's double having
shown both black suits, North's
hand is suddenly very useful.

Contract: 3♠ by N
Opening Lead: ♥A

Tip 56 If you have four/five cards in the two unbid suits, double in preference to
bidding one of them (unless you have a decent five-card major, in which case
prefer the overcall).

Deal 57

Dealer: West **Vulnerability: Neither**

The single most common mistake in doubling auctions is responder neglecting to jump the bidding with a decent hand, in reply to partner's take-out double. Here is the crux for responder, when choosing at which level to bid his best unbid suit:

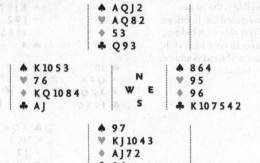

```
              ♠ A Q J 2
              ♥ A Q 8 2
              ♦ 5 3
              ♣ Q 9 3
♠ K 10 5 3              ♠ 8 6 4
♥ 7 6          N        ♥ 9 5
♦ K Q 10 8 4  W   E     ♦ 9 6
♣ A J          S        ♣ K 10 7 5 4 2
              ♠ 9 7
              ♥ K J 10 4 3
              ♦ A J 7 2
              ♣ 8 6
```

Responding to Double Line:

```
0-------------8   9---------12   13-----------
Respond at        Jump          Bid Game
lowest level      a level
```

What happened

South's failure to jump in reply to his partner's take-out double cost his side the opportunity to make a game contract.

In the lowly 1♥ contract, West led ♦K. Declarer won ♦A and immediately finessed ♠J. He was confident that West would hold ♠K from his opening bid (East looked likely to hold a top club because of West's failure to lead from ♣AK, and could hardly hold ♠K in addition). ♠J won, as expected, and now declarer crossed to ♥10 and successfully finessed ♠Q. He cashed ♠A, discarding ♣6, then exited with ♦5 which West took cheaply to lead a second trump (as good as anything).

Declarer won the trump (the even split in the suit revealed), conceded a club, and was able to cross-trump the remaining tricks. 11 tricks, but only a 30 part-score.

What should have happened

The same – but in 4♥. Game made.

S	W	N	E
–	1♦	Dble	Pass
1♥(1)	Pass	Pass(2)	Pass

(1) South would have to reply with absolutely nothing, so must jump when he has 9+ points.
(2) Facing 0–8 points, North is not tempted to bid on. Theoretically a 4♥ game cannot be on.

Contract: 1♥
Opening Lead: ♦K

S	W	N	E
–	1♦	Dble	Pass
2♥(1)	Pass	4♥(2)	End

(1) Correct bid – showing 9–12 points.
(2) Facing a jump response, North is worth game.

Contract: 4♥
Opening Lead: ♦K

Tip 57 Jump in response to partner's take-out double with nine(+) points.

Deal 58

Dealer: North **Vulnerability: East-West**

You suspect the opposing contract may fail. When should you double?

Double: when the opponents have had a faltering auction and you appear to have a nasty surprise about which declarer will be able to do nothing.

Pass: when to double might enable declarer to make a contract (typically because he plays you to have good trumps) in which he would otherwise fail.

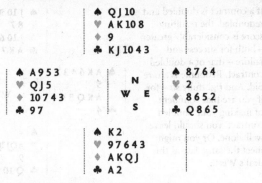

```
                ♠ Q J 10
                ♥ A K 10 8
                ♦ 9
                ♣ K J 10 4 3
    ♠ A 9 5 3              ♠ 8 7 6 4
    ♥ Q J 5         N      ♥ 2
    ♦ 10 7 4 3   W   E     ♦ 8 6 5 2
    ♣ 9 7           S      ♣ Q 8 6 5
                ♠ K 2
                ♥ 9 7 6 4 3
                ♦ A K Q J
                ♣ A 2
```

What happened

West will have wished he had kept his mouth shut! He led ♠A against the doubled slam and followed with ♠3 to declarer's ♠K. Listening to West's double, declarer drew the correct conclusion that West held both the missing trump honours. So he led ♥9 and ran it when West played low. Success! It was now a simple matter to lead to dummy's ♥AK, felling a red-faced West's ♥QJ, and to claim the remainder in top tricks. Doubled slam made.

S	W	N	E
–	–	1♣	Pass
1♥	Pass	3♥	Pass
6♥(1)	Dble(2)	End	

(1) Worth a punt at the small slam, facing jump support from opener.
(2) Unwisely giving away the trump position.

Contract: 6♥ (Doubled)
Opening Lead: ♠A

What should have happened

Had West kept quiet, declarer would not have run ♥9. Instead he would have led to dummy's ♥AK, hoping for an even split. He would have gone down one.

If West's double had worked he would have won 100 points instead of 50. But by allowing declarer to make his slam, when he would otherwise have failed, his double turned +50 into -1210 (Chicago/Duplicate scoring). Gaining 50 (net) but losing 1260 (net) means he would need to defeat the contract 25 times out of 26 to profit by his double. Poor odds!

S	W	N	E
–	–	1♣	Pass
1♥	Pass	3♥	Pass
6♥	Pass(1)	Pass	Pass

(1) Sensibly keeping quiet.

Contract: 6♥
Opening Lead: ♠A

Tip 58 Do not double a contract (for penalties) when to do so will tip declarer off and possibly enable him to make a contract in which he would otherwise have failed.

Deal 59

Dealer: West

Vulnerability: Both

If a contract is doubled and redoubled, the resulting score is considerably greater – both for success and failure – than that of a doubled contract. Redouble is a rare bid. And rightfully so – for if you are that confident of making your doubled contract, you should leave well alone. Or you might meet the same fate as this deal's West...

```
              ♠ J 10 9 8
              ♥ 8 7
              ♦ J 10 6 3
              ♣ A K 7
♠ A K 6 4 3 2              ♠ Q 7 5
♥ 5            N          ♥ K 4
♦ A K Q 8 4  W   E        ♦ 7 5 2
♣ 4            S          ♣ J 8 6 3 2
              ♠ —
              ♥ A Q J 10 9 6 3 2
              ♦ 9
              ♣ Q 10 9 5
```

What happened

Once he received support, West felt certain he could make 4♠ (doubled). But it was a mistake to redouble: South quickly ran back to hearts.

Defending 5♥ (unwisely doubled), West led ♦A and followed with ♦K. Declarer trumped, crossed to ♣K, then led ♥8, running it successfully, and a second heart to ♥K and ♥A. After cashing all bar one trump, he moved to clubs.

Declarer led to dummy's ♣A and saw West discard. So he took the marked finesse against East's ♣J, leading to his ♣10. Able to claim the rest in top tricks, he had notched up a doubled overtrick. N–S +1050 (Chicago/Duplicate scoring).

S	W	N	E
–	1♠	Pass	2♠
4♥	4♠	Dble(1)	Pass
Pass	Redble(2)	Pass	Pass
5♥(3)	Dble(4)	End	

(1) Reasonable – with three likely defensive tricks in the form of ♠J and ♣AK.
(2) Greedy. West should pass and collect!
(3) Tipped off by the redouble.
(4) Reluctantly. Regretting his redouble!

Contract: 5♥ (Doubled) by S
Opening Lead: ♦A

What should have happened

Had West left well alone, he would have declared 4♠ doubled. North would lead ♣A and try to cash ♣K. After trumping, declarer (West) leads to ♠Q (South discarding). He then switches to diamonds, cashing ♦AKQ and trumping ♦4 in dummy, North following helplessly. He leads to ♠AK and plays the established ♦8. All the defence make is master ♠J and ♥A to go with the earlier ♣A. 10 tricks and East-West +790 (Chicago/Duplicate scoring).

West's redouble swung an enormous 1840 points to North-South!

S	W	N	E
–	1♠	Pass	2♠
4♥	4♠	Dble	End

Contract: 4♠ (Doubled) by W
Opening Lead: ♣A

Tip 59 Do not redouble, even if confident of making, if the opponents might then run to cheaper havens.

Deal 60

Dealer: East   **Vulnerability: North-South**

Redouble may be a rare
bid. But it does have a
function. If you redouble
partner's opening bid
(when doubled) you show
10+ points. This can pave
the way for a lucrative
penalty.

```
              ♠ 10 9 7 6 3
              ♥ 8 4
              ♦ 10 7 3
              ♣ Q 7 4

    ♠ J 4                      ♠ A K 5 2
    ♥ A 7 5 3         N        ♥ K J 2
    ♦ A J 6 5 2    W     E     ♦ 9 4
    ♣ 8 5             S        ♣ K J 10 9

              ♠ Q 8
              ♥ Q 10 9 6
              ♦ K Q 8
              ♣ A 6 3 2
```

What happened

West omitted to redouble, and his side sailed into 3NT,
declared by East. This contract made easily, South
leading ♣2 to ♣Q and declarer's ♣K. ♣J was returned
and South won ♣A and switched in desperation to ♥6.
This ran to ♥J and declarer now had nine top tricks via
♠AK, ♥AKJ, ♦A and ♣K109. He actually made a tenth.
East-West +430 (Chicago/Duplicate scoring).

S	W	N	E
–	–	–	1♠
Dble	2♦(1)	Pass	2NT
Pass	3NT	End	

(1) Missed opportunity. West
should redouble.

Contract: 3NT by E
Opening Lead: ♣2

What should have happened

Had West redoubled his partner's 1♠ opener, North-
South would have had no way out of trouble, ending
up in 2♣ doubled declared by South. West would lead
♣5 (best to lead a trump when partner has doubled a
part-score) to ♣4, East's ♣9 and declarer's ♣2 (best).
♦9 switch (best) goes to ♦Q and West's ♦A; ♣8 return
goes to ♣7, ♣10, ♣A. With nothing appealing to
do, declarer leads back ♣3 to ♣Q and East wins ♣K,
cashes ♣J (West discarding two hearts), then leads ♦4.
Declarer wins ♦K but that is his last trick! Say he exits
with ♦8. West wins ♦J, cashes ♦65, and the defence
take the last four tricks with ♠AK and ♥AK.

   Declarer makes just two tricks – six down and 1700
points to East-West. Rather better than collecting a
non-vulnerable game!

S	W	N	E
–	–	–	1♠
Dble	Redble(1)	Pass	Pass
2♣	Pass	Pass	Dble
End			

(1) 10+ points, generally
without a prime fit for
partner (or you would simply
support). By redoubling,
you hope to penalise the
opponents.

Contract: 2♣ (Doubled) by S
Opening Lead: ♣5

Tip 60 Redouble of partner's opening bid when doubled shows 10+ points and good
defence.

Deal 61

Last deal we saw the redouble of an opening bid (when doubled) pave the way for a 1700 point penalty. But it is not right to make such a redouble every time you hold 10+ points. With a good suit, you should simply bid it (natural and forcing – as though there had been no double). And with a fit for partner, you should immediately support to the requisite level – as East learned to his cost!

```
              ♠ A Q 10 5
              ♥ 6
              ♦ Q 9 7 6 4
              ♣ A J 9
  ♠ K 7                      ♠ 6 3
  ♥ K J 10 9 4       N       ♥ A Q 5 2
  ♦ K 3          W       E   ♦ A 5
  ♣ K 10 4 2         S       ♣ Q 8 7 6 3
              ♠ J 9 8 4 2
              ♥ 8 7 3
              ♦ J 10 8 2
              ♣ 5
```

What happened

By redoubling, East allowed North-South to find their spade fit, enabling South to bid on to 4♠ over 4♥. After doubling, West led ♥J to East's ♥A and East switched to ♦A and ♦5 to West's ♦K. West next led ♣2 but declarer rose with ♣A, trumped ♣9, then ran ♠9. When it held, he led ♠4 to ♠K and ♠A and was able to claim the rest using the winning diamonds. North-South +790 (Chicago/Duplicate scoring).

S	W	N	E
–	1♥	Dble	Redble(1)
1♠	Pass	2♠	4♥(2)
4♠	Double	End	

(1) What's the point? North-South are bound to bid and you will have to bid 4♥ next time...

(2) ...but next time is too late as South now knows to try 4♠ (having heard North's support).

Contract: 4♠ (Doubled) by S
Opening Lead: ♥J

What should have happened

When holding a good fit with partner's opening (such as East), there is no reason not to jump support immediately. It is not a misfit deal so there will be no juicy penalty waiting. A jump to 4♥ would silence North-South.

Declaring 4♥, West wins ♦6 lead with ♦A, draws trumps in three rounds, then leads ♣2 to ♣9 and ♣Q. He returns ♣3 and North can make ♣AJ but cannot attack spades from his side. Eventually declarer discards a spade on dummy's established fifth club. 10 tricks and East-West +620 (Chicago/Duplicate scoring). Big swing!

S	W	N	E
–	1♥	Dble	4♥
End			

Contract: 4♥ by W
Opening Lead: ♦6

Tip 61 Do not redouble partner's opening bid (when doubled) if you have a good fit. Instead support to your limit.

Deal 62

Our new topic is
Preemptive Bidding. In
the dictionary, the word
'preemption' means 'the
taking of something before
it is offered to others'. That
'something' in Bridge is
bidding space. When you
hold a weak hand and a
very long suit (typically
seven cards), you do not
need a dialogue in the
auction with partner.
Rather, there is only one

```
              ♠ J 10 5 3
              ♥ Q 8 6 4
              ♦ K Q J
              ♣ 6 5
♠ A K                        ♠ Q 9 8 6
♥ 10 9 7 2         N         ♥ A 5 3
♦ 9 6 4 3 2    W     E       ♦ 10 8 7 5
♣ Q 3             S          ♣ 4 2
              ♠ 7 4 2
              ♥ K J
              ♦ A
              ♣ A K J 10 9 8 7
```

suit which you desire to be trumps. By immediately bidding that suit at a high level (when
opening, this is typically the three-level), partner will realize your lack of interest in other
suits; and crucially your opponents, who rate to hold good cards (you do not), will have
to start bidding at an uncomfortably high level.

What happened

South preempted with far too strong a hand. West
led ♠A against the 3♣ contract. He cashed ♠K, then
switched to ♥10. East took ♥A, cashed ♠Q (West
discarding ♦2), then found the key play of leading his
fourth spade. West's ♣Q now had to score a trick via a
trump promotion (if declarer trumped low, West would
overtrump with ♣Q; if declarer trumped with ♣A or
♣K, West would discard and wait to score ♣Q later).
Down one.

S	W	N	E
3♣(1)	End		

(1) Wrong. A three-level
opener should contain less
than opening points.

Contract: 3♣ by S
Opening Lead: ♠A

What should have happened

Correct bidding sees North declare 3NT. With ♣Q
dropping under ♣AK, he scores up his contract via
seven clubs, ♦A, and a heart. The best the defence can
do is score ♠AKQ and ♥A. Game made.

S	W	N	E
1♣(1)	Pass	1♥	Pass
3♣(1)	Pass	3NT	End

(1) By opening 1♣ and
rebidding with a jump to
3♣, South shows six/seven
clubs and 16 or so points.
This enables North to try
for game, and he sensibly
chooses 3NT as it requires
two fewer tricks than 5♣.

Contract: 3NT by N
Opening Lead: ♠6

Tip 62 An opening bid at the three-level shows less than opening points.

Deal 63

An opening bid at the three-level is preemptive – designed to make life awkward for the opposition. It shows a hand with less than opening points but a good seven-card suit. The bid is made with the expectation of failing in the contract, but losing fewer points than a likely successful opposing contract. However, whereas failing by a trick or two is good Bridge, failing

```
                  ♠ K 10 7 3 2
                  ♥ K 6 5 3 2
                  ♦ 7 5 4
                  ♣ -
  ♠ 9 6 5                      ♠ A Q 8 4
  ♥ J 10            N          ♥ A Q 9 8
  ♦ A K J       W     E        ♦ 10 9 6 2
  ♣ K J 10 9 4      S          ♣ Q
                  ♠ J
                  ♥ 7 4
                  ♦ Q 8 3
                  ♣ A 8 7 6 5 3 2
```

by more is too expensive. Holding a good suit ensures against the latter possibility.
Question: Which suit would you prefer to hold for a preempt? AK65432 or QJ109876?
Answer: The second. It provides five certain tricks whatever the opposing split. The first holding is totally dependent on their split – if one opponent holds five cards you have three losers.

What happened

South preempted with too poor a suit. Declaring the unfortunate contract of 3♣ doubled, he received ♦A lead. With East signalling discouragement with ♦2 ('throw low means no'), West switched to ♥J to ♥K and ♥A. East returned ♦10 to ♦Q and West's ♦K. West cashed ♦J and ♥10, then switched to ♠9 to ♠K and ♠A. Declarer still had four trump losers to come and that meant he ended up with just three tricks. Down six and 1400 points to East-West!

S	W	N	E
3♣(1)	Pass	Pass	Dble(2)
Pass	Pass(3)	Pass	

(1) 'Aces and spaces'. Just one honour in the suit is inadequate for a three-level opener.
(2) Take-out...
(3) ...but converted into penalties by West.

Contract: 3♣ (Doubled) by S
Opening Lead: ♦A

What should have happened

Left to their own devices, East-West would have a quiet Stayman auction to 3NT and would make 11 – even 12 – tricks. East-West +460.

S	W	N	E
Pass	1NT	Pass	2♣(1)
Pass	2♦(2)	Pass	3NT
End			

(1) Stayman – asking for four-card majors.
(2) No four-card major.

Contract: 3NT by W
Opening Lead: ♠3

Tip 63 You always need a good suit in order to preempt: look at the tens and nines too.

Deal 64

Dealer: East   **Vulnerability: North-South**

We have observed that
an opening bid at the
three-level is preemptive:
designed to rob the
opponents of bidding
space; perhaps to steal
the bidding from them;
perhaps to push them too
high. The bid shows a hand
with less than opening
points and a good suit.
A good guideline for suit
quality is at least two of
the ace, king and queen or

```
              ♠ Q J 7 5
              ♥ A 8 6 5 3
              ♦ Q J 10
              ♣ 3
  ♠ 4 2                      ♠ 9
  ♥ J 10 9          N        ♥ K Q 4
  ♦ K 8 6 5     W     E      ♦ 7 2
  ♣ A K 7 6        S         ♣ Q J 10 9 8 5 2
              ♠ A K 10 8 6 3
              ♥ 7 2
              ♦ A 9 4 3
              ♣ 4
```

at least three of the ace, king, queen, jack and ten. Thus AQxxxxx and QJ10xxxx are OK;
but AJxxxxx and Q10xxxxx are not. There is a rumour – from I know not where – that an
'outside ace' is required to preempt. Frankly, this is nonsense!

What happened

East gave as his excuse for failing to open 3♣, 'but I had
no outside ace'. Why is that of relevance? South ended
up defending 4♠. West led ♣A and switched to ♥J.
Declarer won dummy's ♥A, drew trumps finishing in
dummy then ran ♦Q. This lost to ♦K and West led a
second heart to East's ♥Q. The defence had scored three
tricks but that was it. Declarer could trump the third
heart and claim the remainder. North-South +620.

S	W	N	E
–	–	–	Pass(1)
1♠	Pass	4♠(2)	End

(1) Wrong. The lack of an
'outside ace' is not a proper
reason not to preempt. East
should open 3♣.
(2) Seven Losing Tricks.
Enough to jump to game.

Contract: 4♠ by S
Opening Lead: ♣A

What should have happened

Had East opened 3♣, West would have bid 5♣ and
pushed North-South overboard. Yes – 5♣ would have
failed by one trick – but it is natural for North-South
to try for the vulnerable game. 5♠ would lose the same
three tricks as 4♠ – ♣A, ♦K and a heart. East-West
+100. Big swing!

S	W	N	E
–	–	–	3♣(1)
3♠	5♣(2)	5♠	End

(1) Correct. A perfect hand for
preempting.
(2) With an 11-card fit, West
puts the pressure on by
bidding for 11 tricks, the
'level of the fit'.

Contract: 5♠ by S
Opening Lead: ♣A

Tip 64 You do NOT need an outside ace in order to preempt.

Deal 65

Dealer: East

Vulnerability: Neither

When opening preemptively – to show a very long suit and fewer than opening points – you can open at a higher level than three. With a seven-card suit, it is sensible to open at that three-level. To open higher would be too rash. But with an eighth card, a four-level preempt is preferable (provided the suit quality is good). That extra level of bidding space you take away from the opponents can make all the difference.

```
                    ♠ A 9
                    ♥ 6 4 2
                    ♦ Q J 10 7
                    ♣ K 9 8 4
         ♠ 5 3                    ♠ K Q J 10 8 7 4 2
         ♥ 10 9 8        N        ♥ J
         ♦ A K 6 5 2   W   E      ♦ 9 4
         ♣ Q 10 6        S        ♣ J 5
                    ♠ 6
                    ♥ A K Q 7 5 3
                    ♦ 8 3
                    ♣ A 7 3 2
```

What happened

East opened just 3♠ with his good eight-card suit. This allowed South to overcall 4♥ and play there. West led ♦A, followed with ♦K, then led a third diamond. This was best defence – as was East ruffing with ♥J. The crux had arrived.

Had declarer fallen for the temptation to overtrump with ♥Q, he would have failed. West's trump holding would have been promoted into a trick and the defence would also have scored a third-round club trick with ♣Q.

But, craftily, declarer did not overtrump, instead discarding a club (key play). He won East's ♠K switch with dummy's ♠A. He drew West's trumps with his ♥AKQ, then cashed ♣A, crossed to ♣K and discarded his last low club on the master ♦Q. 10 tricks and game made. North-South +420. (Chicago/Duplicate scoring).

What should have happened

Had East opened 4♠, he would probably have stolen the pot. He would have lost just ♠A, ♥A and ♣AK. Down one – North-South +50. An excellent sacrifice.

S	W	N	E
–	–	–	3♠(1)
4♥	Pass	Pass	Pass(2)

(1) Mistake. With eight very good spades, a 4♠ opening bid is indicated.
(2) But at least he is consistent. Once you have preempted, you should not bid again.

Contract: 4♥ by S
Opening Lead: ♦A

S	W	N	E
–	–	–	4♠(1)
End			

(1) Correct. If his partner has absolutely nothing, this contract will go three down (doubled). But in that scenario East-West can make a Grand Slam!

Contract: 4♠ by E
Opening Lead: ♥A

Tip 65 Open at the four-level with a weak hand and a good eight-card suit.

Deal 66

Dealer: East **Vulnerability: Neither**

You are ready to preempt – by opening the bidding at the three (four) level – when an opponent opens in front of you.

Question: Can you preempt any more and, if so, at what level?

Answer: Yes, but you must miss out two lower levels of your suit.

E.g. you hold

```
        ♠ K765
        ♥ K832
        ♦ K932
        ♣ 5

♠ QJ              N         ♠ A10432
♥ QJ7                       ♥ A1095
♦ J1076      W       E      ♦ AQ4
♣ AQ108           S         ♣ 2

        ♠ 98
        ♥ 64
        ♦ 85
        ♣ KJ97643
```

E.g. you hold ♠ 73
            ♥ 94
            ♦ KQJ10632
            ♣ 72

Your right-hand opponent opens (a) 1♣, (b) 1♥. What do you bid?

(a) Overcall 3♦. Because this is a double jump, it is preemptive. It shows the same hand-type as an opening 3♦, i.e. seven good cards and less than opening points.

(b) Pass. To preempt, you would have to miss two lower levels (2♦ and 3♦) and hence bid 4♦. Like an opening bid of 4♦, this would imply eight cards so, lacking the high-card strength for a simple overcall, you should opt out.

What happened

South knew he had to bid 4♣ in order to preempt over East's 1♠ opener. But the wisdom (or lack of it) of this manoeuvre was soon self-evident.

West led ♠Q to ♠K and ♠A. East returned ♠3 to ♠J and West switched to ♥Q. This went to ♥K and ♥A and ♥5 was returned to ♥J. West switched to ♦J to ♦K and ♦A and East cashed ♦Q. With West unavoidably having to score all his four trump tricks, the contract ended up down seven! 1700 points to East-West!

S	W	N	E
			1♠
4♣(1)	Dble	End	

(1) With a broken suit and the overrated 7222 shape, it is a marginal 3♣ opener. Unable to bid 3♣ after East's opener (the single jump overcall would show strength), South should pass.

Contract: 4♣ (Doubled) by S
Opening Lead: ♠Q

What should have happened

East-West bid peacefully to 3NT and make their non-vulnerable game (with overtricks). Somewhat cheaper for North-South.

S	W	N	E
			1♠
Pass(1)	2♣	Pass	2♥
Pass	3NT	End	

(1) Correctly goes quietly.

Contract: 3NT by W
Opening Lead: ♦2

Tip 66 You can preempt after an opposing opener – provided you miss out two lower levels of your bid – but must have the same quality and length of suit as a preemptive opening bid at that level.

Deal 67

Dealer: West **Vulnerability: Neither**

You can only preempt after an opponent has opened if you miss out two lower bids of your suit. Thus, over a 1♦ opener, you can bid 3♥ but not 3♣. A single-jump overcall (e.g. 1♥ – 3♣) shows a good opening bid (about 14–16 points) with an excellent six (seven) card suit.

```
                 ♠ 7
                 ♥ 8 3 2
                 ♦ 9 2
                 ♣ K Q 10 8 5 3 2

    ♠ A 10 8 2          N          ♠ Q J 6 5
    ♥ K Q J 10 5                   ♥ 7 6
    ♦ K 10         W       E       ♦ A J 8 7 6
    ♣ A 4                          ♣ 7 6
                        S
                 ♠ K 9 4 3
                 ♥ A 9 4
                 ♦ Q 5 4 3
                 ♣ J 9
```

What happened

North forgot that he needed to miss out two levels in order to preempt over West's 1♥ opener. South naturally played North to have a much better hand than he actually held and the whole episode ended in tears (metaphorically speaking – it was actually laughter being a light-hearted game).

Defending 3NT doubled, West led ♥K. Declarer kept ♥A back, but West continued with ♥Q and then ♥J, ♥A winning the third round as East discarded an encouraging ♦8. At Trick Four declarer led ♣J, hoping the defence would take ♣A. No: West was going for a big set, so ducked. Declarer forlornly led a second club to West's ♣A, but he was now severed from dummy's clubs, having no more cards in the suit in his hand.

West cashed his two winning hearts, then switched to ♦K (in response to his partner's positive signal in the suit). When this held the trick he continued with ♦10 to ♦A. East switched to ♠Q through declarer's ♠K and declarer could not win a single further trick! All he scored was ♥A and ♣J. Down seven – a loss of 1700 points!

What should have happened

North keeps quiet and East-West sail into 4♠, almost certain to make, with at most a trump, ♥A and a club to lose. Somewhat cheaper for North-South, however.

S	W	N	E
–	1♥	3♣(1)	Pass
3NT(2)	Dble	End	

(1) Mistake. Theoretically this single-jump overcall shows 14–16 points with an excellent suit.
(2) Worth a go facing what he ought to be facing!

Contract: 3NT (Doubled) by S
Opening Lead: ♥K

S	W	N	E
–	1♥	Pass(1)	1♠
Pass	4♠	End	

(1) The preemptive bid is 4♣ (missing two lower levels). Not worth this (no eighth card); North passes.

Contract: 4♠ by E
Opening Lead: ♦3

Tip 67 A double jump overcall (missing out two lower levels) is preemptive but a single jump overcall is (without prior arrangement) a strong bid.

Deal 68

Dealer: North **Vulnerability: Neither**

When you have bid preemptively – such as opening 3♠ or making a double-jump overcall of 3♠ – you have revealed your hand. You are saying, 'This is what I've got. Now you take over, partner'. So, after preempting, you should not bid again.

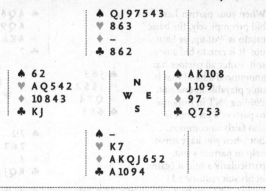

```
              ♠ Q J 9 7 5 4 3
              ♥ 8 6 3
              ♦ –
              ♣ 8 6 2
  ♠ 6 2                      ♠ A K 10 8
  ♥ A Q 5 4 2        N       ♥ J 10 9
  ♦ 10 8 4 3      W     E    ♦ 9 7
  ♣ K J              S       ♣ Q 7 5 3
              ♠ –
              ♥ K 7
              ♦ A K Q J 6 5 2
              ♣ A 10 9 4
```

What happened

North did not envisage tabling his hand as dummy to a 3NT contract – his hand was most unsuited. But, and this is the crux, South knew what North held and decided to play 3NT. It was not up to North even to think, let alone to bid.

East was delighted to double North's erroneous removal to 4♠. This contract stood no chance. East's ♥J lead went to ♥K and West's ♥A. West returned ♥4 to East's ♥9. East continued with ♥10 and West overtook it with ♥Q to lead ♥2. Declarer trumped with ♠7 and East overtrumped with ♠8. He switched to ♣3 and declarer won dummy's ♣A, cashed ♦AK discarding his two remaining clubs, trumped ♣4, and led ♠Q. East won ♠K and exited with ♣Q. Declarer ruffed but had to lose two more trump tricks to East's ♠A10. Down four – 800 points to East-West.

What should have happened

Had North passed 3NT, West would have led ♥4, to East's ♥9 and declarer's ♥K. Declarer would cash his seven diamonds and ♣A. Nine tricks – game made. Admittedly an opening spade lead from West and a heart switch through ♥K would defeat 3NT (by four tricks!) but how likely is that?

S	W	N	E
–	–	3♠(1)	Pass
3NT(2)	Pass	4♠(3)	Dble
End			

(1) Minimum values, but just about acceptable.
(2) Good bid. South has nine almost certain tricks on an opening heart lead around to ♥K.
(3) Mistake. Having preempted, it was not up to North to bid again.

Contract: 4♠ (Doubled) by N
Opening Lead: ♥J

S	W	N	E
–	–	3♠	Pass
3NT	End		

Contract: 3NT by S
Opening Lead: ♥4

Tip 68 After preempting, do not bid again.

Deal 69

When your partner has bid preemptively, the basic motto is 'Put up, or Shut up!' It is rare to bid a new suit – after all partner has announced a hand that is only playable in one suit. Bidding 3NT in response to partner's preempt is also fairly uncommon. But when you have some help in partner's suit, particularly a minor (game in his suit requiring 11

```
              ♠ A Q 6 4
              ♥ A Q 9
              ♦ A K 6 5 2
              ♣ 7
  ♠ J 8 3                    ♠ K 10 9 5
  ♥ J 8 5 2        N         ♥ K 10 4
  ♦ Q 7 4      W     E       ♦ J 10 9 8
  ♣ 6 5 3          S         ♣ A 8
              ♠ 7 2
              ♥ 7 6 3
              ♦ 3
              ♣ K Q J 10 9 4 2
```

tricks), 3NT can be a wise choice. That help should mean that his suit can run for its seven tricks; thus only two outside tricks are needed for the nine-trick game. However, when you have no help for partner's suit, 3NT is fraught. Unless you have a running suit of your own (see last deal), how will you garner nine tricks?

What happened

North learnt his lesson. He should have reasoned that he held a useful hand – with his top cards – for a club contract; but not for notrumps with no source of tricks of his own and holding inadequate help in clubs. 3NT drifted two down, the clubs wasted for the lack of an entry, but...

S	W	N	E
3♣	Pass	3NT(1)	End

(1) Mistake. With no fit for clubs, from where will nine tricks come?

Contract: 3NT by N
Opening Lead: ♦J

What should have happened

...5♣ would have played well. In 5♣ on, say, ♥2 lead from West, declarer plays ♥9 from dummy and loses to East's ♥10. Unable to attack either major from his side, East switches to ♦J. Declarer wins dummy's ♦K and trumps ♦2 as a first stage to establishing the length. He then leads ♣K. East wins ♣A and can do no better than return ♣8. Declarer wins, draws the last trump, crosses to ♥A, cashes ♦A (discarding ♥7), trumps ♦5, crosses to ♠A then cashes the established ♦6, discarding ♠7. All his remaining cards are trumps. Game made.

S	W	N	E
3♣	Pass	5♣(1)	End

(1) Correct. Partner's clubs plus his top cards should give a 5♣ contract a chance.

Contract: 5♣ by S
Opening Lead: ♥2

Tip 69 When partner has preempted, 'put up or shut up'.

Deal 70

'Put up or shut up' is the basic motto for a preemptor's partner. Either support or keep quiet. Say partner opens 3♥. What should the following example hands for responder do?

(1)	(2)	(3)
♠KQJ	♠A863	♠A863
♥74	♥74	♥–
♦QJ86	♦A752	♦AK73
♣KQJ8	♣AQ4	♣AQ742

```
              ♠ K Q J
              ♥ 7 4
              ♦ Q J 8 6
              ♣ K Q J 8

  ♠ A 10 4 2          ♠ 9 6 5 3
  ♥ 9 6        N       ♥ A 5
  ♦ A K 9 4  W   E     ♦ 10 5
  ♣ 6 4 3       S      ♣ A 10 9 7 5

              ♠ 8 7
              ♥ K Q J 10 8 3 2
              ♦ 7 3 2
              ♣ 2
```

Give partner, say, ♥KQJ10xxx and nothing outside. See if you can judge the potential of the two hands in each case.

(1) Should Pass. Not 4♥ (see featured deal) and not 3NT. 3NT is almost sure to fail – the defence can hold up their ♥A until the second round to render the preemptor's hand useless; in any event they have four aces plus ♦K to take.

(2) Should bid 4♥. Fewer points than (1) but much more useful ones. Aces are sure to be worth something facing a preempt. Queens and jacks ('quacks') far less so.

(3) Should bid 4♥. Yes; even with a void heart. Partner's 3♥ bid in effect says, 'I've got the hearts, have you got top cards outside?'

What happened

North, holding Hand (1), tried 4♥. He soon saw the error of his ways. West led ♦A and East signalled with ♦10 ('throw high means aye'). West cashed ♦K and led ♦9 for East to trump. East cashed ♣A, led to his partner's ♠A and waited for ♥A. Down three.

S	W	N	E
3♥	Pass	4♥(1)	End

(1) Mistake. Look at all those useless 'quacks' (queens and jacks). Pass is indicated.

Contract: 4♥
Opening Lead: ♦A

What should have happened

North passes 3♥ and the opponents receive fewer penalty points.

S	W	N	E
3♥	Pass	Pass(1)	End

(1) Correct. A useful guideline when deciding whether to 'Put up or shut up' is to count your aces and kings and discount 'quacks' (outside partner's suit); to raise a 3♥/3♠ preempt to 4♥/4♠ when holding at least 12 such points.

Contract: 3♥
Opening Lead: ♦A

Tip 70   Ignore 'quacks' outside trumps when considering raising a preemptor (hoping to make the contract).

Deal 71

We have learnt that the responder to a preemptor should either 'put up or shut up'; that he should put up, say, a 3♥ preempt to 4♥ when he has opening points discounting queens and jacks outside partner's suit. So far so good. But it can also be right for responder to put partner up with far less. If he has a good fit and a weak hand, he knows that his partner is

```
              ♠ K 6 3
              ♥ A 7
              ♦ J 3
              ♣ 9 7 6 4 3 2
    ♠ 9 5                    ♠ 7
    ♥ Q 6 4 3      N         ♥ K J 10 9 5 2
    ♦ K Q 10 7 6  W   E      ♦ A 9 8
    ♣ K Q         S         ♣ A 10 5
              ♠ A Q J 10 8 4 2
              ♥ 8
              ♦ 5 4 2
              ♣ J 8
```

on the right track in trying to spoil the bidding for the opposition (who are, under those circumstances, sure to have a big contract on their way). In these situations, responder should raise to increase the barrage effect. An easy and effective rule of thumb is to 'bid to the level of the fit'. In other words work out how many cards are held by your partnership in that suit (assuming partner for seven) and bid for that number of tricks.

What happened

By passing his partner's preempt, North let the cat out of the bag. Though he bid later, the opponents had already found their fit and could now bid on to 5♥. This contract made easily – declarer (East) drawing trumps as soon as possible, and losing just ♠A and ♥A. East-West +650 (Chicago/Duplicate scoring).

S	W	N	E
3♠	Pass	Pass(1)	4♥
Pass	Pass	4♠(2)	Pass
Pass	5♥	End	

(1) Mistake. North's pass lets the opponents in the auction.
(2) Too late!

Contract: 5♥ by E
Opening Lead: ♠A

What should have happened

Had North immediately raised to 4♠, he would probably have stolen the pot. His partner would lose two diamonds and two clubs to go one down – but big deal. Losing 50 points in 4♠ is rather better than seeing East-West notch up game.

S	W	N	E
3♠	Pass	4♠(1)	End(2)

(1) Correct to increase the preempt. Holding ten trumps, North bids for ten tricks. Ergo, 4♠.
(2) Reluctant passes by East-West, but they do not know whether or not North has a good hand.

Contract: 4♠ by S
Opening Lead: ♦K

Tip 71   Bid to the level of the fit facing a preempt, when holding a hand unsuited to defence.

Deal 72

Dealer: East **Vulnerability: Neither**

What should your strategy be if an opponent preempts? Say you are contemplating overcalling a suit: should you be bold, cautious, or in-between? The preemptor is weak with little defence so your partner is likely to have a suitable hand. That augurs in favour of boldness. But don't go wild – you are bidding at a high level; the suits rate to split poorly;

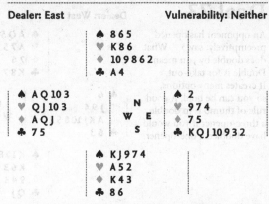

♠ 865
♥ K86
♦ 109862
♣ A4

♠ AQ103
♥ QJ103
♦ AQJ
♣ 75

♠ 2
♥ 974
♦ 75
♣ KQJ10932

♠ KJ974
♥ A52
♦ K43
♣ 86

and the partner of the preemptor will know exactly what to do (including doubling you!) because he knows his partner's hand. With a good suit and/or a good hand, go ahead and make your bid. But don't be reckless!

What happened

The lack of wisdom of South's overcall can be measured by the fact that dummy was quite suitable – three trumps and a useful ace and king – yet the doubled contract still went crashing down.

West led ♣7 and declarer won dummy's ♣A to lead and run ♠8. West took ♠10, led ♣5 to East's ♣9, and received ♦7 return (best) to ♦3 and his ♦J. He switched to ♥Q to dummy's ♥K and ♠6 was passed to his ♠Q. He continued with ♥J to declarer's ♥A and declarer led ♠K to his ♠A. He cashed ♥10 and led ♥3, declarer trumping. Declarer cashed ♠J but at Trick 12 had to lead from ♦K4 to ♦AQ. West took both tricks – down four. 800 points to East-West.

S	W	N	E
–	–	–	3♣
3♠(1)	Dble	End	

(1) Unwise. South has a broken suit and a flattish hand with less than opening bid values.
(2) Had South passed, West would wonder whether to try 3NT. Now he has an easy double.

Contract: 3♠ (Doubled) by S
Opening Lead: ♣7

What should have happened

Had South passed, West would have passed (3NT is tempting but would fail assuming North did not win his ♣A on the first round). The 3♣ contract would make a peaceful overtrick, losing ♣A and ♥AK. 130 points to East-West (Chicago/Duplicate scoring).

S	W	N	E
–	–	–	3♣
End			

Contract: 3♣ by E
Opening Lead: ♠7

Tip 72 Beware of bad splits when an opponent has preempted.

Deal 73

Dealer: West   **Vulnerability: Both**

An opponent has opened preemptively, say 3♦. What does double by you mean? Double is for take-out. It creates many options, so you can be bold. A good rule of thumb is to double a three-opener if you would have doubled a one-opener.

```
                  ♠ A Q 5 4
                  ♥ A 7 5 2
                  ♦ 7 6
                  ♣ K 8 7
  ♠ 6                          ♠ J 9 7
  ♥ J 9 4            N         ♥ Q 10 8
  ♦ A K J 10 8 5 2  W   E      ♦ Q
  ♣ 6 3                 S      ♣ A 10 9 5 4 2
                  ♠ K 10 8 3 2
                  ♥ K 6 3
                  ♦ 9 4 3
                  ♣ Q J
```

What happened

North missed an opportunity. He left West to declare his 3♦ opening, and led a trump (for want of anything better). Declarer won (overtaking ♦Q with ♦K), trumps were drawn, and ♥AK flushed out. Nine tricks made – seven trumps, a heart and ♣A. East-West +110.

S	W	N	E
–	3♦	Pass(1)	Pass
Pass(2)			

(1) North should double for take-out – he would have doubled a 1♦ opener so should double 3♦.
(2) Overcalling 3♠ would work here, but is crazy!

Contract: 3♦ by W
Opening Lead: ♦6

What should have happened

Had North made a take-out double, South would have jumped to 4♠ (he might have to bid 3♠ on nothing, so must jump to 4♠ with his nine points and decent five-card major). West leads ♦A, felling East's ♦Q, and continues with ♦K and ♦J (best). Declarer trumps with ♠Q to avoid an overtrump, cashes ♠A, then leads ♠4 to East's ♠9 and his...

Declarer reflects that West rates to have a singleton somewhere for his preempt (7321 being the likely shape); and that with a singleton heart or club he might have led/switched to it. Playing West for a singleton trump, declarer finesses ♠10 (key play). West discards so he cashes ♠K, felling East's ♠J, and leads ♣Q. East's ♣A is flushed out and declarer can win ♥8 return in hand with ♥K, cash ♣J, cross to ♥A and discard ♥6 on ♣K. 10 tricks and game made. North-South +620.

S	W	N	E
–	3♦	Dble(1)	Pass
4♠(2)	End		

(1) Conforms to the 'SOS' criteria for a take-out double: Shortage in the suit opened; Opening points or more; Support for all unbid suits.
(2) With 9+ points South must jump in reply.

Contract: 4♠ by S
Opening Lead: ♦A

Tip 73
If you would double a one-opener, you should double a three-opener (both for take-out).

Deal 74

Dealer: East   **Vulnerability: North-South**

An opponent has bid
preemptively. Do you fancy
your chances in 3NT? The
instinctive answer is No,
for fear of the preemptor's
suit. But bear in mind that
he is unlikely to have an
outside entry. Provided you
have a 'stopper' in his suit
(a way of stopping the flow
of the suit, i.e. A(x), Kx,
Qxx, Jxxx), bidding 3NT
over a three-opener is a fair
shot. The key will be to

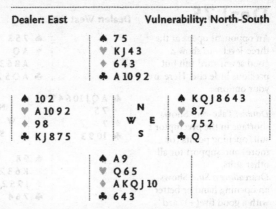

```
              ♠ 7 5
              ♥ K J 4 3
              ♦ 6 4 3
              ♣ A 10 9 2

  ♠ 10 2              ♠ K Q J 8 6 4 3
  ♥ A 10 9 2     N    ♥ 8 7
  ♦ 9 8      W   E    ♦ 7 5 2
  ♣ K J 8 7 5    S    ♣ Q

              ♠ A 9
              ♥ Q 6 5
              ♦ A K Q J 10
              ♣ 6 4 3
```

exhaust his partner of his cards in the suit, in which case you can take him out of play
altogether. Overcalling 3NT over a three-opener is particularly appealing with a trick-source
of your own – a goodish five- or six-card suit. In terms of high-card strength, put the
preemptor with, say, six points; if you have 16, then there are 18 points between the other
two hands; give partner half of those (nine) and you have the 25 points needed for game.

What happened

South missed his chance. With 16 points, a stopper
in the preemptor's suit and a running suit of his own,
a 3NT overcall was indicated. Instead South chose to
overcall a 'nothing' 4♦. I'd even prefer to make a take-
out double to this (though it would result in North
bidding a doomed 4♥). 4♦ made the same nine tricks
as 3NT – down one.

What should have happened

In 3NT on ♠10 lead, declarer ducks and wins the
second spade with ♠A. He leads ♥Q, flushing out
West's ♥A and wins, say, ♣5 return with ♣A. He cashes
♥KJ and ♦AKQJ10. Game made.

S	W	N	E
–	–	–	3♠
4♦(1)	End		

(1) What was South hoping
to achieve? The most likely
game contract is surely 3NT,
which will now be impossible
to reach. Overcalling 4♣/♦
over a three-opener is seldom
best.

Contract: 4♦
Opening Lead: ♠10

S	W	N	E
–	–	–	3♠
3NT(1)	End		

(1) The percentage action –
with 16 good points including
a trick-source and a spade
stopper.

Contract: 3NT
Opening Lead: ♠10

Tip 74 Overcall 3NT over a three-level opener when holding 16+ points and a stopper
in the preemptor's suit. Be especially keen with a trick source of your own.

Deal 75

Dealer: West **Vulnerability: Both**

An opponent opens at the three-level – to show a good seven-card suit but precious little else. Here are your options:

Double: Take-out. Shows shortage in the preemptor's suit, opening points (or more) and support for all other suits.

Overcalling a Suit: Shows an opening hand or better with a good five(+) card suit, or slightly less than an opening hand or better with a good six(+) card suit. Note that an overcall over a preempt does NOT show the same hand-type as the preemptor (a common misunderstanding).

Overcalling 3NT: Shows about 16 or more points and a stopper in the preemptor's suit. If you have a trick-source (a good five/six card suit) so much the better.

```
                    ♠ 7 5 3
                    ♥ A Q
                    ♦ A 8 6 3
                    ♣ A Q 5 2
  ♠ A Q J 10 6 4 2          ♠ K
  ♥ 7 5            N        ♥ J 10 9 8 4
  ♦ 7          W     E      ♦ K Q 10 4
  ♣ 10 9 3         S        ♣ K J 8
                    ♠ 9 8
                    ♥ K 6 3 2
                    ♦ J 9 5 2
                    ♣ 7 6 4
```

What happened

North held a hand that didn't fit into any of the above categories: inadequate length in the other major to make a take-out double, no suit to overcall, and no stopper in the preemptor's suit to bid 3NT. Though passing with 16 points seems feeble, it was certainly the winning action.

West led his singleton ♦7 against 4♥ doubled and declarer rose with dummy's ♦A, cashed ♥AQ and led ♦3 (best). East won ♦Q, cashed ♦K, then switched to his singleton ♠K. West overtook with ♠A, led ♠Q (East discarding ♦10) then switched to ♣10. Declarer rose with dummy's ♣A and led ♦8. East trumped and led ♥J. Declarer won ♥K and exited with ♥6 to East's ♥10. East cashed ♣K and had to give dummy the last trick with ♣Q. A small victory for declarer at the end but he had only garnered six tricks. 1100 points to East-West.

S	W	N	E
–	3♠	Dble(1)	Pass
4♥(2)	Pass	Pass	Dble
End			

(1) Only two cards in the unbid major suit is too great a flaw. Pass is indicated.
(2) Expecting support for the unbid major suit.

Contract: 4♥ Doubled by S
Opening Lead: ♦7

What should have happened

How North wished he had passed and watched the opponents quietly make 3♠ (losing two hearts and the two minor-suit aces).

S	W	N	E
–	3♠	End	

Contract: 3♠ by W
Opening Lead: ♠3

Tip 75 Don't be frightened to pass over an opposing preempt, even with a high point-count, if your hand is not suitable for a positive action.

Deal 76

Dealer: North　　　　　　　　　　**Vulnerability: Both**

Our new topic is opening
bids at the Two-level
(which we will assume to
be the more traditional
Strong variety rather than
Weak – which would show
5–10 points and a good
six-card suit, in effect a
mini-preempt).

```
                        ♠ K 4
                        ♥ A 8 3
                        ♦ A K Q 6 4
                        ♣ A J 6
        ♠ Q 10 8 6 3              ♠ A J 9
        ♥ Q 9 5           N       ♥ J 10 6 2
        ♦ 10 3          W   E     ♦ 9 8 5
        ♣ K 9 3            S      ♣ 10 8 5
                        ♠ 7 5 2
                        ♥ K 7 4
                        ♦ J 7 2
                        ♣ Q 7 4 2
```

Meanings of Two-openers
2♣: Any hand with 23+
points, or a hand wishing
to insist on game with
slightly fewer points.

2♦,♥,♠: 20–22 points with a good five/six card suit, or slightly fewer with 'eight playing
tricks' (the suit being trumps).

2NT: 20–22 balanced (4333, 4432, 5332) or occasionally semi-balanced
(e.g. 5422, even 4441 with a singleton honour).

What happened
Our common mistake saw North opening 2♦ rather
than 2NT. This resulted in his partner, the weaker hand,
declaring 3NT. Disaster! West led ♠6 and declarer tried
dummy's ♠K. East won ♠A, cashed ♠J and led ♠9.
West overtook with ♠10 and cashed ♠Q8. Declarer
took the rest (five diamonds, ♥AK and ♣A) but was
down one.

S	W	N	E
–	–	2♦(1)	Pass
2NT(2)	Pass	3NT	End

(1) Mistake. A 2♦ opener
shows an unbalanced hand
with a big wish for diamonds
to be trumps.
(2) The conventional negative
response, indicating any hand
with 0–7 points.

Contract: 3NT by S
Opening Lead: ♠6

What should have happened
Had North opened 2NT, he would have been declarer
in 3NT with ♠K protected from a spade attack. East
would lead ♥2 and declarer would rise with dummy's
♥K in order to lead ♣2 to ♣J. If East had won with ♣K,
he would be unable to attack spades to his advantage.
As it was, ♣J would score (the finesse succeeding), and
declarer could cash five diamonds, ♣A and ♥A. Nine
tricks and game made.

S	W	N	E
–	–	2NT(1)	Pass
3NT	End		

(1) Correct. Showing 20–22
balanced.

Contract: 3NT by N
Opening Lead: ♥2

Tip 76　Open 2NT as opposed to 2♦/♥/♠ when holding a balanced hand with 20–22
points, even with a good five-card suit.

Deal 77

Dealer: South　　　**Vulnerability: North-South**

An opening bid of 2♦, 2♥ or 2♠ shows a very good hand with a very good suit: 20–22 points with a good five/six card suit, or slightly fewer points with 'eight playing tricks' (the suit being trumps). In the strict Acol of last century, these openers said less about points and more about the hand containing (at least) 'eight playing tricks'. How many playing tricks do these suits contain?

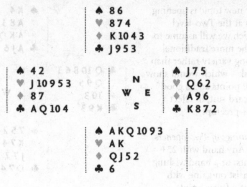

(i) AKQJ32

(ii) QJ10982

(i) contains six – assume no foul split.

(ii) contains four – once the ace-king have been removed. These days there is more stress on the overall point-count (a simpler and more practical approach). But do not lose sight of the trick-taking potential of the hand. If you are slightly short of 20 points, do not be frightened to open at the Two-level with a large trick-taking potential.

What happened

South had a far stronger hand than most 20–22 point hands with his fine suit and distribution. Not to open 2♠ ('I only had 19, points partner') cost his side the chance to bid and make game.

In his lowly 1♠, declarer won ♥J lead with ♥K. He cashed ♠AKQ, drawing the missing trumps, then led ♦Q. The defence scored ♦A and a club trick, but declarer could trump the second club and claim the remainder. He had made 11 tricks.

S	W	N	E
1♠(1)	End		

(1) Though South does not have 20 high-card points, he has a very powerful hand. He has six spade tricks (assuming ♠J is cooperative) and ♥AK. That's eight playing tricks, not even counting the potential in diamonds.

Contract: 1♠
Opening Lead: ♥J

What should have happened

How he wished he had opened 2♠ and so reached game, via the featured auction.

S	W	N	E
2♠	Pass	2NT(1)	Pass
3♦	Pass	4♦	Pass
4♠(2)	End		

(1) The negative response (0–7 points).
(2) Offering a choice of games.

Contract: 4♠
Opening Lead: ♥J

Tip 77　Be prepared to upgrade a near-20 point hand with a powerful shape – an 'eight playing trick hand' – and open at the two-level.

Deal 78

Dealer: South **Vulnerability: East-West**

A 2NT opener shows 20–22 balanced (4333, 4432, 5332). Occasionally the distribution will be 'semi-balanced' (5422, 6322 with a six-card minor, even 4441 with a singleton honour). But it should not be more unbalanced than that.

```
                    ♠ 10 8 5
                    ♥ J 8 3
                    ♦ K 7 4 2
                    ♣ Q 3 2
    ♠ K 9 7 6 2              ♠ A Q 4 3
    ♥ K 9 6 4        N       ♥ 10 7
    ♦ Q 9         W     E    ♦ 10 8 6 5 3
    ♣ 9 4            S       ♣ 10 6
                    ♠ J
                    ♥ A Q 5 2
                    ♦ A J
                    ♣ A K J 8 7 5
```

What happened

South would have liked to open 2♣. But a 2♣ opener is not like a 2♦, 2♥ or 2♠ opener. It shows any hand with 23+ points. Instead South unwisely tried opening 2NT. He was to regret it.

In 3NT, declarer received ♠6 lead. East won ♠A and returned ♠3. West won ♠K (declarer sheepishly discarding), returned ♠2 to East's ♠Q, won ♠4 with ♠7 and cashed ♠9. Declarer took the rest with his clubs and red suit top-tricks but was down one.

What should have happened

Had South opened the recommended 1♣, he would have reached 5♣. Game in a minor is generally undesirable, but his singleton spade – facing a partner that can neither bid spades nor notrumps – is a sufficient disincentive to try notrumps.

Defending 5♣, West would lead ♠6 (the unbid suit) to East's ♠A and declarer would trump ♠3 return. Declarer cashes ♣AK, pleased to observe the 2–2 split, then leads ♦J to ♦Q and ♦K, followed by ♥3 to ♥Q. West takes ♥K and leads ♠K, but declarer can trump, lead ♥2 to ♥J, ♥8 to ♥A (East discarding), then trump ♥5 with dummy's ♣Q. He crosses back to ♦A and takes the last two tricks with his last two trumps. 11 tricks and game made.

S	W	N	E
2NT(1)	Pass	3NT	End

(1) South's hand is not even 'semi-balanced'. To open with a bid that shows a notrumpy hand was a costly mistake.

Contract: 3NT
Opening Lead: ♠6

S	W	N	E
1♣(1)	Pass	1♦	Pass
2♥(2)	Pass	3♣	Pass
5♣	End		

(1) Unable to open 2♣ (or 2NT), South has no choice but to open 1♣. If partner cannot respond, there may not be a making game.
(2) Catching up. A jump rebid in a new suit by opener is forcing to game.

Contract: 5♣
Opening Lead: ♠6

Tip 78 Open 1♣ – not 2NT – holding a profoundly unbalanced 20–22 point hand with strong clubs.

Deal 79

Question: Should an opening bid of 2♦, 2♥ or 2♠ by partner force you to respond?

Answer: Yes. Partner opened at the two-level (rather than at the one-level) to be sure of eliciting a response. Even if you have seemingly nothing for him, you must respond.

```
              ♠ 3
              ♥ 8 6 4 3 2
              ♦ 8 6 2
              ♣ 8 6 3 2
  ♠ 9 5 2              N          ♠ J 8 7 6
  ♥ 9                             ♥ Q 10
  ♦ A 9 7 5 3     W       E       ♦ Q J 10
  ♣ A K 9 4              S        ♣ Q J 10 5
              ♠ A K Q 10 4
              ♥ A K J 7 5
              ♦ K 4
              ♣ 7
```

What happened

When North passed 2♠, West led ♣A and continued with ♣K. Declarer trumped, cashed ♠AKQ (both opponents following but no ♠J appearing), then, leaving the master ♠J outstanding, turned to hearts. He cashed ♥AK, felling ♥Q, then followed with ♥J. East trumped with ♠J and switched to ♦Q. Declarer covered with ♦K and West took ♦A and led back ♦5. East won ♦10 and tried ♦J. But declarer trumped with his last trump (♠10) and cashed his last two hearts. Nine tricks.

S	W	N	E
2♠	Pass	Pass(1)	Pass

(1) Mistake. This is a forcing bid. Though North has nothing for South in a spade contract, South could have a two-suited hand (as he does). In that case, North's hand might prove very useful in support of the second suit.

Contract: 2♠
Opening Lead: ♣A

What should have happened

Had North responded – bidding the negative (any 0–7 points) 2NT – South would have introduced his second suit. Had South merely repeated his spades, North would have passed. But North would have an easy raise of 3♥ to 4♥ with his five-card support.

Against 4♥, West would lead ♣A and follow with ♣K. After trumping, declarer would cash ♥AK, then follow with ♠AKQ, discarding ♦62 from dummy. He would trump ♠4, trump ♣6, then cash the established ♠10, discarding ♦8. He would cross-trump the last three tricks. Game made with two overtricks.

S	W	N	E
2♠	Pass	2NT(1)	Pass
3♥	Pass	4♥(2)	End

(1) The conventional negative response, showing a hand with 0–7 points.
(2) Suddenly North's hand has leapt in value.

Contract: 4♥
Opening Lead: ♣A

Tip 79 You should respond to a Two-of-a-suit opener. Even with nothing.

Deal 80

Dealer: North   **Vulnerability: Both**

An opening bid of 2♦, 2♥
or 2♠, shows 20–22 points,
or slightly less with 'eight
playing tricks'. It forces
partner to respond, even
with nothing. Responder's
first message is to state
whether he has a 'positive'
hand – eight(+) points – in
which case there is a chance
of a slam; or a 'negative'
hand – 0–7 points – in
which case there will
almost certainly not be a
slam, and the issue will be
whether to play game and/
or which game to play.
With a negative hand he
responds 2NT; all other
bids show positives.

```
              ♠ A K J 5 3
              ♥ K 3
              ♦ A K Q 7 5
              ♣ 7
♠ Q 7 4                      ♠ 10 8 6 2
♥ A Q 8           N          ♥ 7 4
♦ J 6         W     E        ♦ 10 9 4 2
♣ J 10 9 6 4      S          ♣ A 8 3
              ♠ 9
              ♥ J 10 9 6 5 2
              ♦ 8 3
              ♣ K Q 5 2
```

What happened

South made a positive with insufficient values.
This induced his partner to look for slam and the
partnership inelegantly ground to a halt in 5♥ when the
response to Blackwood revealed two missing aces. Sadly
there was a third trick to lose.

West led ♣J to ♣A and East continued with ♣8.
Declarer won ♣Q and needed ♥Q onside with precisely
one other card to restrict his trump losers to one. He
led ♥J, but West rose with ♥A and led ♣10. Declarer
won ♣K, crossed to ♥K (bad news: no ♥Q), then
cashed ♠AK discarding ♣5. He later lost to ♥Q. Down
one.

S	W	N	E
–	–	2♠	Pass
3♥(1)	Pass	4♦	Pass
4♥	Pass	4NT(2)	Pass
5♣(3)	Pass	5♥(3)	End

(1) Too weak for a 'positive'.
(2) Facing a 'positive' with
rebiddable hearts, a heart slam
looks good. He asks for aces.
(3) No aces, so North
hurriedly signs off.

Contract: 5♥
Opening Lead: ♣J

What should have happened

How South wished he had slowed his partner down
by starting with the negative response of 2NT before
introducing his hearts. Then his partner would not have
been tempted to go slamming and they would settle in
the making 4♥.

S	W	N	E
–	–	2♠	Pass
2NT(1)	Pass	3♦	Pass
3♥	Pass	4♥	End

(1) Negative response: any
hand with 0–7 points.

Contract: 4♥
Opening Lead: ♣J

Tip 80 When responding to 2♦/♥/♠, you must bid
a negative 2NT with 0–7 points.

Deal 81

Dealer: South **Vulnerability: Both**

The 'negative response' to a strong opening of 2♦, 2♥ or 2♠ is 2NT. This shows any hand with 0–7 points, and tells partner that slam is unlikely. The same principle applies when partner opens 2♣ (23+ points) – there is a negative response that shows 0–7 points. However, in the interest of conserving bidding space, the negative response to a 2♣ opener

```
              ♠ Q 5
              ♥ J 4 2
              ♦ K J 6 4 3 2
              ♣ J 6
   ♠ A 9 7 2           ♠ J 10 8 6 4
   ♥ 8 6        N      ♥ 9 7 5
   ♦ 10 7    W   E     ♦ Q 9 8
   ♣ 10 9 8 7 3  S     ♣ Q 5
              ♠ K 3
              ♥ A K Q 10 3
              ♦ A 5
              ♣ A K 4 2
```

is different to a 2♦, 2♥ or 2♠ opener. It is 2♦, purely a point count and saying nothing about diamonds. Thus if a 'positive' hand (eight(+) points) with diamonds is held then the response must be 3♦.

What happened

North forgot the need to jump when holding a positive hand with diamonds. The decent slam was therefore missed. West led ♣10 against the 4♥ contract, covered by ♣J, ♣Q and ♣K. Seeking to trump his low clubs in dummy, declarer cashed ♣A and trumped ♣2 with ♥2. East overtrumped with ♥5 and returned ♠J to West's ♠A. Declarer trumped West's ♠9 lead with dummy's ♥J, drew trumps and claimed 11 tricks. Uninspired bidding and play.

S	W	N	E
2♣	Pass	2♦(1)	Pass
2♥	Pass	4♥	
End			

(1) North forgets that this is the conventional 'negative' response (showing 0–7 points and saying nothing about diamonds). Despite his later jump, South cannot envisage slam.

Contract: 4♥
Opening Lead: ♣10

What should have happened

In 6♥ on ♠A lead (normally best to lead an ace against a small slam) and ♠2 to his ♠K, declarer plans to set up dummy's diamonds. He cashes ♥AK and, when he sees both opponents follow, cashes ♦A, crosses to ♦K, trumps ♦3 with ♥Q, then crosses to ♥J and cashes established diamonds. 12 tricks and slam made.

S	W	N	E
2♣	Pass	3♦(1)	Pass
3♥	Pass	4♥	Pass
6♥(2)	End		

(1) 'Positive' showing 8+ points and diamonds...
(2) ...enabling South to go for slam.

Contract: 6♥
Opening Lead: ♠A

Tip 81 The negative (0–8 points) response to a 2♣ opener is 2♦. With a positive hand and five(+) diamonds, you must jump to 3♦.

Deal 82

Dealer: South **Vulnerability: East-West**

Let us formalise the
response structures to
two-level openers.
To 2♦, 2♥, 2♠ (20–22
points + good five(+)
cards). *In order of priority:*
2NT: 'Negative' showing
any 0–7 points.
Support: eight(+) points
and three(+) cards.
New Suits: eight(+) points
and five(+) cards. NB:
prefer support to new suits.
To 2♣ (any 23+ points).
In order of priority:
2♦: 'Negative' showing any 0–7 points.
New Suits: eight(+) points and five(+) cards.
2NT: eight(+) points and no five-card suit.

```
              ♠ Q 8 3
              ♥ 6 3
              ♦ K 9 6 5 2
              ♣ 6 3 2
♠ 9 5 4                    ♠ 10 7
♥ K Q 7 2      N           ♥ 10 9 8 5 4
♦ Q 10 8    W   E          ♦ A J 4 3
♣ Q 10 7       S           ♣ J 9
              ♠ A K J 6 2
              ♥ A J
              ♦ 7
              ♣ A K 8 5 4
```

You will note that the first duty of responder in both cases is to announce whether he has
a 'negative' or a 'positive' hand, enabling opener to know whether or not slam is likely.

What happened

North knew as soon as his partner opened 2♠ that 4♠
was on. But his precipitate leap to that contract showed
a positive hand and South (reasonably) went slamming.
Oops.

Against 6♠ West led ♥K. Facing an impossible task,
declarer won ♥A and led ♦7, hoping vainly to sneak
past ♦A. No good: East beat dummy's ♦K with ♦A
and led back ♦10 to ♦J and West's ♥Q. West exited
passively with ♠4 and, after drawing trumps, declarer
cashed ♣AK and gave West ♣Q. He trumped ♥7
return, and claimed but was down two.

What should have happened

How he wished that he had been in just 4♠. Game
made, play progressing similarly to above.

S	W	N	E
2♠	Pass	4♠(1)	Pass
6♠	End		

(1) Theoretically North's
4♠ shows a 'positive', and
this propels South into the
hopeless slam.

Contract: 6♠
Opening Lead: ♥K

S	W	N	E
2♠	Pass	2NT(1)	Pass
3♣	Pass	4♠	End

(1) North correctly goes via
the negative response of 2NT
before supporting to 4♠. This
ensures that South does not
get ideas above his station.

Contract: 4♠
Opening Lead: ♥K

Tip 82 Remember the negative responses (0–7 points) to 2♣ (2♦) and to 2♦, 2♥, 2♠ (2NT).

Deal 83

Dealer: South   **Vulnerability: East-West**

The starting point for a
slam auction is frequently
a Two-level opener.
The latter stages often
feature the most popular
convention in Bridge,
invented in the 1930s by
an American named Easley
Blackwood. Aces are vital
when bidding a slam –
if the opponents hold
two aces, then any slam
venture will be bound to
fail (barring the presence

```
              ♠ K 6 3
              ♥ K 2
              ♦ J 8 6
              ♣ A 10 6 5 3
  ♠ Q J 10 2            ♠ A 9 8 5 4
  ♥ J 9 7 6 4      N     ♥ 10 8 5 3
  ♦ 10 4 3     W     E   ♦ A 9 7
  ♣ 9              S     ♣ 8
              ♠ 7
              ♥ A Q
              ♦ K Q 5 2
              ♣ K Q J 7 4 2
```

of a void). In the Blackwood convention in its basic form, a bid of 4NT asks partner
how many aces they possess. The lowest response (5♣) shows the lowest number of aces
(none) and each higher step shows one more ace. Blackwood is a useful convention,
but beware when clubs (and to a lesser extent diamonds) are trumps. The response to
Blackwood could carry you overboard.

What happened

North's 5♦ response to South's ill-judged 4NT
Blackwood forced him to 6♣ (in order to make clubs
trumps), in spite of his knowing that two aces were
missing. West led ♠Q against the 6♣ contract and
declarer forlornly covered with dummy's ♠K. East won
♠A and wasted no time in placing ♦A on the table.
Down one.

S	W	N	E
1♣	Pass	3♣	Pass
4NT(1)	Pass	5♦(2)	Pass
6♣(oops)	End		

(1) Blackwood but inadvisable
because...
(2) ...when partner shows one
ace (5♦), South is stymied.

Contract: 6♣
Opening Lead: ♠Q

What should have happened

South avoids Blackwood, and settles safely for 5♣.
Game made.

S	W	N	E
1♣	Pass	3♣	Pass
5♣(1)	End		

(1) Though he has a fine hand,
South realizes he cannot
afford to ask for aces in case
of a 5♦ response. Instead he
sensibly settles for game.

Contract: 5♣
Opening Lead: ♠Q

Tip 83 When clubs are trumps you need at least two aces in your hand to bid Blackwood.
When diamonds are trumps you need at least one ace.

112   TIMES BRIDGE

Deal 84

In the Blackwood convention a bid of 4NT asks partner how many aces they possess. The responses are as follows:

- 5♣ no aces (or all four)
- 5♦ one ace
- 5♥ two aces
- 5♠ three aces.

The convention is designed to prevent a partnership from bidding a (small) slam when missing two aces. To be consistent with

```
              ♠ 8753
              ♥ J762
              ♦ Q8
              ♣ AKJ
♠ –                        ♠ Q104
♥ AQ9            N          ♥ 10543
♦ J97653      W   E        ♦ 10
♣ 10986         S          ♣ Q5432
              ♠ AKJ962
              ♥ K8
              ♦ AK42
              ♣ 7
```

the decision to bid Blackwood, if the response indicates that all or all-but-one of the aces are present, slam should be bid. If there is an ace missing, you must hope that it is the only loser. If you feel that slam may not make, though there is just one missing ace, then bidding Blackwood was probably a mistake in the first place. The convention should be reserved for those hands where the number of aces is the key information needed about partner's hand.

What happened

South mistakenly lost courage when he realised that there was a missing ace. West led ♣10 against 5♠ and declarer won dummy's ♣K (no finesse of ♣). He crossed to ♠K and blinked when West discarded. But at least he held a finesse position against East's ♠Q. So he crossed to ♦Q, finessed ♠J, cashed ♠A, then cashed ♦AK (East discarding), trumped ♦4, cashed ♣A (discarding ♥8) and merely conceded a heart to West's ♥A. 12 tricks.

S	W	N	E
1♠	Pass	3♠	Pass
4NT	Pass	5♦	Pass
5♠(1)	End		

(1) To bottle out – when the Blackwood response indicates that just one ace is missing – is a double-cross. You should only stop short of slam (after Blackwood) if two aces are missing.

Contract: 5♠
Opening Lead: ♣10

What should have happened

Slam bonus!

S	W	N	E
1♠	Pass	3♠	Pass
4NT	Pass	5♦	Pass
6♠(1)	End		

(1) Correct.

Contract: 6♠
Opening Lead: ♣10

Tip 84 If it is right to ask for aces, you should bid small slam when missing one ace.

Deal 85

Dealer: South **Vulnerability: North-South**

Blackwood (the ace-asking slam convention) may be the most popular convention in Bridge. But let's be honest – it is a trifle limited. All it gleans about partner's hand is the number of aces held: not where they are; not whether partner likes his hand; not anything else. There is a time and a place for Blackwood, but to believe that a slam has to be bid via Blackwood is a misconception.

```
            ♠ K J 7 6 3
            ♥ J 6 3
            ♦ J 8
            ♣ K J 10
♠ 2                      ♠ 9 5
♥ 10 9 7         N       ♥ K Q 8 4
♦ K Q 10 7 5   W   E     ♦ 9 6 3 2
♣ Q 8 5 2        S       ♣ 9 7 3
            ♠ A Q 10 8 4
            ♥ A 5 2
            ♦ A 4
            ♣ A 6 4
```

Here are some occasions where slamming via Blackwood is incorrect:

(a) You have three or four aces in your hand alone. Aces are not your concern.

(b) You have a void. The response to Blackwood will not tell you where partner's aces are, merely how many are held.

(c) You have two small cards in a suit. Even though Blackwood may reveal that just one ace is missing (and therefore that slam should be bid), the defence may be able to take the ace and king of this suit.

What happened

South should not go slamming at all with such a flat hand. But if he feels that he is worth a try, a 'do you fancy your hand for slam?' bid of 5♠ would be better than 4NT. After all what does he think his partner is going to reply to 4NT?! 6♠ failed by three tricks when declarer guessed to finesse East for ♣Q, crossing to ♣K and running ♣J.

S	W	N	E
1♠	Pass	3♠	Pass
4NT(1)	Pass	5♣	Pass
6♠	End		

(1) A knee-jerk reaction. What is the point of asking for aces when you hold them all yourself?

Contract: 6♠
Opening Lead: ♦K

What should have happened

With careful play, 4♠ is guaranteed. Win ♦K lead with ♦A, draw trumps, then lead to ♦J. West wins ♦Q and switches to ♥10. Win ♥A and exit with a second heart. East takes ♥KQ but then has to switch to a club to solve your guess in the suit. 10 tricks and game made.

S	W	N	E
1♠	Pass	3♠	Pass
4♠(1)	End		

(1) In fact South is too flat to even try for a slam.

Contract: 4♠
Opening Lead: ♦K

Tip 85 Bid Blackwood only if you are interested in (a) slam *and* (b) how many aces your partner holds.

Deal 86

Dealer: North **Vulnerability: East-West**

Broadly speaking my views for non-experts on bidding grand slams can be summarised in one word. Don't. Unless you think the partnership has at least 37 points between the two hands, small slam should be your goal. After all, it is hard enough making all 13 tricks on a deal, let alone bidding for them (and risking walking away with absolutely nothing should

```
              ♠ A K 7 5 4
              ♥ K
              ♦ A 9 7 6
              ♣ 7 6 4
♠ 9 8 2                      ♠ Q J 6 3
♥ A J 6 4 3 2      N         ♥ Q 10 9 8 5
♦ 5 3          W     E       ♦ 8
♣ J 2              S         ♣ 8 5 3
              ♠ 10
              ♥ 7
              ♦ K Q J 10 4 2
              ♣ A K Q 10 9
```

even just one trick get away). Bearing in mind my views on bidding grand slams, you will not be surprised at my opinion of the optional continuation to the Blackwood ace-ask. If the response to 4NT indicates that all the aces are held, the 4NT bidder can bid 5NT to ask for kings (6♣ showing no kings; 6♦ one; 6♥ two etc.). But because this is only of value for bidding a grand slam (you are already at the six-level), the 5NT king-ask should only very rarely be used. Almost never. Yet I see the 5NT king-ask being used far too often, occasionally even when all the aces are NOT held – a bad error. Is there a misconception in some quarters that the 5NT king-ask must follow the 4NT ace-ask, as night follows day?

What happened

South bid an unnecessary 5NT and found himself overboard when his partner showed two kings. West naturally led ♥A against 7♦. Down one and a red-faced South.

S	W	N	E
–	–	1♠	Pass
2♦	Pass	3♦	Pass
4NT	Pass	5♥	Pass
5NT(1)	Pass	6♥	Pass
7♦ (oops)	End		

(1) As there is a missing ace, there is NO point in bidding 5NT to ask for kings. Plus the location of the major-suit kings is irrelevant to South.

Contract: 7♦
Opening Lead: ♥A

What should have happened

South settles for 6♦ over the 5♥ reply to his Blackwood. Small slam made.

S	W	N	E
–	–	1♠	Pass
2♦	Pass	3♦	Pass
4NT	Pass	5♥	Pass
6♦	End		

Contract: 6♦
Opening Lead: ♥A

Tip 86 Only very rarely follow 4NT (Blackwood – asking for aces) by bidding 5NT (asking for kings). You must be interested in a grand slam and know from the reply to the 4NT that all the aces are held by your side.

Deal 87

Dealer: North **Vulnerability: East-West**

The concept of captaincy is a very important one. As an auction progresses, one player tends to take a dominant role and one a supporting one. The captain of the partnership should be the player who knows more of his partner's hand than his partner knows of his. Thus a player opening 1NT (or 2NT) cedes captaincy to his partner. Even though he may have the stronger

```
                    ♠ A K J 8 6 2
                    ♥ K Q 6 4 2
                    ♦ 8
                    ♣ 5
       ♠ 9 7 3                      ♠ 5 4
       ♥ 9 3            N           ♥ 5
       ♦ 10 5 3 2    W     E        ♦ A J 9 6 4
       ♣ J 10 9 4       S           ♣ A 8 7 6 2
                    ♠ Q 10
                    ♥ A J 10 8 7
                    ♦ K Q 7
                    ♣ K Q 3
```

hand, he has shown it so accurately that he can leave further decision-making to partner. Similarly a player preempting (e.g. opening at the three-level) should let partner decide on the outcome of the auction. In a Blackwood auction, the player bidding 4NT is the captain. His partner simply responds with his number of aces (like a robot) and lets all further decision-making be done by the 4NT bidder. After showing his aces, the partner must NOT under any circumstances overrule the 4NT bidder – are you listening South?

What happened

South might have had eight or nine points for his 2♥ bid; in fact he had a good-looking 17. But when his partner signed off in 5♥ after finding out he held one ace, South should have respected the decision. It was his partner who was boss.

The error of South's ways was soon demonstrated. West led ♣J against 6♥. East won ♣A and in a flash tabled ♦A. Down one.

S	W	N	E
–	–	1♠	Pass
2♥	Pass	4NT(1)	Pass
5♦	Pass	5♥	Pass
6♥(2)	End		

(1) Good bid. All North needs to know about is the number of aces opposite.
(2) South has far more strength than he might have. But North, the Blackwood bidder, is captain and South must not overrule.

Contract: 6♥
Opening Lead: ♣J

What should have happened

South respects North's sign off in 5♥, a making contract (losing those same two aces).

S	W	N	E
–	–	1♠	Pass
2♥	Pass	4NT	Pass
5♦	Pass	5♥	End

Contract: 5♥
Opening Lead: ♣J

Tip 87 Do not overrule a Blackwood bidder. He's in charge.

Deal 88

Love or hate the 4NT
Blackwood convention,
it is very important to
understand that 4NT is not
always the conventional
request for aces. Here is
the crux: if the immediate
preceding bid is in
notrumps, then 4NT is
not Blackwood, rather a
quantitative slam invite.
For example: 1NT–4NT
asks partner to bid 6NT
with a maximum for his
1NT opener but to pass
with a minimum. Facing a
12–14 point 1NT, the 4NT
bidder should have a flattish 19–20 point hand.

```
                    ♠ A 9 7
                    ♥ K 10 5
                    ♦ A 6 5
                    ♣ 10 9 5 4
        ♠ Q 6 4                    ♠ K 8 5 2
        ♥ 8 4 2         N          ♥ 7 6 3
        ♦ 10 9 8 7   W     E       ♦ 4 3 2
        ♣ 8 6 2         S          ♣ A 7 3
                    ♠ J 10 3
                    ♥ A Q J 9
                    ♦ K Q J
                    ♣ K Q J
```

What happened

North jumped to 4NT, but because it followed a
notrump bid, this was not ace-asking. Rather it invited
6NT, asking South to pass with a lower-end-of-the-
range hand for his 2NT opener and bid 6NT with an
upper-end hand. But South mistakenly read the bid as
Blackwood and they overbid to 6NT.

West led ♦10 – top of a sequence – and declarer
won in hand to lead ♣K. East won ♣A and returned
a second diamond. Declarer could win and cash three
established club winners, four hearts, one further
diamond and ♠A. But that was only 11 tricks and there
was no hope for a twelfth. He duly lost a spade at the
very end and was down one in his slam.

S	W	N	E
2NT(1)	Pass	4NT(2)	Pass
5♦(3)	Pass	6NT(4)	End

(1) 20–22
(2) Quantitative slam invite,
asking partner to bid 6NT
with a maximum (22 or a
good 21), and to pass with a
minimum (20 or a bad 21).
(3) South mistakenly reads
4NT as Blackwood. Holding
a minimum, he should have
passed.
(4) Although South's 5♦ bid
was unexpected, North pre-
sumes he is maximum.

Contract: 6NT
Opening Lead: ♦10

What should have happened

How South wished he had remembered that Blackwood
only operates after a suit bid. He would then have rested
peacefully in 4NT and chalked up an easy game.

S	W	N	E
2NT	Pass	4NT	End

Contract: 4NT
Opening Lead: ♦10

Tip 88   4NT is not Blackwood after a notrump bid, rather a quantitative notrump slam
invite.

Dealer: South

Vulnerability: Neither

THE DEALS

Declarer Play

Deal 89

Imagine you are declarer: the opening lead has been made and you have given your thanks to partner for their dummy. What next? What you must NOT do is actually play a card from dummy – yet. If you play without looking ahead, or with reference to your own hand, you may suffer a fate similar to this declarer.

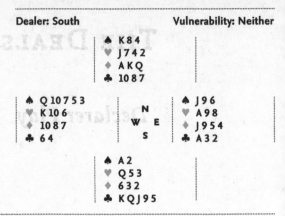

```
              ♠ K84
              ♥ J742
              ♦ AKQ
              ♣ 1087
♠ Q10753              ♠ J96
♥ K106      N         ♥ A98
♦ 1087    W   E       ♦ J954
♣ 64        S         ♣ A32
              ♠ A2
              ♥ Q53
              ♦ 632
              ♣ KQJ95
```

What happened

West led ♠5 against the 3NT contract. Declarer quickly played low from dummy and beat East's ♠J with ♠A. He then looked around, and correctly saw the necessity of removing the opponents' ♣A. At Trick Two he led ♣K.

Can you see what East did? He withheld his ♣A. Declarer followed by leading ♣Q, but East again ducked his ace. He won declarer's ♣5 continuation with his ♣A and then led ♠9. Declarer was now in a complete mess, unable to reach his two remaining clubs. He ducked ♠9, won ♠5 with ♠K, then led ♥2 to ♥Q. West won ♥K, cashed ♠Q10, then led ♥10. Declarer covered with ♥J and East won ♥A and cashed ♥9. Down three.

What should have happened

Declarer should have taken a little time-out before playing from dummy at Trick One. He would realise the need for retaining his ♠A for access to his clubs.

He should have won dummy's ♠K at Trick One (key play), then led ♣10. Assuming East ducks, he follows with ♣8 to ♣9 (East ducking again) and ♣K to East's ♣A. He wins East's ♠9 return with ♠A, cashes ♣QJ, then leads to ♦AKQ. Nine tricks and game made.

S	W	N	E
1NT(1)	Pass	3NT	End

(1) 5332 is a balanced shape, so South is correct to open 1NT rather than 1♣. Open 1NT and he does not need to find a rebid over a change of suit from partner; open 1♣ and he must find a rebid (which he does not have).

Contract: 3NT
Opening Lead: ♠5

Tip 89 Do not play from dummy at Trick One without looking ahead.

Deal 90

Declarer must take a time-out before playing from dummy at Trick One. He should try to form some sort of a plan first:

Stage One: count the top tricks in each suit – just the ones that can be made without losing the lead.

Stage Two: work out how many extra tricks are needed for the contract.

Stage Three: work out where those extra tricks are

	♠ J43	
	♥ K2	
	♦ KQ6	
	♣ A9863	
♠ 107	**N**	♠ 9865
♥ J9863	**W E**	♥ Q1054
♦ A92	**S**	♦ 10875
♣ KJ4		♣ Q
	♠ AKQ2	
	♥ A7	
	♦ J43	
	♣ 10752	

coming from. NB: particularly in notrumps, those extra tricks should be established early. We will concentrate on each stage in more detail over the next few deals, but this deal focusses on the whole process. West leads ♥6 to 3NT. Form a plan (before playing from dummy). *Stage One:* there are four top tricks in spades; two in hearts; none at all in diamonds (without losing the lead) and one in clubs. Total seven.

Stage Two: two extra tricks are required.

Stage Three: though length is often a good source of extra tricks, it is not always.

What happened

Declarer won the ♥6 lead with ♥A, then led ♣2 to ♣A and returned ♣3. East discarded ♠5 and West won ♣J. He followed with ♥3 to ♥K. Declarer then led ♣6. West won ♣K and led ♥8. East won ♣Q and returned ♥10. West overtook with ♥J and cashed ♥9 and ♦A. Down two.

What should have happened

Playing on clubs will work if the suit splits 2–2. But why take the risk? Instead look at diamonds. Flushing out the opposing ♦A MUST create the two extra tricks required.

Win ♥6 lead with ♥A (or ♥K) and lead a diamond (say ♦J). West wins ♦A (if he ducks, then play a second diamond) and continues with ♥3. Win ♥K, cash the promoted ♦KQ and lead out the remaining five top tricks (♠AKQJ and ♣A). Contract made.

S	W	N	E
1NT	Pass	3NT	End

Contract: 3NT
Opening Lead: ♥6

Tip 90   Do not rush to make the seemingly 'obvious' play before following the three key stages.

Deal 91

We are concentrating on forming a plan as declarer. This should occur before playing from dummy to the first trick. The three stages are:

1 Count top tricks;
2 Work out how many extras you need;
3 Decide where to get the extras.

Here we focus on (1) – counting top tricks – only those tricks that can be

```
              ♠ A K J 3
              ♥ K J 10 9
              ♦ K 4 2
              ♣ 7 6 4
♠ 10 5 4 2              ♠ 9 8 7
♥ 8 6          N        ♥ 7 5 4 3 2
♦ 10 8 5    W   E       ♦ A J 9
♣ K 10 8 5     S        ♣ Q 9
              ♠ Q 6
              ♥ A K Q
              ♦ Q 7 6 3
              ♣ A J 3 2
```

made before losing the lead. Look at each suit in turn, taking your hand and dummy in conjunction. If you do not have the ace in either hand, you have no top tricks (having to lose the ace first); if you have the ace but not the king, you have one top trick; if you have the ace and king but not the queen, you have two top tricks; if you have the ace, king and queen but not the jack, you have three top tricks; and so on. Note that you can never have more top tricks than the number of cards held in the longer length (this declarer's common mistake). Count the top tricks on our featured deal. You have four spade tricks, three heart tricks (with only three cards in each hand there can be no more), no diamond tricks (no ace) and one club trick. Total eight.

What happened

Declarer won the ♣5 lead (to East's ♣Q) with ♣A. Excited by holding the six top hearts (expecting six tricks), he cashed ♥AKQ. Sad at only making three tricks, he turned belatedly to diamonds, leading ♦3 to ♦K. East won ♦A and cashed ♥75. He then switched to ♣9. Declarer played low, but West overtook with ♣10 and cashed ♣K. Down one.

What should have happened

Win ♣A and immediately lead ♦3 to ♦K (key play). East wins and returns ♣9. Declarer ducks (best) and say West also plays low. East switches to ♥5. Win ♥Q and, having made an extra trick in diamonds to bring the total to nine, start cashing the top tricks. Cash ♦Q, ♥AK, then turn to spades. Begin with ♠Q (important), then ♠6 to ♠J. Finally cash ♠AK. Nine tricks and game made.

S	W	N	E
1♦	Pass	1♠	Pass
2NT(1)	Pass	3NT	End

(1) 17–18 points and a balanced hand.

Contract: 3NT
Opening Lead: ♣5

Tip 91　Count top tricks first, and remember that you cannot have more top tricks in a suit than the number of cards in your longer length.

Deal 92

Last deal we looked at how to count top tricks. Here we learn how to 'cash' them (play them out) without getting stuck in the wrong hand. Consider the following suit: AQ2 facing KJ43. You have four top tricks, but cashing them correctly may not be trivial. Here is the Unblocking Rule: *If you are leading from the hand with the Longer length, lead the Lowest card (L-L). If you are leading from the hand with the sHorter length lead the Highest card (H-H).* NB: The Unblocking Rule is only to be used when the relevant cards are in sequence, not when there are gaps. Back to AQ2 facing KJ43. The first round should see the ace and three appear (regardless of which hand leads); the second round should see the queen and four; the third the jack and two and the fourth the king. Our featured deal – a small slam – sees West lead ♣K. Following the correct procedure, you count up your top tricks before even playing from dummy. You have four spades, four hearts, three diamonds and one club. Most contracts have fewer top tricks initially than the number of tricks ultimately required to succeed; sometimes many fewer. Here you have the 12 top tricks you need. The only problem is cashing them in the right order.

```
                    ♠ A Q J 3
                    ♥ K Q 2
                    ♦ A 4
                    ♣ 9 8 6 3
     ♠ 10 9 7                      ♠ 8 6 5 4
     ♥ 8 6             N           ♥ 10 9 7 5
     ♦ J 9 5 2       W   E         ♦ 10 8 7 6
     ♣ K Q J 10        S           ♣ 5
                    ♠ K 2
                    ♥ A J 4 3
                    ♦ K Q 3
                    ♣ A 7 4 2
```

What happened

I won't dwell on this, but declarer's last three cards were ♣742 and dummy's were ♠QJ and ♣9. The trouble was that the lead was in declarer's hand.

What should have happened

Win ♣A, cash ♠K, lead ♠2 to ♠J, cash ♠AQ (discarding ♣42). Cash ♥KQ, lead ♥2 to ♥J, cash ♥A (discarding ♣3). Lead ♦3 to ♦A, return ♦4 to ♦Q, cash ♦K. Lose ♣7 at Trick 13. Slam made.

The order of which suit to play first, second and third is irrelevant; but how to play each individual suit matters hugely.

S	W	N	E
1♥	Pass	1♠	Pass
2NT(1)	Pass	6NT(2)	End

(1) 17–18 points and a balanced hand.
(2) 17 + 16 = 33. Enough to try for small slam.

Contract: 6NT
Opening Lead: ♣K

Tip 92 The Unblocking Rule for which order to play out sequential high cards: If you are leading from the hand with the longer length, lead the lowest card. If you are leading from the hand with the shorter length lead the highest card.

Deal 93

Here is the planning process for notrumps:
1 Count top tricks.
2 Work out how many extra tricks are needed.
3 Decide where to get the extra tricks.
4 Go for the extra tricks as soon as possible.

There are three basic methods of establishing extra tricks in notrumps:
1 By Force: flushing out an opposing higher card or cards, using sequential lower cards.

```
              ♠ J 10 5 3
              ♥ K 3 2
              ♦ A Q 4 3
              ♣ 10 4

  ♠ K 4                      ♠ A 8 7 6 2
  ♥ J 9 7 5 4        N       ♥ 10 8
  ♦ J 8           W     E    ♦ 10 9 7 5
  ♣ K 9 7 6          S       ♣ Q 8

              ♠ Q 9
              ♥ A Q 6
              ♦ K 6 2
              ♣ A J 5 3 2
```

2 By Length: exhausting the opponents of all their cards in a suit in which you are longer.
3 By Position ('finessing'): leading from the opposite hand to a card you are trying to promote in the hope that the opponent playing second will have the missing higher card. Force winners do not rely on the opposing split and where the missing high card(s) is located. So, when available (and provided you can afford to lose the lead) Force is usually the preferred method.

What happened

Declarer won ♥5 lead with ♥Q and immediately turned to his long suit, clubs. His ♣2 went to ♣6, ♣10 and ♣Q. East returned ♥8 and declarer won with dummy's ♥K. Declarer then played ♣4 to ♣J and West's ♣K. West led back ♥7 to ♥A (East discarding ♠2) and declarer cashed ♣A. East discarding was a blow and declarer had no winning option at this point. He tried leading the ♠Q but West won ♠K, cashed ♥J9 and ♣9 before leading to East's ♠A. Down three.

What should have happened

First, count top tricks. You have no spades (having to lose the lead first), three hearts, three diamonds and one club. You need two more and they will both come from spades, forcing out ♠AK. 100%.

Win Trick One with ♥Q and lead ♠Q. Say West wins ♠K and leads ♥4. Win ♥A and lead ♠9. Say East ducks his ace (best). Your ♠9 wins and you lead to dummy's ♦Q and lead ♠J. East wins ♠A and leads ♦7. Win ♦K, cross to ♦A, then cash ♠10. ♥K and ♣A are your eighth and ninth tricks. Game made.

S	W	N	E
1♣	Pass	1♦	Pass
1NT(1)	Pass	3NT	End

(1) 15–16 points and a balanced hand.

Contract: 3NT
Opening Lead: ♥5

Tip 93 Look out for Force winners, even in a short suit.

Deal 94

Dealer: South   **Vulnerability: Neither**

Length is possibly the
most important word in
the whole of Bridge, and
certainly in notrumps.
Yet it is easy to neglect
the power of a long suit,
particularly one without
high cards. That was
certainly the mistake
declarer made on this
deal, in which he was also
hypnotised by the strength
in spades.

```
              ♠ K J 10
              ♥ 8 6
              ♦ J 7 4
              ♣ 7 5 4 3 2
  ♠ 7 2                    ♠ 8 6 5 4 3
  ♥ K J 9 5 3      N       ♥ Q 10 7
  ♦ K 10 8      W     E    ♦ A 9 5
  ♣ J 8 6          S       ♣ 10 9
              ♠ A Q 9
              ♥ A 4 3
              ♦ Q 6 3 2
              ♣ A K Q
```

S	W	N	E
2NT	Pass	3NT(1)	End

(1) Partner's 20–22 plus his
five make the 25 for game.

Contract: 3NT

Opening Lead: ♥5

What happened

The opening lead of ♥5 (fourth from the top in his
longest and strongest suit) went to East's ♥Q and
declarer correctly ducked his ♥A. He ducked East's ♥10
continuation and won the third round with ♥A. Though
it was not particularly relevant here, it was good technique
to keep back his ♥A until the third round as it exhausted
one opponent (East) of all their cards of the suit.

Blinded by the riches in spades, he then cashed his
♠A, crossed to dummy's ♠K and returned to his ♠Q.
He cashed his ♣AKQ bringing his trick total to seven,
and then looked around. There wasn't much hope of
any more tricks but he tried ♦2. West rose with ♦K,
cashed ♥KJ, then led ♦10 to East's ♦A. Down two.

What should have happened

Dummy's club suit may look emaciated, but it is the key
to success. Provided the opposing clubs split 3–2 (as
they usually will), declarer's ♣AKQ will remove all the
missing clubs and the way will be clear for declarer to
cross to dummy (in spades so he must must not play
the spades out first) to enjoy the two remaining length
winners in clubs.

There are seven top tricks: three spades, one heart,
no diamonds and three clubs. Aim to score the two
extra tricks with dummy's long clubs.

The correct line is as follows: win the third round of
hearts with ♥A, cash ♣AKQ (observing the 3–2 split), lead
♠9 to dummy's ♠10, cash ♣75 (these are the two extra
tricks) discarding ♦32, then cash ♠K and lead to ♠A.

Nine tricks and contract made.

Tip 94 Do not overlook a long suit, even a weak one.

Deal 95

Dealer: South　　　**Vulnerability: East-West**

Many players are
frightened of declaring
notrumps – without the
security blanket of a trump
suit. Whilst it is true that
notrump contracts can
fall apart (typically if the
opponents are able to
run through a long suit),
they are generally easier
to declare than trump
contracts because there
are fewer options available
(issues such as whether

```
              ♠ 9 7 5
              ♥ Q 5 3 2
              ♦ K J 4 3
              ♣ Q 2
♠ 10 8 6 4 3 2        ♠ J
♥ 9            N      ♥ K J 8 6 4
♦ 7 5 2     W   E     ♦ Q 10 9 6
♣ A K 8        S      ♣ 5 4 3
              ♠ A K Q
              ♥ A 10 7
              ♦ A 8
              ♣ J 10 9 7 6
```

to draw trumps do not arise). Many notrump contracts boil down to a race: can the
opponents set up their long suit before you set up yours? You have the advantage of being
able to play both your hand and dummy; but the opponents have the advantage of leading
the first card. Let us see a typical such race.

What happened

West led ♠4 – fourth from the top of his longest and
strongest suit – and declarer beat East's ♠J with ♠Q.
To pass time, he next cashed ♠K. He then began his
long suit (clubs), leading ♣6 towards dummy's ♣Q.
West stepped in with ♣K and led a third spade, declarer
winning ♠A. Declarer followed with ♣7 but West took
♣A and cashed ♠1086. Down one.

What should have happened

Declarer lost the race because he cashed ♠K
unnecessarily at Trick Two. He should devote all his
attention to setting up his long clubs (very unlikely to
make nine tricks without the suit). After winning ♠Q
he immediately leads ♣6. West wins ♣K and leads ♠2.
He wins ♠K and leads ♣7. West wins ♣A and leads
♠3 but declarer is in control. He wins ♠A, cashes the
established ♣J109, follows with ♥A and ♦AK, and nine
tricks are his. Game made.

S	W	N	E
1♣	Pass	1♦(1)	Pass
2NT(2)	Pass	3NT	End

(1) Respond the cheaper of
two four-card suits.
(2) Jumping a level to show
17–18 balanced.

Contract: 3NT
Opening Lead: ♠4

Tip 95　Notrump contracts are frequently a race between both sides to set up their long
suit. Play your long suit each time you win the lead.

Deal 96

Dealer: North　　　　　　　　**Vulnerability: Both**

The three basic methods of
making extra tricks without
trumps are (1) by Force
(2) by Length and (3) by
Position (The 'Finesse').
A finesse is an attempt
to win a trick with a card
when the opponents
have a higher card in the
same suit. The relative
position of those cards is
all-important. This is the
process:

A. Identify the card that
needs to be promoted.

B. Lead from the opposite hand to that card.

C. Assuming the second hand played low, play – third to the trick – the card that you are trying to promote. You hope that the opponent playing second holds the missing higher card. The most common mistake when finessing is actually to lead the card you are trying to promote. Unless you also have the adjacent card, this gives you no chance of success: the opponent will simply cover.

		♠ K 9 4		
		♥ Q 10 7		
		♦ 8 6 5		
		♣ A K 5 3		
♠ Q J 10 7				♠ 8 6 2
♥ 8 2		**N**		♥ 9 5 4
♦ J 9 4 2	**W**		**E**	♦ Q 10 7
♣ 9 7 4		**S**		♣ Q 10 8 6
		♠ A 5 3		
		♥ A K J 6 3		
		♦ A K 3		
		♣ J 2		

What happened

South declared 6♥ on ♠Q lead. With five trump tricks and three ace-kings, he had 11 top tricks. The twelfth could only come from promoting ♣J. At the table declarer won ♠A, drew trumps finishing in hand, then led ♣J. This passed to East's ♣Q and there was no twelfth trick – down one. Note that even if West had held ♣Q, he would simply have covered ♣J and nothing would have been achieved.

What should have happened

In order to promote ♣J, declarer must lead from the opposite hand (i.e. from dummy), hoping that the player playing second, East, holds ♣Q. He wins ♠A, crosses to ♥10, then leads ♣3 (key play). If East plays low, ♣J wins the trick, and declarer draws the remaining trumps and cashes out for 12 tricks.

Say East rises with ♣Q and leads a second spade. Winning dummy's ♠K, declarer crosses to ♣J, returns to ♥Q, then cashes ♣AK discarding ♠5 and ♦3. He now leads over to ♠AKJ and ♦AK. 12 tricks and slam made.

S	W	N	E
–	–	1NT	Pass
3♥	Pass	4♥	Pass
6♥(1)	End		

(1) South knows he is at most one point short of the 33 point guideline for a small slam. His good heart fit and fine controls should compensate.

Contract: 6♥
Opening Lead: ♠Q

Tip 96　When finessing, lead from the opposite hand to the card you are trying to promote. Do not lead the card itself.

Deal 97

Dealer: South **Vulnerability: Neither**

Notrumps is so often
a battle to prevent the
opponents from setting up
their long suit. Sometimes
– especially if the opening
leader strikes lucky – you
as declarer cannot prevent
one opposing hand from
setting up his long suit.
But all is not lost. If one
opponent has set up his
suit, he becomes the
'danger hand'. You must
try to ensure that you lose

```
              ♠ 9 5
              ♥ K J 2
              ♦ 8 7 5 2
              ♣ A K Q 3
  ♠ Q J 8 7 4           ♠ K 6 2
  ♥ 9 6 4 3       N     ♥ A 8
  ♦ J 6       W     E   ♦ Q 10 9 3
  ♣ 10 4          S     ♣ J 9 6 5
              ♠ A 10 3
              ♥ Q 10 7 5
              ♦ A K 4
              ♣ 8 7 2
```

the lead to the other hand, not to the danger hand. You will then survive if:
(1) The partner of the danger hand has no more cards in the danger hand's suit, and
(2) There is no other suit in which the danger hand can be reached (no 'entry').
This deal we focus on the first point: making sure you have exhausted the partner of the
opening leader of his cards in the danger suit.

What happened

West led ♠7 – fourth from the top in his longest and
strongest suit – to East's ♠K. Unable to resist the
temptation to win a king with an ace, declarer scooped
up the first trick with his ♠A.

Declarer counted up six top tricks (♠A, ♦AK and
♣AKQ – note he has no top tricks in hearts because he
must lose the lead first). Needing three extra, he led ♥5
to dummy's ♥K. East won ♥A and returned ♠6. West
won ♠J, cashed ♠Q, then followed with ♠84. Down
one.

What should have happened

Declarer should have withheld ♠A at Trick One. He
cannot stop the defence from knocking out his ♠A, but
by delaying winning with the card until the third round,
he exhausts East of all his spades. Then, when he knocks
out ♥A (as he must), he has to hope that it is East who
holds the card. This time he is lucky, and East has no
more spades. He has established three heart tricks –
game made.

S	W	N	E
1NT	Pass	3NT	End

Contract: 3NT
Opening Lead: ♠7

Tip 97 Withhold (duck) an ace in notrumps sufficient times in order to exhaust one
opposing hand of their cards in the danger suit.

Deal 98

Dealer: South **Vulnerability: North-South**

When, declaring a notrump contract, the opponents lead a suit in which you have just one 'stopper' (a certain trick such as the ace), the warning light should appear. Withholding the stopper will not see the opponents switch to another suit; they will force out your stopper. But there is nonetheless a very good reason for withholding the stopper:

```
            ♠ 6 4
            ♥ Q 6 5
            ♦ K J 2
            ♣ K J 6 5 2
♠ K J 9 3 2              ♠ Q 10 5
♥ K J 7 3        N       ♥ 10 9 8 2
♦ 7 6        W     E     ♦ A 8
♣ 8 3           S       ♣ Q 10 9 7
            ♠ A 8 7
            ♥ A 4
            ♦ Q 10 9 5 4 3
            ♣ A 4
```

you hope to exhaust the partner of the leader of his cards in the suit. If you can make sure you later lose the lead to him, he now has no further cards in the long suit to lead.

Question: How many times should you withhold your one stopper?

Answer: Try to gauge how many cards each opponent holds. Win your stopper on the final card of the opponent with the shorter holding.

What happened

Declarer won ♠3 led (to East's ♠Q) with ♠A and led ♦3 to ♦K. East won ♦A and followed with ♠10 (top of the remaining doubleton). West overtook ♠10 with ♠J, then cashed ♠K, ♠9 and ♠2. Down one.

What should have happened

The bidding has told declarer that West has five spades (for his overcall) and East three (for his support). He must therefore delay winning his ♠A until the third round, so that East has no more spades. He then flushes out ♦A and, because East holds the card (lucky!), the spade attack is thwarted. He wins East's ♥10 return with ♥A and cashes five diamonds and ♣AK. Nine tricks and game made.

S	W	N	E
1♦	1♠	2♣	2♠
Pass	Pass	3♦	Pass
3NT(1)	End		

(1) Not guaranteed, but South hopes for ♦AK opposite, in which case he can count nine tricks (six diamonds and three aces).

Contract: 3NT
Opening Lead: ♠3

Tip 98 Working out how many cards each opponent has in their long suit will tell you how many times to withhold your stopper. Win it on the shorter holding's last card.

Deal 99

Dealer: South

Vulnerability: Both

You have just one stopper in the suit the opposition lead against your notrump contract. We have learnt that it is correct to withhold ('duck') that stopper enough times to exhaust the opponent with the shorter length of their cards in the suit.

Question: How do you know how many cards the opponent with the shorter length holds?

```
                  ♠ 8 7 4
                  ♥ K Q J
                  ♦ A J 9
                  ♣ Q 10 4 2
   ♠ K J 6 5 2            ♠ Q 9
   ♥ 10 8 4 3      N      ♥ 9 7 2
   ♦ Q 4 3      W   E     ♦ K 10 8 6 2
   ♣ 7             S      ♣ A 9 8
                  ♠ A 10 3
                  ♥ A 6 5
                  ♦ 7 5
                  ♣ K J 6 5 3
```

Answer: The bidding can help you, as can the opening lead. For example, if the lead is a two, the leader has four cards in the suit, assuming he has led the conventional fourth from the top. But sometimes the lengths will be unknown. In those cases you can revert to a useful (but not foolproof) guideline – *The Rule of Seven*: Add up your length in the suit to dummy's. Subtracting the total from seven tells you how many times to duck your stopper.

What happened

West led ♠5 to East's ♠Q. Declarer knew the advantage of ducking so played ♠3. East continued with ♠9 and declarer ducked again, playing ♠10. West won ♠J and, reflecting that he would be most unlikely to regain the lead after knocking out ♠A, alertly switched to ♦3. Declarer tried dummy's ♦9, but East won ♦10 and led back ♦6 to West's ♦Q. Declarer won dummy's ♦A and led ♣Q but East took ♣A and cashed ♦K82. Down three.

What should have happened

Using The Rule of Seven, declarer counts six spades between his two hands. Subtracting from seven means he must duck his ace just once. Letting ♠Q hold Trick One, he wins ♠9 with ♠A. He then leads to ♣Q. If East holds a third spade, the defence can only cash two further spades (splitting 4–3). In fact East has no more spades, so switches to ♦6. Dummy's ♦A beats West's ♦Q and declarer cashes four established clubs and three top hearts. Nine tricks and game made.

S	W	N	E
1NT	Pass	3NT	End

Contract: 3NT
Opening Lead: ♠5

Tip 99 With just one certain stopper in the suit led, use the Rule of Seven. Add up your length in the suit to dummy's. Subtracting the total from seven tells you how many times to withhold your stopper. Warning: this is at best a guide, not a rule.

Deal 100

It is notrumps and the
opponents lead a suit in
which you have just one
stopper. You hold it up
enough times to exhaust
one opponent of his cards
in the suit. If you lose
the lead to him, there is
nothing he can do to hurt
you. He is the 'safe hand'.
His partner, with more
winners in the suit led,
is the 'danger hand'. It is
imperative that if the lead
must be lost it should be
the safe hand who wins
the defensive trick.

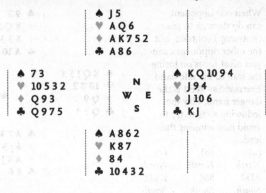

```
              ♠ J 5
              ♥ A Q 6
              ♦ A K 7 5 2
              ♣ A 8 6
 ♠ 7 3                      ♠ K Q 10 9 4
 ♥ 10 5 3 2      N          ♥ J 9 4
 ♦ Q 9 3     W     E        ♦ J 10 6
 ♣ Q 9 7 5       S          ♣ K J
              ♠ A 8 6 2
              ♥ K 8 7
              ♦ 8 4
              ♣ 10 4 3 2
```

What happened

East's overcall marked him with five (six) spades,
leaving West with at most two. So declarer correctly
ducked the first spade – to dummy's ♠J and East's ♠Q
– and won ♠K continuation with ♠A.

Needing to develop two more tricks, declarer
played ♦AK, planning to lose a third round. Had
West retained ♦Q, his plan would have succeeded
because West, the safe hand, would have won the third
diamond. Declarer could win any return from him and
cash two long diamonds.

However, West made the fine defence of throwing
♦Q under ♦K. Now East won the third diamond with
♦J and was able to cash three spade winners. Down one.

What should have happened

You as declarer need to keep East off lead and must
hope West holds ♦Qxx. You must lead through West,
so that if he plays ♦Q on the first or second rounds, you
let him win the trick.

Win ♠A on the second round and lead ♦4. Assuming
West plays low, win ♦K. Then return to ♥K and lead
♦8. If West plays ♦Q, duck in dummy; assuming he
plays low, win ♦A and lead a third round. West wins
♦Q, but dummy wins a club/return return and the two
long diamonds can be cashed. Game made.

S	W	N	E
–	–	1♦	1♠
1NT(1)	Pass	3NT	End

(1) Balanced 6–9 points with
spades well held.

Contract: 3NT
Opening Lead: ♠7

Tip 100   In notrumps, focus on each opponent separately and ask yourself: 'safe hand'
               or 'danger hand'?

Deal 101

Dealer: South   **Vulnerability: North-South**

When one opponent
can do damage to your
(notrump) contract, but
the other opponent cannot,
you must focus on losing
the lead to the safe hand.
Exercise: Say West is the
danger hand. Play the
following suits to try to
avoid him winning the
lead.

| ♠ 92 |
| ♥ KQ5 |
| ♦ 873 |
| ♣ A10532 |

```
      ♠ KQJ53            ♠ 1086
      ♥ 1082      N      ♥ 9764
      ♦ Q9      W   E    ♦ 1065
      ♣ Q74        S     ♣ KJ9

                  ♠ A74
                  ♥ AJ3
                  ♦ AKJ42
                  ♣ 86
```

(a)	(b)	(c)
North	North	North
AJ32	864	K942
South	South	South
K1098	AKJ52	AJ75

(a) Lead the king and run the ten. If West holds the queen, you have not lost a trick; if East holds the queen, the finesse has lost to the safe hand.

(b) Cash the ace-king to catch a doubleton queen in West's hand. If both follow low, lead a third round in the hope that East holds the queen.

(c) Cash the ace, then lead low to North's nine. You only lose a trick to West when he holds Q10x or better.

What happened

Declarer correctly ducked ♠K lead, then ♠Q, and won ♠A on the third round. This had the desired effect of exhausting East of spades (he knows this from West's overcall in the suit – promising five cards).

At Trick Four declarer cashed ♦A but, knowing that the best odds to avoid losing a trick to ♦Q was a finesse, crossed to ♥Q and led back to ♦J. Oops! West won ♦Q and cashed two more spades. Down one.

What should have happened

Declarer only needed four diamond tricks so could afford to lose a trick provided it was to East (who, thanks to holding up ♠A until the third round, held no more spades). So cash ♦AK at Tricks Four and Five. On the actual hand West's ♦Q drops, promoting ♦J42, and ten tricks are made. If only low diamonds appear under ♦AK, lead a third round in the hope that East holds ♦Q.

S	W	N	E
1♦	1♠	2♣	Pass
3NT	End		

Contract: 3NT
Opening Lead: ♠K

Tip 101 Look for ways to prevent the danger hand from winning the lead.

Deal 102

Dealer: South　　　　　　　**Vulnerability: Neither**

Usually you (South, as
declarer in notrumps)
have no choice as to which
opponent is the danger
hand and which is the safe
hand. But consider:

```
             ♠ K 4 3 2
             ♥ A 7 4 2
             ♦ 8 3
             ♣ 10 9 2

North
xx
South
AJx
```

```
♠ Q 9              N          ♠ J 10 8 7
♥ Q 10 6       W     E        ♥ J 9 5 3
♦ Q 10 7 5 2       S          ♦ K 9 6
♣ K 6 5                        ♣ 8 3

             ♠ A 6 5
             ♥ K 8
             ♦ A J 4
             ♣ A Q J 7 4
```

Say West leads this suit
to East's king (marking
West with the queen) and
it looks as if West has five
cards and East three. You have two possible strategies:

(i) Win the ace immediately.

(ii) Duck the ace until the third round.

Strategy (i) makes East the danger hand, leading through your jack.

Strategy (ii) makes West the danger hand, with his two long cards.

Question: Which strategy is better?

Answer: It depends on which opponent (if any) will win a subsequent lead.

What happened

West's ♦5 lead went to East's ♦K and declarer ducked.
He ducked ♦9 to ♦J and ♦Q and won the third round
with ♦A. Needing tricks from clubs, he crossed to ♠K
and ran ♣10. No good: West won ♣K and cashed two
diamonds. Down one.

S	W	N	E
1♣	1♦(1)	1♥	2♦(1)
3NT	End		

(1) It generally pays to
compete aggressively,
especially when non-
vulnerable.

Contract: 3NT

Opening Lead: ♦5

What should have happened

Because the club finesse is being taken through East,
only West can win the lead in the suit. Appreciating the
power of ♦J, you as declarer should immediately win
♦K with ♦A. This makes West into the safe hand, so
that when you cross to ♠K and run ♣10 to West's ♣K,
there is nothing he can do to hurt you. If West follows
with ♦Q and a third diamond, you win ♦J and cash
your winners, emerging with ten tricks. Better for him
is to return a passive major suit, but you still score nine
tricks. Game made.

Note that if you swap your clubs with dummy's, the
club finesse would be taken into East, in which case it
would be correct to duck the ace of diamonds until the
third round to exhaust him of diamonds (making West
into the danger hand).

Tip 102　If you can choose which opponent to make the danger hand, choose the one
who will not win a subsequent lead.

Deal 103

Dealer: South   **Vulnerability: North-South**

There are twins goals when declaring notrumps:
(a) preventing the opponents from setting up their long suit
(b) setting up your long suit.
Concentrating on (a) over the past few deals, we have studied Avoidance Play.
Now we move to (b): how best to set up your suit. In order to establish a suit, it is imperative that entries

```
              ♠ 9 8 2
              ♥ 10 7 3
              ♦ A K 6 4 2
              ♣ 6 3
♠ Q 10 7 6 4          N          ♠ J 5
♥ J 9                         ♥ Q 8 6 4 2
♦ Q 8 7        W       E      ♦ J 10 2
♣ K J 10          S          ♣ Q 8 4
              ♠ A K 3
              ♥ A K 5
              ♦ 9 3
              ♣ A 9 7 5 2
```

(ways of reaching) are preserved in the hand with the long suit. But say there are no entries to that hand, apart from within the long suit itself. All is not lost.

What happened

Declaring 3NT, South won West's ♠6 lead – to dummy's ♠8 and East's ♠J – with ♠K. He crossed to ♦K, cashed ♦A and led a third diamond. With both opponents following to all three rounds, dummy's two long cards were both masters. But there was no way to reach them.

West won ♦Q and pressed on with ♠Q. Declarer (who had by now realized the error of his ways) forlornly won ♠A, cashed his seven top tricks, and resigned. Down two.

What should have happened

Even on a 3–3 diamond split, declarer must lose a round of the suit. And here is the key motto: *if you have to lose a trick in a suit, it is best to lose the first* (for communication purposes).

Declarer wins ♠K and leads ♦9 but, crucially, plays dummy's ♦2 (key play). East wins ♦10 and returns ♠5 but, provided diamonds are 3–3 (a pre-condition of success), declarer is in control. He wins ♠A and leads ♦3 to ♦AK. With the 3–3 split revealed, he is in dummy and so able to enjoy ♦64. The two long diamonds added to his seven give nine. Game made.

Question: why establish diamonds rather than clubs – both have seven cards?

Answer: even on a 3–3 split, playing clubs means losing the lead twice. The defence would be able to set up spades and a 5–2 split in the suit would lead to defeat.

S	W	N	E
1♣	Pass(1)	1♦	Pass
2NT(2)	Pass	3NT	End

(1) Might bid 1♠.
(2) 17–18 balanced.

Contract: 3NT
Opening Lead: ♠6

Tip 103   If you have to lose a trick in a suit, it is best to lose the first round.

Deal 104

Dealer: South   **Vulnerability: East-West**

You are declaring a notrump contract and seek to make a long suit good. If there are outside entries to the hand with the long suit, they must be preserved. If there are no outside entries, then the entries within the suit must be used at precisely the right moment. The only entry to dummy's clubs on this deal is ♣A. When should the crucial card be played?

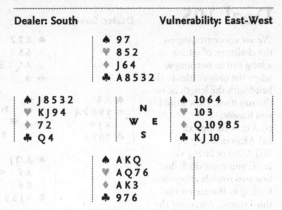

```
                    ♠ 9 7
                    ♥ 8 5 2
                    ♦ J 6 4
                    ♣ A 8 5 3 2
    ♠ J 8 5 3 2              ♠ 1 0 6 4
    ♥ K J 9 4          N     ♥ 1 0 3
    ♦ 7 2          W     E   ♦ Q 10 9 8 5
    ♣ Q 4             S     ♣ K J 10
                    ♠ A K Q
                    ♥ A Q 7 6
                    ♦ A K 3
                    ♣ 9 7 6
```

What happened

Declarer won the spade lead with ♠Q and counted seven top tricks (♠AKQ, ♥A, ♦AK and ♣A). Correctly choosing clubs as the best route to the two extra tricks needed, at Trick Two he crossed to ♣A and...

No need to divulge the rest of the play. Dummy's ♣A had not been used as an entry – it might just as well have been in his hand – and declarer only managed to score his top tricks. Down two.

What should have happened

For ♣A to be a meaningful entry, it needed to be played on declarer's last club. Another way of looking at things is to consider the motto: if you have to lose a trick in a suit, it is best to lose the first or, extending it, if you have to lose two tricks in a suit, it is best to lose the first two.

The correct line, after winning ♠Q, is to duck a club altogether, playing low from both hands. Win the spade return with ♠K and duck a second club. Win the spade return with ♠A and lead your last club to ♣A. You are now in dummy to cash the two long clubs (thanks to the 3–2 split). Game made.

Question: Why go for the extra tricks in clubs rather than hearts?

Answer: Clubs only need a 3–2 split to work (probable), whereas hearts need a finesse and a 3–3 split (very improbable).

S   **W**   **N**   **E**
2NT(1)   Pass   3NT   End

(1) 20–22 points.

Contract: 3NT
Opening Lead: ♠3

Tip 104   For a high card in a long suit to be an effective entry in the establishment process of that suit, it must be used on the last card of the other hand.

Deal 105

We are concentrating on the challenge of setting up a long suit in notrumps, when the only entries to the hand with the length lie in the suit itself. How would you handle:

(i) Axxxx facing xxx
(ii) AKxxxx facing xx
(iii) AQxxxx facing xx?

In (i) you must duck the first two rounds altogether, leading to the ace on the third round. Assuming the

```
                    ♠ 872
                    ♥ 652
                    ♦ A Q 7 5 4 2
                    ♣ 9
     ♠ K 6                      ♠ 10 9 5 4 3
     ♥ J 9 8 7 4         N      ♥ Q 10
     ♦ K J 9         W     E    ♦ 10 3
     ♣ 10 7 4           S       ♣ K Q 8 6
                    ♠ A Q J
                    ♥ A K 3
                    ♦ 8 6
                    ♣ A J 5 3 2
```

suit splits 3–2, you can now cash the two remaining cards in the five-card holding. In (ii) you must duck the first round completely, then lead to the ace-king. If the suit has split 3–2, you can enjoy three more winners. This deal features combination (iii) – see the diamond suit.

What happened

West led ♥7 to East's ♥Q, and declarer won ♥K. Naturally turning his attention to dummy's diamonds – without which he had little chance of garnering nine tricks, at Trick Two declarer led ♦6 to West's ♦9 and dummy's ♦Q. Pleased that the finesse against ♦K succeeded, declarer cashed ♦A and led a third round to West's ♦K.

Declarer had established three diamond winners in dummy... but there was no way to reach them. West continued hearts and declarer struggled on, finally emerging with seven tricks. Down two. Where did he go wrong?

What should have happened

Even with diamonds splitting as favourably as possible (3–2 and ♦K with West), declarer has to lose a trick in the suit. To maintain communications with dummy he must follow the normal procedure of losing the first round.

After winning ♥K, declarer leads ♦8 but ducks West's ♦9 (key play). East overtakes with ♦10 to fire back ♥10, but declarer takes ♥A and leads ♦6. West follows with ♦J, and this time he (successfully) finesses ♦Q. It is now a simple matter to cash ♦A, felling ♦K, and to continue with ♦754. ♠A and ♣A bring the total to nine tricks.

S	W	N	E
1♣	Pass	1♦	Pass
3NT	End		

Contract: 3NT
Opening Lead: ♥7

Tip 105   Ducking, sometimes in conjunction with finessing, retains communications.

Deal 106

Dealer: South   **Vulnerability: Both**

Question: How would you play a suit of AKQxx facing xx?

Answer: It depends. Normally it will be correct to bang down the ace-king-queen. But not always.

```
              ♠ 62
              ♥ 95
              ♦ 9642
              ♣ AKQ52
   ♠ KJ984              ♠ 107
   ♥ J1063       N      ♥ Q87
   ♦ J8      W     E    ♦ KQ73
   ♣ 107         S      ♣ J943
              ♠ AQ53
              ♥ AK42
              ♦ A105
              ♣ 86
```

What happened

West led ♠8 which went to East's ♠10 and declarer's ♠Q. Naturally excited by dummy's clubs, declarer led to dummy's ♣AKQ. West discarded on the third round, so declarer conceded to East's ♣J. He won East's ♠7 continuation with ♠A and looked for a way to reach dummy's established fifth club. As you can see, there was none. All he could do was to cash ♥AK and ♦A then resign. Down one.

What should have happened

The first thing declarer should do is to count his top tricks. ♠AQ (♠Q has been promoted because of West's lead), ♥AK, ♦A and ♣AKQ give him eight top tricks. He only needs one more. Clubs is the right place to garner that extra trick but he can afford to cater for a 4–2 split (more likely than the 3–3 split he needed in any event). If clubs are 4–2 he will have to lose a trick and, as we know, the right time to lose a trick in a suit is the first round.

The correct line, after winning ♠Q, is to duck a club altogether (key play). The defence win and lead a second spade but you can win ♠A, lead over to ♣AKQ (removing all East's clubs), then enjoy ♣5. ♥AK and ♦A bring the total to nine. Game made.

Question: Pretend ♠Q was a low spade. How would you play 3NT now?

Answer: With only seven top tricks, you need two extra tricks from clubs. A 3–3 split is required and the clubs should simply be led from the top.

S	W	N	E
1♥(1)	Pass	2♣	Pass
3NT	End		

(1) Open with the higher ranking of two equal length suits except on this one occasion: prefer 1♥ to 1♠ with 4–4 in both majors.

Contract: 3NT
Opening Lead: ♠8

Tip 106   Count your top tricks before embarking. Knowing how many extra tricks you need may affect how you broach your long suit.

Deal 107

Dealer: South **Vulnerability: Both**

Most so-called 'Rules' in Bridge are merely guidelines. Take the Rule of 20 (open the bidding when your high-card points added to the number of cards in your two longest suits reach 20). I would open ♠KQ1097 ♥AJ108 ♦1085 ♣5 but not ♠AKQ ♥KJ ♦Q862 ♣97532.

However, the Rule of 11 is much more than

	♠ A K 4	
	♥ A K 10	
	♦ 8 7 5	
	♣ 8 6 4 2	
♠ J 8	**N**	♠ Q 10 5 3 2
♥ Q J 8 6 5	**W E**	♥ 3 2
♦ J 4	**S**	♦ 10 9 6 3
♣ K J 9 5		♣ Q 10
	♠ 9 7 6	
	♥ 9 7 4	
	♦ A K Q 2	
	♣ A 7 3	

a guideline – it is mathematically foolproof. It is tremendously useful when declaring notrumps and I shall be spending a few pages divulging all. The Rule of 11 is only to be used at Trick One in notrumps, when the opening lead is 'fourth highest of the longest and strongest suit'. Here is how it works:

(a) Subtract the size of the lead from 11.

(b) The answer tells you how many higher cards than the lead are in the other three hands (apart from the leader's).

(c) Look at your hand and dummy's and count up how many cards are higher than the lead. From this work out how many higher cards are in the partner of the opening leader's hand.

What happened

West led ♥6 and declarer rose with dummy's ♥K. He led to his ♦AKQ but, with the suit failing to split 3–3, soon found that he could not make more than his eight top tricks. Down one.

Have you spotted the trick that got away?

S	W	N	E
1NT	Pass	3NT	End

Contract: 3NT
Opening Lead: ♥6

What should have happened

Apply the Rule of 11 to West's ♥6 lead.

(a) 11 – 6 = 5.

(b) There are thus five higher cards than ♥6 in the other three hands.

(c) You can see three higher in dummy; and two higher in your hand. Ergo, East cannot have any higher heart than ♥6.

So play dummy's ♥10 at Trick One, confident that it will hold the trick. Indeed it does and you can now cash your remaining eight top tricks. Game made.

Tip 107 The Rule of 11 is a foolproof rule for Trick One in notrumps (provided the lead is fourth highest).

TIMES BRIDGE

Deal 108

This declarer was blessed with a favourable lead against his 3NT contract. Could he take advantage?

Dealer: South　　　　　　**Vulnerability: Both**

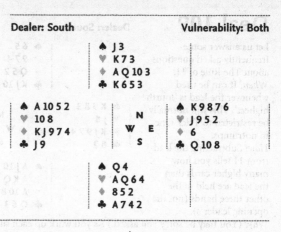

```
              ♠ J 3
              ♥ K 7 3
              ♦ A Q 10 3
              ♣ K 6 5 3

♠ A 10 5 2              N         ♠ K 9 8 7 6
♥ 10 8                            ♥ J 9 5 2
♦ K J 9 7 4        W     E        ♦ 6
♣ J 9                  S          ♣ Q 10 8

              ♠ Q 4
              ♥ A Q 6 4
              ♦ 8 5 2
              ♣ A 7 4 2
```

What happened

After heaving a huge sigh of relief at the lack of a spade lead, declarer never fully focussed himself on the task in hand. Not counting his top tricks (or applying a certain rule), he finessed dummy's ♦Q at Trick One. He was aware that most of the outstanding diamond strength was on his left, but was unwilling to take a deeper finesse for fear of losing the lead and see the defence switch to spades. He next tried the three top hearts. With West discarding (a spade) on the third round, he could only garner seven tricks (♥AKQ, ♦AQ and ♣AK). Down two.

S	W	N	E
1NT	Pass	3NT	End

Contract: 3NT
Opening Lead: ♦7

What should have happened

Declarer had been victim of fuzzy thinking when that mathematically foolproof rule we introduced last deal would have given him all the necessary answers.

At Trick One in notrumps (when the lead is 'fourth highest'), The Rule of 11 should be applied. Subtracting the lead from 11 tells you that there are four higher diamonds than ♦7 in the other three hands (North, East, South). Declarer can see three higher in dummy (♦AQ10) and one higher in hand (♦8), thus he knows there can be no higher diamonds than ♦7 in East's hand.

Declarer confidently plays dummy's ♦3 at Trick One, knowing that he will win the first trick with his ♦8. And so it comes to pass, East following with ♦6. At Trick Two he leads ♦2, to West's ♦4, and dummy's ♦10 (East discarding a spade). He cashes ♥K, crosses to ♥AQ (West also throwing a spade), finesses ♦Q, cashes ♦A and takes his ♣AK. Nine tricks and game made.

Tip 108 Taking the (fourth highest) opening lead from 11 tells you how many (but not which) higher cards than the lead are in the other three hands.

Deal 109

Dealer: South　　　　　**Vulnerability: East-West**

Let us answer some
frequently asked questions
about The Rule of 11.
When? It can be used
whenever the lead is 'fourth
highest'. This will normally
be restricted to Trick One
in notrumps.
How? Subtracting the lead
from 11 tells you how
many higher cards than
the lead are held in the
other hands (not the
opening leader's).

```
              ♠ 6 5
              ♥ 9 7 4
              ♦ Q 5 2
              ♣ K J 10 7 4
♠ K 9 8 3              N       ♠ Q 7 4
♥ J 8                         ♥ 10 6 5 3 2
♦ K J 9 7 4      W       E    ♦ 6 3
♣ 8 2                 S       ♣ A 9 5
              ♠ A J 10 2
              ♥ A K Q
              ♦ A 10 8
              ♣ Q 6 3
```

Why? (You may be sorry you asked.) As you work up each suit, a nine is a nine, a ten is
a ten, a jack is (in effect) an 11, a queen is a 12, a king a 13 and an ace a 14. Take the size
of the lead from 14 (the highest card) and you have the total number of higher cards in
the suit than the card led. But because the opening leader led fourth highest, he has three
of those higher cards. 14 − 3 = 11. So take the lead from 11 and you have the number of
higher cards than the lead in the other three players' hands.

What happened

Declarer won West's ♦7 lead cheaply in hand with ♦8.
He then led ♣Q (ducked) ♣3 to ♣10, ducked again,
and ♣K, taken by East's ♣A. East returned ♦3 to
declarer's ♦10 and West's ♦K, then West led back ♦4
to declarer's ♦A. Declarer had set up two club winners
in dummy but, thanks to East's crafty refusal to win his
♣A until the third round, he had no way to reach them.
All he could do was cash his ♠A and ♥AKQ. Down one.

What should have happened

Declarer needs an entry to dummy's clubs (in case
♣A is held up until the third round). This can only be
♦Q. The Rule of 11 tells him that East has no higher
diamonds than ♦7 (11 − 7 = 4; declarer + dummy have
all four higher diamonds between them). Knowing
that West holds ♦K, declarer must win Trick One with
♦A (key play). East wins the third club with ♣A, but
declarer can subsequently lead towards ♦Q and cash
♣J7. Game made (plus one).

S	W	N	E
2NT(1)	Pass	3NT	End

(1) 20–22 points.

Contract: 3NT
Opening Lead: ♦7

Tip 109　Consider the entry position before automatically winning a trick with the
cheapest card.

Deal 110

Dealer: South   **Vulnerability: North-South**

Last deal we considered
some frequently asked
questions about the Rule
of 11. However, we did not
mention perhaps the most
common query of all: 'Why
lead fourth highest (from
your longest and strongest
suit against notrumps)
and help declarer?' Whilst
it is true that declarer can
draw potentially crucial
clues from the fourth
highest lead, it is still worth

```
                    ♠ K 3 2
                    ♥ K 8
                    ♦ K 6 5
                    ♣ K J 9 7 3
        ♠ Q 9 7              N        ♠ J 8 6
        ♥ J 9 4 3                     ♥ 10 6 2
        ♦ Q 10 8 7      W       E     ♦ A J 9 3
        ♣ 4 2                S        ♣ A 6 5
                    ♠ A 10 5 4
                    ♥ A Q 7 5
                    ♦ 4 2
                    ♣ Q 10 8
```

persevering with that lead. Why? Because partner can take advantage too, also being able
to apply the Rule of 11. Though strictly speaking a test for the defence, I have included
this deal in our Declarer Play section to illustrate the need for the defence to lead fourth
highest, even though it helps declarer.

What happened

West led ♦7 against the 3NT contract, dummy played
low and East won ♦J. At Trick Two he cashed ♦A and
then led ♦3 to dummy's ♦K. Declarer led ♣3 to ♣Q,
returned ♣10 (also ducked) and ♣8, East winning his
♣A on the third round. The defence cashed a fourth
diamond but declarer made the remainder. Nine tricks
and game made – losing three diamonds plus ♣A.

S	W	N	E
1NT	Pass	3NT	End

Contract: 3NT

Opening Lead: ♦7

What should have happened

East should have used the Rule of 11. Subtracting seven
from 11 gives four – the number of higher diamonds
than the lead in the other three hands. With three in his
hand and one visible in dummy, East can work out that
declarer has no higher diamond than ♦7.

At Trick One East makes the key play of ♦3, letting
West's ♦7 win the trick. A second diamond through
dummy's ♦K ensures four diamond tricks for the
defence, with ♣A to come. Down one.

Tip 110   The partner of the opening leader can use the Rule of 11 in exactly the same
way as declarer; but only if partner can be trusted to lead 'fourth highest'.

Deal 111

Dealer: South　　　**Vulnerability: East-West**

This deal we consider
another clue available to
declarer from a 'fourth
highest' opening lead
against notrumps.

Question: What can you
deduce from the lead of
a two?

Answer: Assuming the lead
to be the fourth from the
top, there must be precisely
three higher cards. As there
is no lower card in the pack
than the two, the opening
leader must have precisely
four cards in the suit led.

```
              ♠ A 7 4
              ♥ 8 6 3
              ♦ K Q 10 7 5
              ♣ Q 5
♠ K J 8 2              ♠ Q 10 6
♥ Q 10 5        N     ♥ K 9 7 2
♦ 9 4       W     E   ♦ A 8 6 2
♣ J 8 6 4       S     ♣ 10 9
              ♠ 9 5 3
              ♥ A J 4
              ♦ J 3
              ♣ A K 7 3 2
```

What happened

Declarer ducked West's ♠2 lead in dummy. East won
♠Q and brightly switched to ♥2. In some trouble,
declarer tried ♥J. West won ♥Q and continued with
♥10. Declarer ducked but won ♥5 continuation with
♥A. He led ♦J but East won ♦A and cashed ♥K.
Down one.

What should have happened

West's ♠2 lead indicates a holding of precisely four
cards in spades (assuming ♠2 is his 'fourth highest'). If
declarer ducks, the defence might (indeed did) switch
to hearts, thereby establishing too many winners. If he
wins ♠A immediately and knocks out ♦A, the defence
will be limited to four tricks – three spades and ♦A.

The correct line is to rise with dummy's ♠A at Trick
One (key play), East encouraging the suit by playing
♠10; then to lead ♦5 to ♦J and ♦3 to ♦10 and East's
♦A. East continues with ♠Q (top of a remaining
doubleton) and ♠6. West scores ♠KJ, but his ♥5 exit
(best) is won by declarer's ♥A. Declarer crosses to ♣Q,
cashes ♦KQ7, then leads to ♣AK. Nine tricks and game
made – scoring ♠A, ♥A, four diamonds and ♣AKQ.

S	W	N	E
1NT	Pass	2NT	Pass
3NT(1)	End		

(1) Accepts the invitation to
game with 13 points because
of his five-card suit.

Contract: 3NT

Opening Lead: ♠2

Tip 111　The lead of a two against notrumps indicates that the leader holds precisely
four cards in that suit.

142　　　　　　　　　　　　　　　　　　　　　　TIMES BRIDGE

Deal 112

Dealer: South   **Vulnerability: Both**

We are exploring the
inferences available to
declarer based on the
choice of opening lead
against a notrump contract.
Question: If the opening
lead is a three, which card
do you immediately look
for?
Answer: The two. If you
can see the two in your
hand or dummy, you know
the three was the leader's
lowest card. Assuming his
lead was 'fourth highest',
he must have just four
cards in the suit led.

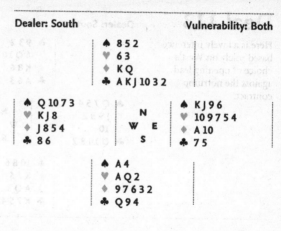

```
              ♠ 8 5 2
              ♥ 6 3
              ♦ K Q
              ♣ A K J 10 3 2

♠ Q 10 7 3              ♠ K J 9 6
♥ K J 8          N      ♥ 10 9 7 5 4
♦ J 8 5 4     W   E     ♦ A 10
♣ 8 6            S      ♣ 7 5

              ♠ A 4
              ♥ A Q 2
              ♦ 9 7 6 3 2
              ♣ Q 9 4
```

What happened

Declarer ducked ♠3 lead to East's ♠K, and won ♠6
continuation with ♠A. He cashed dummy's six clubs
and had a choice for routes for the precious ninth trick.
He could knock out ♦A and establish a diamond trick;
or he could finesse ♥Q and hope that East held ♥K.

Worried about losing the lead and seeing too many
spade winners being cashed (the case if West had begun
with five spades), declarer led ♥3 to ♥Q. No good:
West won ♥K and the defence cashed two more spades
and ♦A. Down one.

What should have happened

Declarer knows that the opposing spades are 4–4.
Why? Because West has led ♠3 yet ♠2 is visible in
dummy. Therefore West has precisely four spades (as
must his partner). Declarer can afford to flush out
♦A, establishing dummy's other honour, because the
opponents will only be able to take three spades and
♦A. What he cannot afford to do is create an extra loser
by finessing ♥Q and losing to ♥K.

The correct line is to win ♠A at Trick One (for fear
of a heart switch), cash six clubs, then lead ♦K. East
wins ♦A and the defence cash three spades. But declarer
has nine tricks: ♠A, ♥A, ♦Q and six clubs.

S	W	N	E
1NT	Pass	3NT(1)	End

(1) No point in mentioning
clubs when 3NT is almost
certain to be a better game
than 5♣.

Contract: 3NT
Opening Lead: ♠3

Tip 112

When the 'fourth highest' opening lead against your notrump contract is a
three, look out for the two. If it is in any other hand but the opening leader's,
he must have precisely four cards in his suit.

Deal 113

Dealer: South　　　　**Vulnerability: Neither**

Here is a lovely inference based solely on West's choice of opening lead against the notrump contract.

```
              ♠ 9 3 2
              ♥ A Q 10 4
              ♦ K 8 6
              ♣ A 6 3
  ♠ Q 7 5 4              ♠ A K J
  ♥ J 9 5 2      N       ♥ 8 3
  ♦ 10       W     E     ♦ J 9 7 5 4 2
  ♣ Q 10 8 2     S       ♣ J 9
              ♠ 10 8 6
              ♥ K 7 6
              ♦ A Q 3
              ♣ K 7 5 4
```

What happened

West led ♣2 to ♣3, ♣J and ♣K. Pleased to have avoided a spade lead, declarer counted eight top tricks: ♥AKQ, ♦AKQ and ♣AK. He correctly assessed that his best (only realistic) chance of a ninth trick was dummy's ♥10. Hoping for ♥J to fall in three rounds, declarer cashed ♥AKQ (the best play taking the suit in isolation). But no ♥J appeared and no ninth trick materialised. Down one.

What should have happened

There was no need to play the key suit immediately. Better to delay matters and seek to gather more information. There is no cost to playing out the top diamonds first and – lo-and-behold – West discards (a spade) on the second top diamond. What do you make of that?

West's lead of ♣2 indicates precisely four cards in the suit (assuming the lead is 'fourth highest'). Presumably he has no five-card suit or he would have preferred that suit to lead. Thus when he turns up with a singleton diamond, his exact distribution must be 4♠4♥1♦4♣.

And now the deal becomes an open book. The correct play is to cash ♥A, cross to ♥K, and lead a third heart towards dummy's ♥Q10. When West plays low a third time, declarer knows to finesse dummy's ♥10 (key play). East discards (as expected), so ♥10 has become declarer's extra trick. He can now cash ♥Q and ♣A. Nine tricks and game made.

S	W	N	E
1NT	Pass	3NT	End

Contract: 3NT
Opening Lead: ♣2

Tip 113　A player leading a two against notrumps (revealing a precisely four-card suit) will not generally have a side five-card suit. If he turns up with a singleton elsewhere, he should have a 4441 shape.

Deal 114

Dealer: South   **Vulnerability: Both**

Question: What is the
universally favoured lead
against notrumps?
Answer: Fourth from the
top of the longest and
strongest suit.
Question: You bid
1NT–3NT. What
deductions can you draw
from the lead of the two
in a known-to-be-feeble
minor?
Answer: He has precisely
four cards in the minor

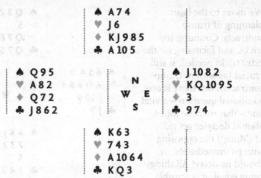

♠ A 7 4
♥ J 6
♦ K J 9 8 5
♣ A 10 5

♠ Q 9 5
♥ A 8 2
♦ Q 7 2
♣ J 8 6 2

♠ J 10 8 2
♥ K Q 10 9 5
♦ 3
♣ 9 7 4

♠ K 6 3
♥ 7 4 3
♦ A 10 6 4
♣ K Q 3

(leading fourth from the top). He will not have a side five-card suit (he would prefer that
lead). Nor is he likely to have another four-card suit (particularly a major – he would
choose a major-suit over a minor suit in marginal cases, as the auction 1NT–3NT often
conceals a good minor-suit fit but rarely a good major-suit fit) because that other four-
card suit would presumably be at least as strong as his weedy choice.
Question: What is his exact distribution.
Answer: 4333.

What happened

Declarer won ♣2 lead – to ♣5, ♣9 and ♣Q. The à
priori odds missing four diamonds including ♦Q are
to 'drop': in other words to cash ♦AK and hope to see
♦Q fall in two rounds. Thinking no further, declarer
cashed ♦A and led to dummy's ♦K. East discarded
an encouraging ♥10, so that when declarer gave West
his ♦Q, West had no trouble in switching to ♥A and
following with ♥8. East cashed three more hearts –
down one.

S	W	N	E
1NT	Pass	3NT	End

Contract: 3NT
Opening Lead: ♣2

What should have happened

Declarer works out from West's ♣2 lead that he has just
four clubs. Unlikely to have another (stronger?) four-
card suit, he is placed with a 3♠3♥3♦4♣ shape. There
is now no problem in diamonds.

The correct line is to win ♣Q, cash ♦A, then run
♦10 (key play), finessing West for ♦Q. ♦4 goes to ♦Q
and ♦K and declarer cashes ten tricks via ♠AK, all five
diamonds and ♣AKQ.

Tip 114   The lead against notrumps from a feeble four-card suit is a strong indication
that the leader's distribution is 4333.

Deal 115

Dealer: South **Vulnerability: East-West**

We move to the basic
planning of trump
contracts. Counting top
tricks, and focussing on the
extra tricks needed, is still
crucial (as with notrump
contracts). But there is one
additional question – a vital
one – that must be asked.
Should declarer get rid
of ('draw') the opposing
trumps immediately, or
should he delay? All things
being equal, it is sensible

```
                ♠ Q 3 2
                ♥ 5
                ♦ Q 7 6 3 2
                ♣ Q 7 5 2
  ♠ 6 5 4                      ♠ 7
  ♥ A Q 9 8 4         N        ♥ K J 10 6
  ♦ J 10 9      W         E    ♦ K 8 5 4
  ♣ J 9                S       ♣ K 10 8 6
                ♠ A K J 10 9 8
                ♥ 7 3 2
                ♦ A
                ♣ A 4 3
```

to remove the opposing trumps, or they will trump his winners. But getting rid of the
opponents' trumps means getting rid of dummy's trumps; and dummy's trumps may be
needed in their own right. Should the missing trumps be drawn immediately on this deal?

What happened

Declarer won ♦J opening lead with ♦A and decided it
would be a good idea to remove the opponents' trumps.
After all, they only held four small ones. He crossed to
♠Q, returned to ♠K (East discarding ♥6) and cashed
♠A (East discarding ♣6). West's trumps were drawn
(the bad news was that so were dummy's trumps).
What next?

Trying to promote dummy's ♣Q, he led ♣3 to ♣9,
♣Q and ♣K. East switched to ♥J, winning the trick,
then ♥K (and ♥10. He next played ♣8 and, though
declarer won ♣A, he had to concede a further trick to
East's ♣10. Down two.

S	W	N	E
1♠	Pass	2♠(1)	Pass
4♠	End		

(1) The best bid, in spite of
the lack of a fourth trump.

Contract: 4♠
Opening Lead: ♦J

What should have happened

You have eight top tricks: six trumps and two aces. The
other two will come from trumping hearts in dummy.
You must not draw trumps yet, or dummy's trumps
will fall helplessly under yours.

Win ♦A and lead ♥2. The opponents win and lead a
trump (best), trying to remove dummy's trumps. Win
♠8, trump ♥3, trump ♦3 (not an extra trick but a way
of returning to hand), trump ♥7 (with ♠Q), and trump
♦6. Only now draw the two remaining trumps. Then
cash ♣A and lead towards ♣Q. It loses to ♣K and East
cashes ♣10, but 10 tricks are made.

Tip 115 Drawing the opponents' trumps also draws dummy's trumps, trumps you
may need for other purposes.

Deal 116

When declaring trump contracts, the key question is 'Should you get rid of the opposing trumps immediately?' Some declarers make the mistake of getting rid of the missing trumps before anything else on virtually every hand, though often dummy's trumps will be needed in their own right to trump his losers (see the previous common mistake). Others

```
              ♠ A J 3
              ♥ J 10 7
              ♦ A Q 10
              ♣ 7 4 3 2
   ♠ 8 6                      ♠ 9 7 2
   ♥ 9 8           N          ♥ 6 5 4 3 2
   ♦ K J 9 8 6   W   E        ♦ 7 3
   ♣ K 8 6 5       S          ♣ Q 10 9
              ♠ K Q 10 5 4
              ♥ A K Q
              ♦ 5 4 2
              ♣ A J
```

make the opposite error. They neglect to get rid of the missing trumps until – disaster – an opponent trumps a winner. Witness this deal.

What happened

West led ♥9 against 6♠ and declarer correctly paused to count top tricks. He had five in trumps; three in hearts (sadly the high cards falling on top of one another); one in diamonds and one in club. Total ten. The extra tricks could only come from promoting both the ♦Q and ♦10.

Having worked this out, declarer won ♥Q, then played ♦2 to ♦10. This was the correct play in the suit, as he needed West to hold both ♦K and ♦J. He got lucky! ♦10 won. He crossed back to ♥K then played ♦4 to ♦Q, also winning. Delighted with his successful finessing, he next tried to cash ♦A... and the roof fell in. East trumped and led ♥4. West trumped ♥A and the defence waited for their club trick. Down two.

What should have happened

Declarer's play in diamonds was impeccable, but there was no reason not to draw the opposing trumps first. The correct line is: win ♥Q, cross to ♠AJ, back to ♠10, ♦2 to ♦10, back to ♥K, ♦4 to ♦Q; then cash ♦A, ♥A and ♣A; just concede one club. 12 tricks. Slam made.

S	W	N	E
–	–	1NT	Pass
3♠	Pass	4♠	Pass
6♠(1)	End		

(1) 33 partnership points are needed for a good slam, less if there is a big fit, good controls (i.e. aces) and some shape. Here South knows that two of those three factors are present: the fit and the controls. He is prepared to take a gamble on slam given that the partnership are at most two points short of that 33.

Contract: 6♠
Opening Lead: ♥9

Tip 116　Get rid of the opposing trumps unless you have a reason not to.

Deal 117

Dealer: South

Vulnerability: Neither

Have a look at this deal. Do you think that declarer's basic strategy should be to draw trumps straight away? Or should he play on the other suits and leave trumps well alone?

```
              ♠ Q J 6
              ♥ 8 7 4 3
              ♦ A Q J 5
              ♣ K 7
♠ 10                          ♠ 9 5 4 3 2
♥ A Q 9          N            ♥ K J
♦ 10 8 6 4 3 2  W   E         ♦ 7
♣ 9 3 2          S            ♣ J 10 8 6 5
              ♠ A K 8 7
              ♥ 10 6 5 2
              ♦ K 9
              ♣ A Q 4
```

What happened

With such lousy trumps, declarer was understandably frightened to try to draw them. Instead he won ♠10 lead with dummy's ♠Q, crossed to ♦K, and led back to dummy's ♦J. At this point the roof fell in.

East ruffed the second diamond, with ♥J. He then correctly led a second spade. West ruffed with ♥9 and led a third diamond. East ruffed with ♥K and led a third spade. West ruffed with ♥Q and his ♥A took the fifth defensive trick. Down two.

Declarer had allowed the defence to score all their five trumps separately.

What should have happened

Declarer should realize that he has a plethora of side-suit winners and that his only losers are in trumps. Leading trumps himself will draw two of the opposing trumps on one trick, and so prevent the opposition from scoring too many of their trumps separately.

Win ♠10 with ♠Q and lead ♥3 to East's ♥J. East leads a second spade for West to trump (with ♥Q) and West switches to a diamond. Win and lead a second trump. ♥K and ♥A crash together. 10 tricks and game made.

S	W	N	E
1♥(1)	Pass	4♥(2)	End

(1) Theoretically the correct choice. In modern English Standard Acol the higher ranking of two equal-length suits is opened except when holding four hearts and four spades.

(2) Again theoretically sound, with the known fit. However, 3NT would be a far superior contract.

Contract: 4♥
Opening Lead: ♠10

Tip 117 With weak trumps between your hand and dummy, it is usually best to draw the opposing trumps early – to prevent them from scoring separately.

Deal 118

Dealer: South **Vulnerability: Neither**

We have been looking at when it is correct to draw all the opposing trumps immediately; and when the missing trumps should be left at bay, whilst declarer has more urgent business to attend to (typically using dummy's trumps for trumping his losers). Can it ever be right to draw some of the opposing trumps, but not all? The answer is yes, and the clearest time is

```
              ♠ A 8 6 5
              ♥ 8 3
              ♦ Q 7 4
              ♣ K J 4 2
  ♠ Q J 9              N      ♠ 3
  ♥ Q J 10 9                  ♥ 7 5 4
  ♦ K 10 2        W      E    ♦ A J 9 6 5
  ♣ 9 7 3              S      ♣ Q 10 8 5
              ♠ K 10 7 4 2
              ♥ A K 6 2
              ♦ 8 3
              ♣ A 6
```

when the opponents have just one trump remaining that is higher than all of yours. Why waste two of your trumps getting rid of a trump that is going to win a trick anyway? The Rule of One states 'Leave a Master Trump Outstanding'. There are very few hands where obeying the Rule will let you down. Conversely disobeying it (our common mistake) can have disastrous consequences.

What happened

Declarer won West's ♥Q lead with ♥K, then crossed to ♠A and returned to ♠K (East discarding ♦5). In order to remove the last missing trump, he next led ♠4. West won ♠Q (East discarding ♦6) and continued with ♥J. Declarer won ♥A and trumped ♥2 with dummy's last trump, ♠8. He crossed to ♣A, but was faced with three further losers, two diamonds and his fourth heart. In an effort to create an extra trick, he next led ♣6 to dummy's ♣J.

The finesse failed, ♣J losing to ♣Q. East then cleverly led ♦9 and West won ♦K, cashed ♥10, and led ♦10 to East's ♦J. Declarer was left with two trumps but was two down.

What should have happened

Declarer's mistake was wasting a trump in each hand to get rid of West's master ♠Q.

The correct line is as follows: Win ♥Q with ♥K, cross to ♠A, back to ♠K, then, leaving ♠Q outstanding, cash ♥A, trump ♥2, return to ♣A, trump ♥6, cash ♣K, trump ♣4, and concede two diamonds and the master ♠Q. Game made.

S	W	N	E
1♠	Pass	3♠	Pass
4♠	End		

Contract: 4♠
Opening Lead: ♥Q

Tip 118 The Rule of One: leave the master trump outstanding.

Deal 119

Declarer holds very good trumps on this deal and the question is: should he draw the opposing trumps straight away or should he delay matters? It might appear sensible to get rid of the opposing trumps immediately – they are very small and should not score tricks unless they trump your winners. Is this correct?

```
              ♠ Q 10 9
              ♥ 7 5
              ♦ 10 8 6 5
              ♣ J 5 3 2
  ♠ 3                        ♠ 7 6 5
  ♥ K 10 3 2        N        ♥ A Q 8 6
  ♦ Q J 9 7 3    W     E     ♦ 4 2
  ♣ Q 9 4           S        ♣ K 10 8 6
              ♠ A K J 8 4 2
              ♥ J 9 4
              ♦ A K
              ♣ A 7
```

What happened

Declarer won ♦Q lead with ♦K and immediately drew trumps. This took three rounds (no surprise as four missing cards are more likely to split 3–1 than 2–2). With dummy now having no trumps left, declarer played out his two minor-suit aces but was left with three losing hearts and a losing club at the end. Down one.

What should have happened

Declarer counts nine top tricks: six trumps: ♦AK and ♣A. He can generate a tenth by trumping a heart in dummy. But this requires dummy to hold a trump. Because drawing the opposing trumps involves drawing dummy's trumps, he must delay drawing trumps.

Win ♦Q with ♦K and immediately lead a heart (key play). The defence win and do best to lead trumps themselves (trying to get rid of dummy's trumps before you can use them to trump hearts). Win dummy's ♠9 and lead a second heart. East wins and leads a second trump. Win in hand and trump your third heart with dummy's last trump (this is the tenth trick). Cross to hand with ♣A and draw the last trump. Game made.

Play hearts early and you lose just two of them as you trump the third in dummy; play hearts late and you lose all three.

S	W	N	E
2♠	Pass	2NT(1)	Pass
3♠	Pass	4♠(2)	End

(1) Negative – showing any hand with 0–7 points.
(2) Just enough to try for game – with three such good trumps.

Contract: 4♠
Opening Lead: ♦Q

Tip 119   Delay drawing trumps when you need dummy's trumps for trumping. This will be possible when you have a side-suit with fewer cards in dummy than in your hand.

Deal 120

Dealer: South   **Vulnerability: East-West**

If dummy has a side-suit that is shorter than yours, there is potential for using dummy's trumps to trump your extra card(s) in that suit.

```
                 ♠ 8 3
                 ♥ K 5 4
                 ♦ 9 5 3 2
                 ♣ A 6 5 2
  ♠ K J 9                      ♠ A 10 6 5 2
  ♥ 10 8 7 3         N         ♥ 9
  ♦ J 8           W     E      ♦ Q 10 7 6
  ♣ Q J 10 7         S         ♣ 9 8 4
                 ♠ Q 7 4
                 ♥ A Q J 6 2
                 ♦ A K 4
                 ♣ K 3
```

What happened

In 4♥, declarer won ♣Q lead with ♣K, and counted nine top tricks (wishing he was in 3NT). Spotting the potential length winner of dummy's fourth diamond, he crossed to ♥K, returned to ♥AQJ (drawing the missing trumps – splitting four-one – and discarding ♣5 from dummy), then cashed ♦AK and led ♦4.

Even had diamonds split three-three, establishing dummy's thirteenth card, the defence could cash three quick spades when in with the third diamond. In fact, East won with ♦10 and returned ♦Q, but nothing mattered. After ruffing and crossing to dummy's ♣A, declarer had no way to avoid three spade losers. Down one.

What should have happened

If declarer was going to concentrate on the potential length winner in diamonds, he needed to play ♦AK and ♦4 before dummy's trumps were gone (with dummy able to trump the third spade).

But dummy's ability to trump the third spade presents a far better opportunity than three-three diamonds. The correct line is to forget diamonds, rather to lose two spades early and trump the third spade in dummy.

Win ♣K, lose a spade. The defence return a trump (best to try to remove dummy's trumps). Win ♥K, lose a second spade. West wins and returns a second trump. Win ♥J and trump a third spade with dummy's last trump (the extra trick). Cross to ♦K, cash ♥AQ and claim in top tricks. Game made.

S	W	N	E
1♥	Pass	2♥(1)	Pass
4♥	End		

(1) Likely to be more helpful than the 'dustbin' 1NT response, even without the fourth trump.

Contract: 4♥
Opening Lead: ♣Q

Tip 120   If dummy has a short side-suit that has fewer cards than you, try to void it a.s.a.p whilst dummy still has trumps to trump your extra card(s).

Deal 121

Look at the trump suit, hearts, on our featured deal. How many trump tricks are available? Right, there are five. Would you be creating a sixth trump trick if you lead a non-trump card from dummy and trump ('ruff') it with your two of hearts? *Answer*: NO. It is a pure illusion. You will now only make four heart tricks (in addition to the ruff).

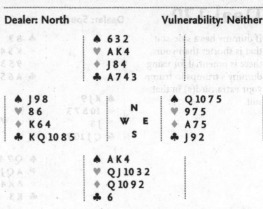

```
             ♠ 6 3 2
             ♥ A K 4
             ♦ J 8 4
             ♣ A 7 4 3
♠ J 9 8                      ♠ Q 10 7 5
♥ 8 6            N           ♥ 9 7 5
♦ K 6 4      W     E         ♦ A 7 5
♣ K Q 10 8 5     S           ♣ J 9 2
             ♠ A K 4
             ♥ Q J 10 3 2
             ♦ Q 10 9 2
             ♣ 6
```

You have gained nothing. Needlessly trumping in the hand with the longer trump length (usually your hand) is at best pointless and at worst dangerous. As this declarer found out to his cost.

What happened

Declarer won West's ♣K lead with ♣A. At Trick Two he led ♣2 and trumped it with ♥2, seemingly a terrific trick for his side. He then set about drawing the opposing trumps. He led ♥3 to ♥K, cashed ♥A (both opponents following to reveal the 3–2 split), then led ♥4 to ♥J. The opposing trumps drawn, declarer now (correctly) turned his attention to diamonds. He led ♦2 to ♦4, ♦J and ♦A and East shrewdly returned his last club, ♣J.

Declarer, feeling a little uneasy, trumped with his last trump, ♥Q (discarding ♠4 would only prolong the agony). But when he led ♦Q, West won ♦K and cashed ♣Q and ♣10, declarer helplessly discarding. Down one.

What should have happened

Declarer dug his own grave by trumping the club at Trick Two. If he followed his actual line of play exactly, but without that trick (trumping ♣2 with ♥2), he would have had one more trump.

The correct line is as follows: Win ♣A, cash ♥A, cash ♥K, lead ♥4 to ♥10; lead ♦2 to ♦J and East's ♦A; trump ♣J with ♥J, lead ♦Q to ♦A; trump ♣Q with ♥Q, cash ♦109, cash ♠AK, concede ♠4. Game made.

S	W	N	E
		1NT	Pass
3♥	Pass	4♥	End

Contract: 4♥

Opening Lead: ♣K

Tip 121   Do not trump needlessly in the long trump hand (typically yours).

Deal 122

Dealer: South **Vulnerability: Both**

The importance of trumping in dummy (the short trump hand) cannot be over-stressed. Conversely trumping in hand is not inherently a good policy (those trumps will score tricks anyway as a result of their length). However, as the means to an end, trumping in hand can be essential. Typically that end is setting up length winners in dummy.

```
              ♠ 10 8 2
              ♥ 8 4
              ♦ A K 6 4 2
              ♣ 6 4 2
  ♠ 9 7 4                    ♠ 6 5
  ♥ K Q J 5         N        ♥ 10 9 7 6
  ♦ Q 10 5      W     E      ♦ J 8 3
  ♣ A 8 7          S         ♣ K J 10 3
              ♠ A K Q J 3
              ♥ A 3 2
              ♦ 9 7
              ♣ Q 9 5
```

What happened

Declarer won ♥K lead with ♥A and counted eight top tricks in his 4♠ contract. At Trick Two he led back ♥2 (to void the dummy in preparation for trumping his third heart). This would only give him one extra trick (he needed two), but there was an even more pressing problem with the plan. For East won ♥9 and returned ♣J. Declarer ducked his ♣Q, but the defence quickly followed with ♣3 to ♣A and ♣7 back to ♣K. Down one.

What should have happened

Declarer's only chance lies in dummy's diamonds. Having bid aggressively, he needs to be lucky – the suit must split three-three (with trumps three-two) for the two extra tricks to be generated.

The correct line is: win ♥A, cross to ♦AK (♠AK can be cashed first), trump ♦2 with ♠J (noting the even split), cash ♠AK, lead ♠3 to ♠10 (drawing the last trump), then cash the established ♦64 (discarding two losers from hand). 10 tricks (five trumps, ♥A, ♦AK plus established ♦64) and game made.

S	W	N	E
1♠	Pass	2♠(1)	Pass
3♠(2)	Pass	4♠(3)	End

(1) The single major raise with just three trumps is acceptable in a hand that lacks the values to bid a new suit at the two-level. But a jump-raise (e.g. 1♠ – 3♠) requires 4+ trumps.
(2) Invitational to game.
(3) Marginal (you could say very optimistic). North hopes his fine diamonds will set up.

Contract: 4♠
Opening Lead: ♥K

Tip 122 Trumping in your hand as an end in itself is generally pointless. But as a means to the end of setting up a suit in dummy, it can be most worthwhile.

Deal 123

Dealer: South **Vulnerability: North-South**

Setting up a long suit in dummy is a wonderful way of making extra tricks. Because it takes time and often requires several ways of reaching dummy ('entries'), the process should begin as soon as possible.

```
              ♠ Q 10 2
              ♥ 7 5 3
              ♦ J 8
              ♣ K 6 4 3 2
  ♠ 9 6 3                    ♠ 8
  ♥ K Q 10 4       N         ♥ J 6 2
  ♦ K 9 5 3     W     E      ♦ A 7 6 4 2
  ♣ J 9            S         ♣ Q 10 8 7
              ♠ A K J 7 5 4
              ♥ A 9 8
              ♦ Q 10
              ♣ A 5
```

What happened

Declarer had nine top tricks in his 4♠ contract: six trumps, ♥A and ♣AK. He won ♥K lead with ♥A, crossed to ♠Q and returned to ♠J, East discarding.

Belatedly turning his attention to dummy's clubs, declarer cashed ♣A, crossed to ♣K, then trumped ♣3 (remembering to trump high, with ♠K). West discarded to reveal the 4–2 split. Declarer crossed to ♠10 (drawing West's last trump), trumped ♣4, and had only to cross to dummy and he would have been able to enjoy the established ♣6. But sadly he had no way of reaching dummy and so had to lose two tricks in each red suit – as ♣6 remained stranded. Down one.

What should have happened

In order to conserve dummy's entries (♠10 and ♠Q), declarer should start establishing dummy's clubs immediately. At Trick Two he cashes ♣A; he then crosses to ♣K and trumps ♣3 (with ♠J). He crosses to ♠10 and trumps ♣4 (with ♠K). Needing to reach dummy's ♠Q on the third round of trumps (in case of a three-one split), he first cashes ♠A (East discarding), then crosses to ♠Q (drawing West's third trump), then cashes the established ♣6, discarding a red-suit loser. He loses three red-suit tricks but ten tricks are his – via six trumps, ♥A, ♣AK and, crucially ♣6. Game made.

S	W	N	E
1♠	Pass	2♠(1)	Pass
4♠	End		

(1) Partner is most unlikely to have a minimum opener with just four spades: he would have opened a weak 1NT. Hence the single raise without a fourth trump will rarely backfire.

Contract: 4♠
Opening Lead: ♥K

Tip 123 It is usually correct to start setting up a side-suit as soon as possible – and that means before drawing the opposing trumps.

Deal 124

Dealer: North   **Vulnerability: Neither**

Entries are crucial in the
setting up of a long suit.
Consider:

Dummy
Axxxx
Declarer (you)
xx

If you lead to dummy's ace
on the first round and lose
the second round, you have
not used the ace as an entry
and will need to get back to
dummy to trump the third
round. However, if you

```
              ♠ K J 2
              ♥ A 6 5 4 2
              ♦ A 8
              ♣ 7 6 3
♠ 9 7 4                      ♠ 8
♥ J 7          N            ♥ K Q 10 9
♦ Q 10 7 4   W   E          ♦ K J 6 5 2
♣ K 10 8 5      S           ♣ Q 9 4
              ♠ A Q 10 6 5 3
              ♥ 8 3
              ♦ 9 3
              ♣ A J 2
```

lose the first round of the suit, the ace takes the second round and you are in dummy to
trump the third round. You have gained an entry.

What happened

Declarer withheld dummy's ♦A at Trick One, but
East won ♦K and cleverly returned ♦5 to remove the
dummy entry. Declarer won and knew about setting
up suits before drawing trumps (to preserve the trump
entries). He cashed ♥A and led ♥2. East won and
returned ♣4.

Winning ♣A, declarer crossed to ♠J and trumped ♥3
(with ♠10), West discarding. He cashed ♠A, crossed to
♠K and trumped ♥5. ♥6 was now set up but there was
no way to reach it. Declarer had to lose two clubs at the
end – down one.

What should have happened

You as declarer must use ♥A as an entry. After winning
♦A, lead ♥2 (without cashing ♥A – key play). East
wins and switches to ♠8 (best at this point). Win ♠A
(preserving dummy's ♠KJ). Lead ♥8 to ♥A, trump
♥4 (with ♠10), cross to ♠J, trump ♥5 (with ♠Q),
cross to ♠K (drawing West's last trump), and cash the
established ♥6. 10 tricks and game made.

S	W	N	E
–	–	1NT(1)	Pass
4♠(2)	End		

(1) More descriptive of
strength and shape than
opening 1♥ – and avoids the
rebid problem.
(2) No way to invite to 4♠
(3♠ offers a choice of games)
so South simply blasts and
hopes.

Contract: 4♠
Opening Lead: ♦4

Deal 125

Some long suits beg to
be set up. Others look so
feeble that they can all-too-
easily be ignored. Take:

Dummy
65432
Declarer (you)
7

Bearing in mind that the
most likely split of the
seven missing cards (by far)
is four-three, dummy has a
potential fifth round length
winner. It will be far from

```
              ♠ Q 9 7
              ♥ 8 3
              ♦ 6 5 4 3 2
              ♣ A 3 2
♠ 5 2                      ♠ 4
♥ Q J 10 5        N        ♥ K 9 7 6 2
♦ A J 9 8     W       E    ♦ K Q 10
♣ K 10 8          S        ♣ Q 7 6 5
              ♠ A K J 10 8 6 3
              ♥ A 4
              ♦ 7
              ♣ J 9 4
```

trivial to score the trick, however. No less than four entries will be needed (trumping the
second, third and fourth rounds then returning to dummy to enjoy the fifth).

What happened

Declarer won ♥Q lead with ♥A and counted nine
top tricks (seven trumps, ♥A and ♣A). Overlooking
dummy's diamonds, declarer could see little hope for a
tenth trick. He drew trumps in two rounds, finishing in
dummy, then led a low club, playing for a miracle in the
suit. Say East held ♣K10 doubleton and rose with ♣K.
Declarer could subsequently lead ♣J and pin his ♣10,
so setting up his ♣9. It was not to be. East played low,
declarer tried ♣9 and West won ♣10. No tenth trick
materialized and 4♠ went down one.

What should have happened

Spotting the potential of dummy's five-card diamond
suit, you as declarer win ♥A and immediately lead ♦7
(key play). The defence win, cash a heart, and switch to
a club (best). Win ♣A (on the first or second round),
trump ♦3, cross to ♠7, trump ♦4 (with ♠10), cross to
♠9, trump ♦5 (with ♠K), cross to ♠Q, then cash the
established ♦6. 10 tricks and game made.

Note that an opening lead of either black suit
would defeat the game, by removing a dummy entry
prematurely.

S	W	N	E
1♠	Pass(1)	2♠	Pass(1)
4♠	End		

(1) Both players are close to
a take-out double, but recall
the motto: 'Don't fight the
spade suit'.

Contract: 4♠
Opening Lead: ♥Q

Tip 125 Do not overlook a long suit, however weak, in a hand with entries.

Deal 126

Dealer: North **Vulnerability: Both**

We have been looking at the process of using trumps to set up a long side-suit in dummy. Preservation of entries – often in the trump suit itself – is vital. Here are two pointers that will save you from the embarrassment of blocking yourself from dummy in trumps:

(a) Retain trumps in your hand that are lower than dummy's.

(b) Lead to the lowest trump entry in dummy first.

```
              ♠ J 9 7
              ♥ Q 4
              ♦ K Q 9
              ♣ A 7 5 4 2
♠ 2                         ♠ 5 4
♥ J 10 9 8 7      N         ♥ K 6 3 2
♦ 10 7 5 3    W     E       ♦ A 8 6
♣ J 9 6           S         ♣ K 10 8 3
              ♠ A K Q 10 8 6 3
              ♥ A 5
              ♦ J 4 2
              ♣ Q
```

S	W	N	E
–	–	1NT	Pass
6♠(1)	End		

(1) Hard to bid scientifically, but facing most balanced 12–14 point hands, a 6♠ slam should have a decent play.

Contract: 6♠
Opening Lead: ♥J

What happened

West's ♥J lead went to dummy's ♥Q, East's ♥K and declarer won ♥A. Staring at a loser in each red suit, declarer needed to set up a long club in dummy to discard his heart and would need a four-three split.

Declarer led ♣Q to ♣A (West would cover with ♣K if he had it so there was no point in running ♣Q). He ruffed ♣2 (with ♠3), then led ♠6 to ♠J. He ruffed ♣3 (with ♠8) and realized to his horror that his last four trumps were ♠AKQ10 and dummy's were ♠97. He had squandered two of his three trump entries to dummy, flouting both (a) and (b) above. With no quick way back to dummy he tried ♦2 to ♦Q but East won ♦A and the defence cashed a heart. Down one.

What should have happened

Win ♥A, lead ♣Q to ♣A, and trump ♣2 with ♠A (preserving the lower trumps – see (a)). Lead ♠3 to ♠7 (lowest trump entry – see (b)), trump ♣4 with ♠K, lead ♠6 to ♠9, trump ♣5 with ♠Q, then lead ♠8 to ♠J and enjoy the established ♣7, discarding ♥5. Finally lead to ♦Q and flush out ♦A. Trump East's heart return (with ♠10) and cash ♦K and ♦J. 12 tricks and slam made.

Tip 126 To avoid squandering entries, cross to the lowest trump entry in dummy first.

Deal 127

In a perfect world, you would count up both your winners and your losers when declaring a trump contract. Counting winners (after all, it is a game of making tricks) is more important. But a quick tally of your losers can make all the difference.

You might think that adding up winners to losers will always give you 13, the number of tricks; in which

```
                ♠ A K 4
                ♥ Q J 10 8
                ♦ 7 4 2
                ♣ 8 7 5
   ♠ J 9 7                    ♠ Q 10 8 5 3 2
   ♥ 7 3           N          ♥ A
   ♦ A 9 6 5   W     E        ♦ 10 8 3
   ♣ K Q J 3       S          ♣ 10 9 4
                ♠ 6
                ♥ K 9 6 5 4 2
                ♦ K Q J
                ♣ A 6 2
```

case counting winners will always give you the number of losers (by subtracting from 13). But look at this deal. Winning West's ♣K lead with ♣A, you count ten winners (♠AK, five trumps: all bar ♥A, two easily established diamonds, plus ♣A). That would suggest getting on with drawing trumps, knocking out the ace, before any of your winners are trumped, expecting to emerge with ten tricks.

What happened

And that is precisely what declarer did, leading to ♥Q at Trick Two. But the defence won ♥A, cashed two clubs, and later came to ♦A. Down one.

What should have happened

Declarer did indeed have ten winners. But he had four losers (♥A, ♦A and two clubs). Total 14.

Question: why did the total of winners + losers = 14?

Answer: because there was a winner that wasn't used (effectively it was used at Trick 14): ♠K.

The crux is that there was an overlapping winner in spades that needed to be cashed to discard a loser. Put another way, there are more spade winners than the number of spades in your hand.

The correct line after winning ♣A is to cross to ♠AK discarding a club (key play), and only then to draw trumps. That way you have 10 winners and only three losers (two club losers have become one).

S	W	N	E
1♥	Pass	3♥	Pass
4♥	End		

Contract: 4♥

Opening Lead: ♣K

Tip 127   Though counting winners is more important in a trump contract, a quick tally of losers can help.

Deal 128

When declaring a trump contract it is vital that you look to see if dummy has an overlapping winner. This will happen when there are more winners in a suit than you have cards in your hand.

Examples are:

Dummy	Dummy
AKx	AKQ
Declarer	Declarer
x	xx

Dummy	Dummy
AQx	Ax
Declarer	Declarer
Kx	K

```
                ♠ Q 5 3 2
                ♥ 8 4 2
                ♦ A Q 5
                ♣ 8 7 6
     ♠ 8                        ♠ A 4
     ♥ A 10 6 3        N        ♥ K Q J
     ♦ K 10 6 4    W       E    ♦ J 9 8 7 2
     ♣ J 10 9 5        S        ♣ 4 3 2
                ♠ K J 10 9 7 6
                ♥ 9 7 5
                ♦ 3
                ♣ A K Q
```

In such situations it is advisable to cash your winners in the suit early, for it will enable you to discard a loser from hand. This will be particularly vital when you have too many fast losers. On our featured deal, declarer escaped the heart lead that would have doomed his ambitious 4♠ contract (three fast heart losers plus ♠A). Could he take advantage?

What happened

At the table declarer won ♣Q and led a trump, hoping the defence would not find the heart switch. No good. East won ♠A and promptly cashed ♥KQJ. Down one.

What should have happened

Declarer's only hope is to discard a heart from hand before losing to ♠A. He needs dummy to have an overlapping winner in diamonds, which means taking the finesse and hoping West holds ♦K.

The correct line is to win ♣Q and lead ♦3 to ♦Q (key play). With West holding ♦K (a 50% chance, but that is all you've got) you have created an overlapping winner in the form of ♦A. You cash it, discarding a heart loser, and only now knock out ♠A. You lose just two hearts and ♠A. Or, put another way, you score five trumps, ♦AQ, and ♣AKQ.

S	W	N	E
1♠	Pass	2♠	Pass
4♠(1)	End		

(1) (Over) optimistic facing a weak (6–9 point) raise.

Contract: 4♠

Opening Lead: ♣J

Tip 128   When the recommended quick tally of losers indicates that there are too many, you must look to see if there are any actual or potential overlapping winners in dummy.

Deal 129

Dealer: South **Vulnerability: Both**

When declaring a trump contract, a look to see if dummy has any overlapping winners is essential. On this deal, the heart suit presented declarer with two overlapping winners (♥AQ). Greed was to be his downfall.

```
              ♠ 8 5
              ♥ A Q 3
              ♦ 9 7 6 3
              ♣ 5 4 3 2
♠ Q J 10 6              ♠ K 9 7 3 2
♥ 10 8 6 5 4      N      ♥ J 9 7 2
♦ K J 2      W     E     ♦ Q 5
♣ 10             S       ♣ J 7
              ♠ A 4
              ♥ K
              ♦ A 10 8 4
              ♣ A K Q 9 8 6
```

What happened

Declarer won ♠Q lead with ♠A and cashed ♣AK, drawing the three missing trumps. He cashed ♥K and then looked for a way of reaching dummy to score ♥AQ. The infuriating trump pips meant that there was no quick route, so he cashed ♦A and led ♦4, vainly hoping that the defence would win and lead a heart.

No such luck! East beat West's ♦J with ♦Q and made the fine play of leading a low spade to West's ♠10, enabling West to cash ♦K. Declarer had the rest – his fourth diamond was good – but was down one.

What should have happened

Given that the fourth round of diamonds will be a winner (unless one opponent holds ♦KQJx of the suit), there is only one loser that declarer needs to dispose of: the second spade. He does not need both dummy's overlapping heart winners, just one. And that is just as well, for the only way to reach dummy involves overtaking ♥K with dummy's ♥A, so reducing the number of overlapping winners in the suit to one.

The correct line is to win ♠A, cash ♣AK, then overtake ♥K with ♥A (key play); next to cash ♥Q discarding ♠4 and to play on diamonds, leading to ♦A and following with ♦4. The defence win and try to cash a spade, but you trump and lead ♦8 to establish your fourth card as a length winner. 11 tricks and game made.

S	W	N	E
1♣(1)	Pass	2♣	Pass
5♣(2)	End		

(1) Unable to open 2♣ (any hand with 23+ points), South chooses 1♣, preparing to...
(2) ...catch up. But perhaps he should have thought about 3NT (an easy make).

Contract: 5♣
Opening Lead: ♠Q

Tip 129 Examine the entry-to-dummy situation. If there is a scarcity, you may have to overtake winners.

Deal 130

Dealer: North **Vulnerability: East-West**

A blocked suit is one which
requires transportation
in another suit in order
to score all the tricks. By
definition there will be
overlapping winner(s). E.g.
(i) K facing AQ2
(ii) AQ facing K32
(iii) KQJ facing A432
In (i) the king is cashed,
then a card of another suit
led to reach the hand with
its stranded ace-queen.
Note: if there is no way

```
              ♠ K 6 2
              ♥ Q J 5 3
              ♦ A 5 2
              ♣ Q 8 6
   ♠ 9 7                    ♠ 10 8 5
   ♥ 10 7 4         N       ♥ 9 8 6 2
   ♦ K Q J 9    W     E     ♦ 7 6 3
   ♣ A 9 5 4        S       ♣ K 10 7
              ♠ A Q J 4 3
              ♥ A K
              ♦ 10 8 4
              ♣ J 3 2
```

to reach the other hand (see previous deal), overtake the king with the ace and cash the
queen, at least scoring two tricks in the suit.
In (ii) the ace-queen are cashed, and then a card of another suit led to reach the stranded
king.
In (iii) the king-queen-jack are cashed, then a card of another suit led to reach the ace.
Note: with no entry, the third round must be overtaken, hoping for a 3–3 split. On our
featured deal the heart suit was blocked. Declarer failed to cope.

What happened

Declarer won ♦K lead with ♦A, cashed ♠K, crossed to
♠AQ (drawing the trumps), followed with ♥AK, then
led ♣2, trying to reach dummy's ♥QJ via ♣Q. No good.
East beat ♣Q with ♣K and led back ♣10 (best). West
beat declarer's ♣J with ♣A and cashed ♣9 plus ♦QJ.
Down two.

What should have happened

With ♦A removed at Trick One, declarer's only entry
to dummy's ♥QJ is ♠K. After winning ♦A, he crosses
to ♠AQ (retaining ♠K). He then unblocks ♥AK before
leading to ♠K (drawing the last trump). Key play. He
cashes ♥QJ discarding two diamonds, and merely loses
three clubs at the end. 10 tricks and game made.

S	W	N	E
–	–	1NT	Pass
3♠	Pass	4♠	End

Note that, though 3NT would
be easier, it is normal for
South to jump to 3♠ to show
a game-going hand with
five spades and for North to
raise to 4♠ with three-card
support.

Contract: 4♠
Opening Lead: ♦K

Tip 130 Spot a blocked suit at the beginning of a hand. Provision may need to be
made early.

Deal 131

Dealer: South **Vulnerability: Neither**

The issue of whether to begin a trump contract by drawing trumps is not a simple one (sorry). Here are the major situations where you should delay drawing the missing trumps, and why.

(1) When dummy has a short side-suit with fewer cards than you. Your first priority should be to void dummy of that suit and then to trump your extra card(s) with dummy's trumps.

```
                    ♠ Q 8 4
                    ♥ K J 8 6
                    ♦ K Q 7
                    ♣ 10 7 4
    ♠ A 10 7 2               ♠ 9 6
    ♥ 7 5 2          N       ♥ 9 4
    ♦ 9 8         W     E    ♦ J 10 6 4 3 2
    ♣ K 9 6 5        S       ♣ A Q 3
                    ♠ K J 5 3
                    ♥ A Q 10 3
                    ♦ A 5
                    ♣ J 8 2
```

Reason for delaying: Drawing the missing trumps involves drawing dummy's trumps, which are needed to trump your side-suit losers.

(2) When there is a long suit in dummy that needs to be established.

Reason for delaying: Frequently the entries to dummy are in trumps; draw trumps first and those entries are wasted.

(3) When there is an overlapping winner(s) in dummy and the quick tally of losers reveals you have too many.

Reason for delaying: Lose the lead in trumps and the opposition will cash too many winners. You must first discard a loser(s) on dummy's overlapping winner(s). NB: you can afford to draw trumps if it does not involve losing the lead: see this deal.

What happened

Declaring 4♥, South won ♦9 lead (top from two) with ♦A and couldn't wait to get rid of one of his three club losers. He immediately crossed to ♦KQ (discarding ♣2). Oops. West trumped and the defence took ♣AK and ♠A. Down one.

What should have happened

Though dummy had an overlapping winner in diamonds, declarer could afford to draw trumps first, for it did not involve losing the lead.

Win ♦A, draw the missing trumps in three rounds (key play), and only then cash ♦KQ, discarding ♣2. Next lead ♠Q. The defence win ♠A and cash two clubs, but you can trump the third club, cash ♠KJ, then trump ♠5 in dummy. Game made.

S	W	N	E
1♥(1)	Pass	3♥	Pass
4♥	End		

(1) Open 1♥ with 4–4 in the majors. Otherwise open higher ranking of two equal length suits.

Contract: 4♥
Opening Lead: ♦9

Tip 131 If you can draw the opposing trumps without losing the lead, then you can delay throwing losers on dummy's overlapping winner(s) until trumps have been drawn.

Deal 132

Dealer: South **Vulnerability: Neither**

Be honest. How many of
you have found yourself
declaring the contract you
wished you were declaring,
rather than the one you
were actually declaring?
South deliberated whether
to open Two Spades or
Two Notrumps. In the
end he decided (correctly
– for 5332 is a balanced
shape even with a five-
card major) to open Two
Notrumps.

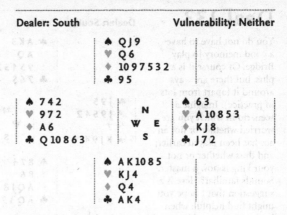

♠ Q J 9
♥ Q 6
♦ 10 9 7 5 3 2
♣ 9 5

♠ 7 4 2
♥ 9 7 2
♦ A 6
♣ Q 10 8 6 3

W E
N S

♠ 6 3
♥ A 10 8 5 3
♦ K J 8
♣ J 7 2

♠ A K 10 8 5
♥ K J 4
♦ Q 4
♣ A K 4

What happened

Declarer won East's ♣J with ♣K, then cashed ♣A and
led ♣4. A slightly surprized West won ♣8 and dummy
'trumped' (in fact discarded) ♠9. Can you see what has
happened?

As soon as declarer saw dummy, he wished he was
in Four Spades (the contract he would have reached
had he opened 2♠). And dummy tabled his hand with
spades on his right (take note: don't table your dummy
with a plausible trump suit on the right). So declarer
mentally began to declare 4♠ instead of 3NT! In 4♠ his
line of play was eminently reasonable. He was trumping
his third club in dummy and so generating an extra
trick.

He only realized his folly when West led first to Trick
Four, having won ♣8 (declarer thought it was dummy
to lead, having 'trumped' with ♠9). Anyway, the
defence lost no time in cashing ♣Q10, ♥A and ♦AKJ.
Down three.

What should have happened

Remembering he is in Three Notrumps, declarer first
counts his top tricks: five spades, no hearts or diamonds
(no ace) and two clubs. Total seven. He can garner the
extra two tricks by flushing out ♥A – two force winners.

The correct line is: win East's ♣J with ♣K and lead
♥4 (going for the extra tricks early). East beats ♥Q with
♥A and returns ♣7. Win ♣A, then cash the five spade
winners and the promoted ♥KJ. Contract made.

S   W   N   E
2NT(1) Pass 3NT(2) End

(1) 5332 is a balanced hand so
South is correct to open 2NT
rather than 2♠.

(2) No point in mentioning
diamonds – 5♦ is a long way
away.

Contract: 3NT
Opening Lead: ♣6

Tip 132 Don't declare the contract in which you wish you were, as opposed to the one
in which you really are.

Deal 133

Dealer: South **Vulnerability: Both**

You do not have to have
a good memory to play
Bridge. Of course it is a
plus, but there are ways
around it (apart from lots
of practice). Imagine a
scenario in which you are
worried whether or not an
ace has been played earlier;
and thus whether or not
your king is now a master.
Sounds familiar? Here is a
suggestion that I hope you
might find helpful: when

	♠ A K 3	
	♥ A Q	
	♦ 9 5 4 3 2	
	♣ 7 6 5	

♠ J 9 5	**N**	♠ Q 10 6 2
♥ J 9 5 4 2	**W E**	♥ K 10 7 3
♦ 7	**S**	♦ K 10 6
♣ K J 9 4		♣ 10 8

	♠ 8 7 4	
	♥ 8 6	
	♦ A Q J 8	
	♣ A Q 3 2	

leading to an ace-king combination, lead to the king (not the ace). Though the cards are
of equal value, leaving the ace for later is wiser than leaving the king for later. You know
the ace will score a trick, regardless of whether the king is still outstanding. Leaving the
king for later relies on your memory of whether the ace has gone. Why take the risk?

What happened

West led ♥4 and declarer tried ♥Q from dummy.
Disappointingly, East won ♥K and returned ♥3 to
dummy's ♥A. Declarer now needed to make his nine-
trick contract without losing the lead.

At Trick Three declarer led ♦2 to East's ♦6 and his ♦J
and West's ♦7. Relieved that East held ♦K, he sought
to return to dummy to repeat the finesse. At Trick Four
he led to ♠A. He then led ♦3 to ♦10 and ♦Q (West
discarding). He cashed ♦A felling ♦K, led ♦8 to ♦9,
then cashed ♦5. With seven tricks made and ♣A to
come, the question was, where was his ninth trick?

Now you can probably tell me that ♠K is that ninth
trick. But the problem was that declarer had forgotten
whether ♠A had already been played. He deliberated a
while, but eventually decided not to risk leading it (♠K).
Instead he tried to promote ♣Q and led dummy's ♣5 to
that card, hoping East held ♣K (a finesse). Disaster –
West won ♣K and led ♥J. East carefully unblocked ♥10
and West followed with ♥95. Down one.

What should have happened

Instead of leading to dummy's ♠A at Trick Four, declarer
should have led to ♠K. After playing the diamond suit
for five tricks as above, he would be left with ♠A in
dummy and ♣A in hand with two tricks required.

S	W	N	E
1NT	Pass	3NT	End

Contract: 3NT
Opening Lead: ♥4

Tip 133 If you are prone to forgetfulness, win with the king from ace-king (as declarer).
At least you will know later that the ace is high.

Deal 134

Dealer: South   **Vulnerability: Neither**

The ability to count is essential in Bridge. It is not too hard provided you count the *missing* cards in the relevant suit, and not the cards held by you and dummy. Obviously it is best to count all the four suits when declaring; but set yourself realistic goals and begin by counting merely the trump suit:

(1) Work out how many cards are missing.

(2) Reduce that number by one each time you see an opponent play a trump.

(3) When the answer is zero, you know there are no more trumps left out.

```
                 ♠ 87
                 ♥ J975
                 ♦ A98
                 ♣ AK42
     ♠ 965                  ♠ 104
     ♥ K6          N        ♥ AQ2
     ♦ QJ1042   W     E     ♦ K63
     ♣ J97          S        ♣ Q10863
                 ♠ AKQJ32
                 ♥ 10843
                 ♦ 75
                 ♣ 5
```

What happened

Declarer won West's ♦Q lead with ♦A and cashed ♣A and ♣K (discarding ♦7). Realising that to trump a minor suit card was at best pointless (his trumps would score anyway), he began drawing trumps.

He crossed to ♠A, and cashed ♠KQ (West following and East discarding). In case West held another trump he led ♠J 'for lurkers' (he had not counted). Fatal!

He then cut loose with a heart. West won ♥K and led ♦J. Declarer trumped (with his penultimate trump) and led a second heart. East won ♥Q and led ♦K. Declarer trumped (with his last trump) and led a third heart. No good – East won ♥A and cashed ♣Q as declarer and dummy followed helplessly with hearts. Down one.

What should have happened

Declarer would have made his contract had he not played that extra round of trumps.

The correct line is: win ♦A, cash ♣AK discarding ♦7 (this should perhaps be delayed until trumps have been drawn); lead ♠A (five missing trumps reduced to three); cash ♠K (three missing trumps reduced to one); cash ♠Q (one missing trump reduced to zero). Now lead ♥3 to West's ♥K and trump ♦J. Lead ♥4 to ♥J and ♥Q and trump ♦K. Lead ♥10 to ♥A, trump ♣Q with your last trump and table the established heart winner. Game made.

S	W	N	E
1♠(1)	Pass	2♣	Pass
2♠	Pass	3♠(2)	Pass
4♠(3)	End		

(1) Using the Rule of 20: Open the bidding when your high-card points added to the length in your two longest suits gets to 20.

(2) South has implied six spades so it is reasonable to support, although 3NT has nine top tricks.

(3) Optimistic.

Contract: 4♠
Opening Lead: ♦Q

Tip 134   Count only the missing trumps – down to zero.

Deal 135

The simplest method
of counting is by only
thinking about the *missing*
cards in the relevant suit.
Thus if you and dummy
have eight trumps, the
number to focus on is five
– the missing trumps.
The best way to use that
information is to think in
terms of the most likely
split of the opposing cards.
Missing five cards, by far
the most likely split is
three-two.

```
              ♠ K742
              ♥ A96
              ♦ QJ105
              ♣ 62

  ♠ 10                    ♠ J983
  ♥ Q10853        N       ♥ J72
  ♦ 764        W     E    ♦ A8
  ♣ QJ105         S       ♣ K973

              ♠ AQ65
              ♥ K4
              ♦ K932
              ♣ A84
```

When one opponent shows out of a suit, you can work out precisely how many cards
his partner started with and therefore the split. Thus if one opponent shows out on the
second round of the eight-card trump fit, you know the split to be four-one.
So try to focus on these patterns; the more familiar you will become with the common
patterns, the easier the process will become.

What happened

Declarer knew that three-two was the most likely split
missing five cards. But he failed to reassess after one
opponent discarded on the second round of the suit.
He ducked ♣Q lead – good technique as he has to lose
a club trick sooner or later. He won ♣5 to ♣K with ♣A
and set about drawing trumps.

Assuming a three-two split of the five missing cards,
he drew three rounds with ♠K, then ♠Q and ♠A (not
noticing West discard on the second round). He then
led ♦K. East won ♦A, cashed ♠J (drawing the last two
trumps) and led to his partner's ♣J10. Down two.

S	W	N	E
1♠	Pass	3♠	Pass
4♠	End		

Contract: 4♠
Opening Lead: ♣Q

What should have happened

Declarer revises his assessment of the trump break when
West discards on the second round. Knowing of the
four-one split, he leaves trumps well alone and flushes
out ♦A.

The correct line is: duck ♣Q, win the second club
with ♣A; cross to ♠K, back to ♠Q; then lead ♦K. East
can do no better than win ♦A and lead ♠J. Win ♠A
and play winning diamonds; then trump the third
heart/club in the other hand. East just scores his master
♠9. Contract made.

Tip 135 Think of the missing cards in terms of their likely split.

THE DEALS

Defence

Deal 136

Dealer: North　　　　　　　**Vulnerability: Both**

Look at West's hand. If someone asked you what would be your opening lead against a 5♦ contract, what would be your answer? If you are choosing between your sequential holdings in hearts and clubs then you are missing the point. You must first ask: 'What was the auction?' West must ask himself why North-South did not choose 3NT. The answer is that both

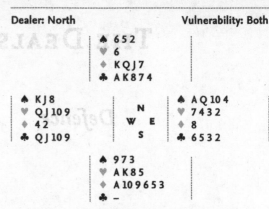

```
                    ♠ 652
                    ♥ 6
                    ♦ KQJ7
                    ♣ AK874

        ♠ KJ8                     ♠ AQ104
        ♥ QJ109        N          ♥ 7432
        ♦ 42        W     E       ♦ 8
        ♣ QJ109        S          ♣ 6532

                    ♠ 973
                    ♥ AK85
                    ♦ A109653
                    ♣ —
```

of them, by bidding every other suit, have advertized weakness in the spade suit. And because a wide-open suit is very dangerous in notrumps, they ended up instead in 5♦ (ironically 3NT would have made, losing just four spade tricks). However, West was too focussed on his hand, and not focussed enough on the opponents' auction (the common mistake).

What happened

Beguiled by his sequences, West shuffled his ♥Q and ♣Q around before eventually selecting ♥Q. ♣Q would have been equally fatal.

Declarer won ♥Q with ♥K, crossed to dummy's ♦J, cashed ♦K (drawing the last remaining trump), cashed ♣AK (discarding ♠3 and ♠7), trumped ♣4, trumped ♥5, trumped ♣7, trumped ♥8, then tabled the established ♣8 (a winner because of the 4–4 split in the suit). He discarded ♠9 from hand, trumped ♠2 and took the last two tricks with ♥A and ♦A. All 13 tricks made!

What should have happened

West should have led the unbid suit, the suit both his opponents were clearly worried about in the auction. Normally KJ8 is a most unattractive holding to lead from, likely to give declarer two fast tricks with the ace and queen. But here the auction told West to lead a spade *whatever his holding in the suit.*

His ♠8 lead is won by East's ♠A. ♠4 is returned and West wins ♠J and cashes ♠K. The defence have taken the first three tricks and the contract is down one.

What a swing an opening lead can make!

S	W	N	E
–	–	1♣	Pass
1♦	Pass	3♦	Pass
3♥	Pass	4♦	Pass
5♦	End		

Contract: 5♦
Actual Opening Lead: ♥Q
Correct Opening Lead: ♠8

Tip 136　Do not overlook the auction when selecting your opening lead.

Deal 137

Dealer: North   **Vulnerability: Neither**

Question: When does the
defence begin?
Answer: In a sense, it begins
before the opening lead,
during the auction. Make
a skimpy overcall in order
to attract a lead from
partner and you are already
shaping the defence. Take
this deal.

```
              ♠ J 5 3
              ♥ 6
              ♦ A J 10 8 6
              ♣ A K 5 3
  ♠ 8 7                        ♠ K Q 10 4 2
  ♥ K J 7 4 2         N        ♥ 10 8 5 3
  ♦ K 5 4        W         E   ♦ Q 9
  ♣ 10 8 2           S        ♣ 6 4
              ♠ A 9 6
              ♥ A Q 9
              ♦ 7 3 2
              ♣ Q J 9 7
```

What happened

With no squeak from his partner, West naturally began
with his fourth highest heart, ♥4. Declarer won East's
♥10 with ♥Q and led ♦2 to ♦10. East won ♦Q and
continued with ♥3 (too late for spades). Declarer won
♥A and led ♦3 to ♦J. This won, so he could cash ♦A86
and follow with the four club winners and ♠A. 11 tricks
and game made plus two.

What should have happened

If East overcalls 1♠, West obediently leads ♠8. (You
should be even more keen to lead partner's suit when it
is an overcall – as opposed to an opening bid/response
– for he has guaranteed at least five good cards and has
often bid primarily to attract a lead of the suit.) East
plays ♠10 on dummy's ♠3 and, even if declarer ducks
♠A, East can force ♠A out with ♠K and regain the lead
with ♦Q to cash ♠Q42. Down one.

S	W	N	E
–	–	1♦	Pass(1)
2♣	Pass	3♣	Pass
3NT	End		

(1) Not a great hand, but how
is partner supposed to know
to lead a spade if you do not
overcall in the suit? A 1♠
overcall is indicated.

Contract: 3NT
Actual Opening Lead: ♥4
**Correct Opening Lead (with
East overcalling 1♠): ♠8**

Tip 137   Don't forget the lead-directing one-level overcall – either to make one yourself
or to lead the suit if partner makes one.

Deal 138

Dealer: North　　　　　**Vulnerability: East-West**

There are various sayings
in Bridge that are at best
misleading and at worst
just plain wrong. Perhaps
they were the accepted
wisdom in the early days
of the game, but they have
proved over the years not
to work. One such saying is
'Lead top of your partner's
suit': that if partner has bid
a suit, you should lead your
top card in it, regardless of
your length and honours.

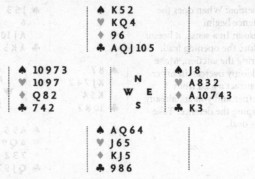

```
              ♠ K 5 2
              ♥ K Q 4
              ♦ 9 6
              ♣ A Q J 10 5
  ♠ 10 9 7 3              ♠ J 8
  ♥ 10 9 7        N       ♥ A 8 3 2
  ♦ Q 8 2      W   E      ♦ A 10 7 4 3
  ♣ 7 4 2        S        ♣ K 3
              ♠ A Q 6 4
              ♥ J 6 5
              ♦ K J 5
              ♣ 9 8 6
```

Now whilst you should lead the ace (if holding it), and there may be the odd occasion
where to lead, for example, the king from king and two small cards, may work well as this
clarifies matters for partner. However, it is generally inadvisable. There are many layouts
where the honour simply cannot afford to be released. On our featured deal, West's
choice of card in his partner's diamonds was to prove critical.

What happened

West led ♦Q, East played low and declarer won the
trick with ♦K. At Trick Two he ran ♣9, correctly
seeking to make extra tricks from his long suit. East won
♣K and led ♦4 (nothing works better). Declarer won
♦J, cashed dummy's ♣AQJ10, and then led out ♠AKQ.
Game made, scoring three spades, two diamonds and
four clubs. Total nine.

What should have happened

West should lead ♦2 not ♦Q. Lest he should be worried
that he is not conveying a positive message about his
holding in the suit, he should bear in mind that the lead
of a low card indicates an honour (a defender should
try to lead a high spot card from 'rubbish').

　　East would win Trick One with ♦A and return ♦4.
Declarer has two options at this point, both losing.

　　(1) He plays ♦K. He then runs ♣9 to East's ♣K. East
returns ♦3 to ♦J and ♦Q, wins ♥10 return with ♥A,
then cashes ♦107. Down two.

　　(2) He plays ♦J. West wins ♦J with ♦Q and returns
♦8. Declarer wins ♦K and runs ♣9. East wins ♣K,
cashes ♦107, then ♥A. Also down two.

S	W	N	E
–	–	1♣	1♦
1♠	Pass	2♠(1)	Pass
2NT	Pass	3NT	End

(1) North cannot make
his planned rebid of 1NT
(15–16 balanced) as he has
no stopper in the opponents'
suit.

Contract: 3NT
Actual Opening Lead: ♦Q
Correct Opening Lead: ♦2

Tip 138　Do not normally lead top of partner's suit (unless from a sequence or a
doubleton).

Deal 139

Dealer: South **Vulnerability: Neither**

About half of all contracts that start life in the balance are decided one way or the other by the opening lead. It is that important. No-one, not even a world expert, can hope to make the best opening lead on all hands. But certain guidelines will help you to make sensible opening leads, and avoid silly ones. Usually, although not always, the best way to

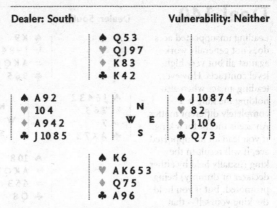

defeat a contract is to sit back and wait. One particularly misguided strategy against all but very high-level contracts is to bash out unsupported (i.e. no king held in the suit) aces.

What happened

West was in a hurry to defeat the 4♥ contract – as though there was a bonus for winning tricks early. At Trick One he cashed ♦A. When a sight of dummy revealed ♦K, he switched to ♠A. Both these aces (predictably) attracted low cards from the other players – not good value for the ace. It was all over. At Trick Three he led ♠9. Declarer won ♠K, crossed to ♥QJ, drawing the missing trumps, cashed ♠Q discarding ♣6, and won the remainder, using ♦KQ and ♣AK. 11 tricks.

S	W	N	E
1♥	Pass	3♥(1)	Pass
4♥	End		

(1) 10–12 with 4+ card support.

Contract: 4♥
Actual Opening Lead: ♦A
Correct Opening Lead: ♣J

What should have happened

West should keep his aces back, preferring the top of an honour sequence lead, ♣J (showing ♣10). Declarer would win ♣A, cross to ♥QJ (drawing the trumps), then lead ♠3 to ♠K. This time West takes a king with an ace, much better value. He then leads ♣5. Winning with dummy's ♣K, declarer's best play is to cash ♠Q, trump ♠5, then exit with ♣9.

East wins ♣Q, then switches to ♦J. Declarer plays low from hand and West refrains from playing ♦A, keeping it back to catch an honour. Dummy's ♦K wins the trick and declarer can do no better than lead to his ♦Q. This time West wins ♦A and then leads to East's ♦10. Down one.

A patient defence wins four tricks. An ace-cashing defence wins two (the aces).

Tip 139 Cashing unsupported aces at the beginning is usually a poor defensive strategy. They will only catch low cards, not kings and queens.

Deal 140

Dealer: South **Vulnerability: East-West**

Leading unsupported aces does not generally work against all but very high-level contracts. However, leading an ace when also holding the king is a completely different matter. An ace is meant for a king. If you lead an unsupported ace, it will result in the king (usually held by either declarer or dummy) being promoted. But if you hold the king yourself – that won't happen.

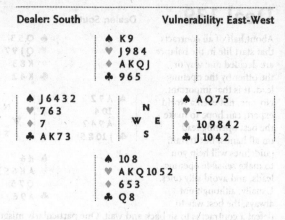

♠ K 9
♥ J 9 8 4
♦ A K Q J
♣ 9 6 5

♠ J 6 4 3 2
♥ 7 6 3
♦ 7
♣ A K 7 3

♠ A Q 7 5
♥ —
♦ 10 9 8 4 2
♣ J 10 4 2

♠ 10 8
♥ A K Q 10 5 2
♦ 6 5 3
♣ Q 8

Leading a singleton (not trumps) is a very attractive defence. If the suit is led again before your trumps have been drawn, you can trump. But if you are lucky enough to hold an ace-king combination in another suit, it should be preferred (leading the ace) to the singleton. Why?

Answer: Because it gives you the opportunity to look at dummy and to choose whether to follow with the king, to switch to the singleton, or perhaps to broach the other suit (or even to lead trumps).

What happened

West looked no further than his singleton ♦7 to lead. Declarer won in dummy, drew West's trumps in three rounds, then cashed dummy's three remaining top diamonds. On the fourth round he discarded ♣8. He crossed to his hand in trumps and then led towards dummy's ♠K. East won ♠A, cashed ♠Q, then led to his partner's ♣K. But declarer trumped ♣A and showed his last card, a trump. 10 tricks and contract made.

What should have happened

West should have kept his options open by leading ♣A. A glance at dummy reveals that a switch to his singleton ♦7 is not a sensible choice. Instead he switches to dummy's weakest suit, spades. His ♠3 goes to dummy's ♠K and East's ♠A. East cashes ♠Q and reverts to clubs, leading ♣J to declarer's ♣Q and West's ♣K. The defence takes the first four tricks and declarer is one down.

By the way – note how well East-West do in a spade contract. But neither of them has a safe entry into the bidding.

S	W	N	E
1♥	Pass	4♥(1)	End

(1) Enough strength to go straight to game in the known fit – and no point in mentioning diamonds.

Contract: 4♥
Actual Opening Lead: ♦7
Correct Opening Lead: ♣A

Tip 140 Ace from ace-king is the best lead of all – against a trump contract.

Deal 141

We have observed that
the lead of an ace almost
invariably implies the king
(it is generally losing Bridge
to lead an unsupported ace,
even from just two cards).
Similarly the lead of a king
implies the queen; the lead
of a queen implies the jack;
the lead of a jack implies
the ten; and the lead of a
ten implies the nine.
NB: the lead of a non-
honour (nine or below)

```
              ♠ K 4
              ♥ Q J 6
              ♦ A Q 10 3 2
              ♣ 7 6 3
♠ Q J 10 3 2          N          ♠ A 7 6
♥ 7 5                             ♥ 4 3 2
♦ 8 6          W    E             ♦ 9 7 5
♣ A 10 8 5          S            ♣ Q J 4 2
              ♠ 9 8 5
              ♥ A K 10 9 8
              ♦ K J 4
              ♣ K 9
```

does not imply the card immediately below.
These honour sequence leads are both informative to partner and potentially devastating
for declarer. But remember to lead the *top* of your sequence (of two or more cards) – our
common mistake. Though it does not matter to you (the cards in sequence are all equals),
it may matter to partner.

What happened

West led ♠10 against the 4♥ contract and declarer
cleverly played ♠4 from dummy (it would be most
unusual for West to lead 'away from an ace' at Trick
One). Now East 'knew' that declarer must hold ♠J from
his partner's lead of ♠10. So he went up with ♠A in
order to attack clubs (right in theory).

He led ♣Q (top of the sequence), covered by
declarer's ♣K and West's ♣A. West returned ♣5 to
East's ♣J, but declarer trumped ♣4 continuation. He
drew trumps, cashed his diamonds, and claimed 10
tricks. Game made.

What should have happened

West should have led ♠Q (top of the sequence –
showing ♠J). If declarer plays low from dummy, East
knows to play low. Say dummy's ♠K is played. East
wins with ♠A and switches correctly to ♣Q. Note
that his partner's spade winner can wait, but that it is
important for East to lead clubs from his side.

East's ♣Q goes to ♣K and West's ♣A. West cashes
♠J and leads ♣5 to East's ♣J. Declarer trumps ♣4
return, draws trumps, then runs his diamonds. But he
has lost four tricks. Down one.

	S	W	N	E
	–	–	1NT	Pass
	3♥	Pass	4♥	End

Contract: 4♥
Actual Opening Lead: ♠10
Correct Opening Lead: ♠Q

Tip 141

Lead top of a sequence of two or more touching cards, where the highest is
the ten or above.

Deal 142

Dealer: South   **Vulnerability: Neither**

It is a mistake to 'lead away from an ace' at Trick One to a trump contract. This means that leading from a suit headed by the ace (without the king) should be avoided. Why? By leading from an ace, the king becomes the boss card in the suit for the rest of the trick. Declarer may very well be able to score a trick with that card, when the ace was meant to 'chop

```
              ♠ Q 9
              ♥ 7 6 4 3
              ♦ J 6 4 3
              ♣ K Q 7
  ♠ 8 6 4                    ♠ A 7
  ♥ A J 9 5         N        ♥ Q 10 2
  ♦ K 9 5      W       E     ♦ Q 10 8 2
  ♣ 10 9 6         S        ♣ 5 4 3 2
              ♠ K J 10 5 3 2
              ♥ K 8
              ♦ A 7
              ♣ A J 8
```

the king's head off'. Though it has much appeal for its simplicity, the 'Lead your strongest suit and have partner return it' school is not a winning one. Leading from a suit such as West's fine hearts on this deal is too dangerous. Far better to let the lead of the suit come to you. As West found to his cost.

What happened

West led ♥5, which went to East's ♥Q and declarer's ♥K. Declarer led ♠2 to ♠Q and East won ♠A and returned ♥10. West overtook with ♥J and tried to cash ♥A. But declarer trumped, drew the remaining trumps, cashed his club winners, and merely conceded the second round of diamonds. 10 tricks and game made.

What should have happened

West should have kept his heart holding firmly in his hand. Rejecting a diamond lead – again too dangerous – he adopts a more passive approach.

His ♣10 lead is won by declarer's ♣J and ♠2 led to dummy's ♠Q. Dummy's club holding suggests that there is no future in continuing with the suit (except in the unlikely scenario that West's ♣10 is a singleton). Dummy's hearts are slightly weaker than his diamonds, so the natural return for East is ♥2 (actually a club or low diamond return would lead to the beating of the contract too, eventually).

Declarer has to try ♥K on ♥2 return, in the hope that East holds ♥A. No good: West beats ♥K with ♥A and returns ♥5 to East's ♥Q. Declarer trumps ♥10 continuation and draws trumps, but is forced to concede a diamond at the end. By not scoring ♥K, he scores just nine tricks instead of ten. Down one.

S	W	N	E
1♠	Pass	1NT	Pass
3♠(1)	Pass	4♠(2)	End

(1) When repeating your six-card suit, remember to jump the bidding with 16+ points

(2) At worst one point short of the 25 point guideline for game.

Contract: 4♠
Actual Opening Lead: ♥5
Correct Opening Lead: ♣10

Tip 142 Do not lead away from ace at Trick One against a trump contract.

Deal 143

Dealer: South **Vulnerability: Both**

There are various strategies for opening leads against trump contracts, the most attractive of which being tops of sequences and singletons. However, against notrump contracts there is a standard ploy – to lead 'fourth from the top of your longest and strongest suit'. 'Fourth highest of the longest' is a good strategy, and has been around since the days of whist. The

```
              ♠ A 4
              ♥ 7 6 2
              ♦ A K J 8 3
              ♣ J 8 4
♠ K Q 10 6 2              ♠ 8 5 3
♥ 9 5 4          N        ♥ K Q J 3
♦ 9 4        W     E      ♦ Q 10 5
♣ 10 3 2         S        ♣ 9 6 5
              ♠ J 9 7
              ♥ A 10 8
              ♦ 7 6 2
              ♣ A K Q 7
```

principle is to exhaust the opponents of their cards in that suit, and so establish length winners. However, there are exceptions. If your longest suit has been bid by an opponent, you might well try another suit; if partner has bid a suit, then you would tend to lead his suit. Even if you are leading your longest suit (no inferences to the contrary), you should not always lead 'fourth'. Take a suit headed by three touching high cards (e.g. KQJx, QJ10x); or two touching high cards, a gap of one card and then a third high card (e.g. KQ10x, QJ9x). In these situations the top card should be led.

What happened

West erred by leading his fourth highest spade, ♠6. Declarer played low from dummy and was pleased to see that he could win his ♠9. He crossed to ♦K, returned ♣Q, then finessed ♦J. East won ♦Q and switched to ♥K, but declarer could win ♥A, cross to ♦A83, ♣J, across to ♣AK, and finally back to ♠A. 11 tricks and game made in some comfort.

What should have happened

West should lead ♠K – promising ♠Q and either ♠J or ♠10. Declarer does best to win ♠A immediately, protecting ♠J, then play to avoid East winning the lead. He bangs down ♦AK, hoping ♦Q will drop. When it does not, he must lead a third round. If West holds ♦Q, he cannot continue spades to his advantage (without promoting ♠J) and the contract is home. However, East wins ♦Q and a second spade through declarer's ♠J ensures four defensive tricks in the suit. Down one.

S	W	N	E
1NT	Pass	3NT	End

Contract: 3NT
Actual Opening Lead: ♠6
Correct Opening Lead: ♠K

Tip 143

Prefer to lead top of your longest suit against notrumps (rather than 'fourth') with three successive high cards (KQJ, QJ10, J109) or two, a gap of one, then the next card (KQ10, QJ9, J108).

Deal 144

One of the most popular
mottoes in Bridge is 'fourth
highest of your longest
and strongest suit against
notrumps'. But it must not
be adhered to willy-nilly.
It is correct to lead the top
card from KQJx, KQ10x,
QJ10x, QJ9x, J109x, J108x
etc. It is also correct to lead
an honour from KJ10x,
Q109x, although this time
it is correct to lead the top
of the sequential bit, i.e.
the jack from KJ10x and
the ten from Q109x. This is
referred to as leading 'top
of an internal sequence'.

```
              ♠ 7 5 2
              ♥ Q 8 3
              ♦ A Q J 10 5
              ♣ A 6
    ♠ A 9              ♠ 10 8 6 4
    ♥ K J 10 5 2    N   ♥ A 7 6
    ♦ K 4 3     W    E   ♦ 8 7
    ♣ 10 5 2         S   ♣ 9 7 4 3
              ♠ K Q J 3
              ♥ 9 4
              ♦ 9 6 2
              ♣ K Q J 8
```

What happened

West led ♥5 and, although it is tempting for declarer to
rise with dummy's ♥Q as the best chance of scoring a
trick in the suit, declarer knew his customer and played
low. East won ♥A (he had to or South would score ♥9)
and returned ♥7. West took ♥K and led a third heart to
dummy's ♥Q.

Declarer cashed ♣A, crossed to ♣KQJ, then,
unwilling to flush out ♠A and see the opponents take
more heart tricks, played West for ♦K by running ♦9.
When this card held the trick, he led to dummy's ♦10,
then cashed ♦A (felling West's ♦K). ♦QJ followed and
declarer had scored 10 tricks. Game made plus one.

What should have happened

On the recommended ♥J lead – top of an internal
sequence – declarer's goose is cooked. Say he ducks in
dummy. East also ducks; a second heart goes to East's
♥A and a third heart sees West score the ♥K and follow
with his two remaining hearts. With ♠A to come,
declarer is down two.

S	W	N	E
1NT(1)	Pass(2)	3NT	End

(1) Technically you have a
balanced 12–14 – a 1NT
opener. But it is tempting to
treat the hand as a two-suiter
and open 1♣, planning to
rebid 1♠.
(2) Vulnerable Two-level
overcalls should rarely contain
less than opening bid values.

Contract: 3NT
Actual Opening Lead: ♥5
Correct Opening Lead: ♥J

Tip 144   Versus notrumps, lead top of an internal sequence (KJ10x, Q109x) in your
longest suit in preference to fourth highest.

Deal 145

Dealer: South   **Vulnerability: Neither**

One of my absolute
favourite maxims for the
Bridge table – applying to
defenders – is 'Lead High
for Hate and Lead Low for
Like'. This applies to Trick
One and throughout the
play on the first round of
each suit, both in notrumps
and suits. So if you are
leading from a lousy suit,
then lead a high spot card
such as an eight or a nine.
This even overrides leading
fourth highest at Trick One against notrumps. Thus you should lead fourth highest if you
are leading from an honour, and highest/second highest from 'rubbish'.

```
              ♠ 7 3 2
              ♥ Q 10
              ♦ A K J 9 7 3
              ♣ A 8
♠ A Q 10 4              ♠ J 6 5
♥ 8 7 6 3 2      N      ♥ A J 9
♦ 8          W     E    ♦ 6 4 2
♣ J 7 3          S      ♣ 10 9 6 4
              ♠ K 9 8
              ♥ K 5 4
              ♦ Q 10 5
              ♣ K Q 5 2
```

What happened

West led ♥3 against the 3NT contract, and dummy
played ♥Q. East won ♥A and unsuspectingly returned
♥J – if his partner held ♥Kxxxx then the defence would
score the first five tricks. But declarer won ♥K and
could cash six diamonds and three clubs. 10 tricks and
game made plus one.

What should have happened

West should lead ♥8 – 'Lead High for Hate'. Now East
knows that West has led hearts because of length not
strength. A look at dummy reveals that the defence
must take tricks quickly (or declarer will romp home via
dummy's diamonds), so it is clear for East to win Trick
One with ♥A and switch to dummy's weakness, spades.

In order for the defence to score the necessary four
spade tricks before declarer wins the lead (and runs
diamonds), East needs his partner to hold spades
at least as good as ♠AQ10x. But, in that case, it is
imperative that he switch to specifically ♠J (key play).
If he erroneously switches to a low spade, then declarer
can insert ♠8/9 and force West (who cannot profitably
continue the suit) to win.

♠J lead at Trick Two stymies declarer. If he ducks,
♠J wins and ♠6 follows. If he covers ♠J with ♠K, West
takes ♠A and follows with ♠Q10 and ♠4. Down one.

S	W	N	E
1NT	Pass	3NT(1)	End

(1) Prefer 3NT to looking for
5♣/♦, unless VERY shapely
(e.g. with a seven-card suit or
a void).

Contract: 3NT
Actual Opening Lead: ♥3
Correct Opening Lead: ♥8

Tip 145   'Lead High for Hate; Lead Low for Like' – even at Trick One in notrumps.

Deal 146

Dealer: South **Vulnerability: Neither**

When I am teaching a class on defence and ask my students if they, like me, enjoy defence more than any other part of the game, a surprisingly large number agree. But there are always at least as many who enjoy defence least, and would much rather hurry up and get on with the next deal. My task is to convert those people; and to make you all into 'TOP' defenders. The

```
            ♠ 6 5 3
            ♥ J 10 9 3
            ♦ A Q J 8
            ♣ K 7
♠ K J 4 2           N       ♠ A 9 8
♥ A Q          W       E    ♥ 7 5 4 2
♦ 10 9 6 5          S       ♦ 7 3 2
♣ J 10 9                    ♣ 6 3 2
            ♠ Q 10 7
            ♥ K 8 6
            ♦ K 4
            ♣ A Q 8 5 4
```

'T' of being a TOP defender stands for focussing on your Trick Target. It is much easier to forget your trick target when you defend than when you declare. If you are defending a 4♠ contract, your target is four; if you are defending a 2♣ contract, your target is six. This deal's West fell from grace by not being aware of his trick target. Cover up South and East's cards before reading on.

What happened

West led ♠2 to East's ♠A, and East returned ♠9 (top of two remaining). South covered with ♠10 and West won ♠J, cashed ♠K (felling South's ♠Q) and tabled ♠4. North discarded ♥3, East discarded ♥2 and South discarded ♦4 (trying to encourage West to switch to a diamond). West then switched 'safely' to ♣J. By discarding ♦4, declarer was unable to disentangle his minor suit winners. But watch what happened.

He rose with dummy's ♣K, crossed to his ♣AQ (noting the 3–3 split), then cashed his ♣85. West discarded ♥Q on the penultimate club but had to discard ♦5 on the last club in order to retain ♥A. Dummy's last four cards were ♦AQJ8 and declarer overtook his singleton ♦K with ♦A, cashed ♦QJ felling West's ♦109, then, at Trick 13, tabled ♦8. Game made.

What should have happened

After taking the first four spade tricks, West needed just one more trick to beat the contract. What could be simpler than cashing ♥A! Down one.

S	W	N	E
1NT	Pass	2NT(1)	Pass
3NT	End		

(1) Are you minimum (12) or maximum (14)?

Contract: 3NT
Opening Lead: ♠2

Tip 146 When defending, never lose sight of how many tricks you need to defeat the contract.

Deal 147

Dealer: North　　　**Vulnerability: North-South**

The 'O' of being a 'TOP' defender stands for Observe Dummy. As soon as it has been tabled, have a good look. You will not be able to see all its 13 cards again, so try to commit at least the distribution to memory. Next, look for dummy's weakness(es). If it has a side suit of three or four small cards, it will almost certainly be right for you as a defender to attack

```
              ♠ Q
              ♥ A K J 3
              ♦ 7 6 4
              ♣ K Q J 10 9

♠ A K 10 8              N              ♠ J 9 6 3 2
♥ 9 6           W             E       ♥ 8 4
♦ K 10 5 2             S              ♦ Q 8 3
♣ 8 5 3                              ♣ A 4 2

              ♠ 7 5 4
              ♥ Q 10 7 5 2
              ♦ A J 9
              ♣ 7 6
```

that suit (in a trump contract). And if the dummy has a long, strong suit somewhere else, you had better attack that weak suit FAST!

What happened

West led ♠A against declarer's 4♥ contract. Correctly realising that continuing spades was futile (dummy would trump), West switched to a trump (presumably to cut down declarer trumping spades in dummy). Do you think this was a good strategy? Let us see what happened.

Declarer won with dummy's ♥K, and cashed dummy's ♥A. He then led ♣K. East won ♣A and switched to ♦3. Too late! Declarer rose with ♦A, then crossed to dummy's ♣QJ109. He discarded ♦J9 and ♠5. He trumped ♦6, trumped ♠7, then claimed the remainder, holding all trumps in hand. Game made with an overtrick.

What should have happened

After cashing ♠A, West should have looked at dummy's club suit with fear and trepidation. In the normal course of events, declarer would establish dummy's clubs, knocking out ♣A if necessary, and dump his other losers on the club winners. How can West prevent this from happening? He must attack the weakness in the dummy: diamonds. Immediately!

At Trick Two West switches to ♦2 (key play). This goes to East's ♦Q and declarer wins ♦A. Declarer draws the trumps in two rounds, then knocks out ♣A. East wins his ♣A and returns ♦8 (top of two remaining). Declarer tries ♦9 but West wins ♦10 and cashes ♦K. The game is down one. What a difference!

S	W	N	E
–	–	1♣	Pass
1♥	Pass	3♥	Pass
4♥(1)	End		

(1) Just worth a try at game with five decent trumps and an outside ace.

Contract: 4♥
Opening Lead: ♠A

Tip 147　Observe dummy: if in doubt lead dummy's weakest suit.

Deal 148

Dealer: South

Vulnerability: Both

There is a misguided motto that has blighted defenders for decades. I'm referring to 'Lead through Strength'. If dummy has a long, strong suit, then it is *almost never* right for a defender to lead that suit (even if he is leading 'through' rather than 'around to' dummy). Indeed quite to the contrary: when dummy has a long, strong suit, the defence must attack the *other* suit(s) and fast. Otherwise declarer will dump his losers in those suits on dummy's winners in the long, strong suit.

```
                 ♠ J 10 7 6
                 ♥ J
                 ♦ A Q J 8 6
                 ♣ 6 5 2
    ♠ 8 4 2                      ♠ 9 3
    ♥ A K 4 2         N          ♥ 10 9 7 6 5
    ♦ 7 3         W       E      ♦ K 9 4
    ♣ Q 10 4 3        S          ♣ K J 7
                 ♠ A K Q 5
                 ♥ Q 8 3
                 ♦ 10 5 2
                 ♣ A 9 8
```

What happened

West led ♥A and observed dummy (the 'O' of being a 'TOP' defender stands for Observe). Hoping for partner to hold ♦K, and utilizing that motto 'Lead through Strength' (yuk!), West switched to ♦7. Declarer took no chances (in case ♦7 was singleton).

He rose with dummy's ♦A and drew the opposing trumps in three rounds finishing in his hand. He then led and ran ♦10, and East won ♦K. East switched to ♣7, but declarer was in control. He rose with ♣A and led to dummy's ♦QJ8. He discarded both his club losers and was now able to trump a club, trump a heart, and merely concede the last trick. Game made.

What should have happened

After cashing ♥A, West should reason as follows: 'I must attack clubs (dummy's weakness) before declarer discards his club losers on dummy's diamonds. There is absolutely NO need for me to attack diamonds. If my partner holds ♦K, then he will make it in the fullness of time'.

At Trick Two West switches to ♣3 (key play) to East's ♣K and declarer's ♣A. Declarer draws trumps in three rounds finishing in hand, then runs ♦10. East wins ♦K, and leads ♣J (top of two remaining). In case ♣J is his only remaining club, West alertly overtakes ♣J with ♣Q and cashes ♣10. Down one.

S	W	N	E
1♠	Pass	3♠	Pass
4♠	End		

Contract: 4♠

Opening Lead: ♥A

Tip 148 It is almost never right to lead dummy's long, strong suit.

Deal 149

Dealer: North **Vulnerability: Neither**

We are currently learning to be 'TOP' defenders. The 'T' of 'TOP' stands for Trick Target – focus on the number of tricks you need in order to defeat the contract. The 'O' stands for Observe Dummy. When dummy is first tabled, have a good look and try to commit as much as possible about the distribution and high cards to memory. If in doubt as

```
              ♠ Q 10 9 3
              ♥ 6 4
              ♦ K J 4 3 2
              ♣ A K
  ♠ 6 5 2                    ♠ A 7
  ♥ Q J 9 7          N       ♥ A K 10 8 3 2
  ♦ 5            W       E   ♦ 9 7 6
  ♣ Q 10 8 5 2       S       ♣ 9 7
              ♠ K J 8 4
              ♥ 5
              ♦ A Q 10 8
              ♣ J 6 4 3
```

to what to lead during the defence, the lead of dummy's weakest suit is often best. Now we look at the 'P'. It stands for that most important person to you, the one opposite, your Partner. He is on your side and has exactly the same goal as you. So try to work out why he is doing what he is doing: there is usually a good reason. East did not ask that key question: why did West lead a diamond and not a heart (the suit East bid)?

What happened

West's opening lead against the 4♠ contract was ♦5. East suppressed a wince – why had he bothered to overcall 1♥? Declarer won with ♦A and led ♠4 to dummy's ♠Q. East won ♠A and quickly laid down ♥A and followed with ♥K. Declarer trumped, drew the remaining trumps in two further rounds, then cashed all his diamonds and, finally, ♣AK. 11 tricks and game made at a breeze.

What should have happened

East's reaction to his partner's opening diamond lead had been a critical, unconstructive one: 'Why do I play with someone who can't even remember the bidding?'. Instead he should have asked himself 'Now why did my partner lead dummy's suit instead of my suit? He must have a very good reason. Aha! That ♦5 must be a singleton'.

On winning ♠A at Trick Two, East should return a second diamond for his partner to trump. He wins West's heart return with ♥K and leads a third diamond for West to trump again. Declarer has lost four tricks and is down one.

S	W	N	E
–	–	1♦	1♥
1♠	3♥	3♠	4♥
4♠	End		

Contract: 4♠
Opening Lead: ♦5

Tip 149 Ask yourself why partner is defending in the way that he is – try to follow his defence.

Deal 150

Dealer: South **Vulnerability: Both**

We are becoming 'TOP'
defenders –
T = Trick Target: focus
on it.
O = Observe Dummy.
P = Partner: cooperation
needed.
Now it is time to look at
more specific situations.
This deal we will begin
looking at defensive plays
by the second player.

```
              ♠ 86
              ♥ A K 7 4
              ♦ Q 6 4
              ♣ A 8 6 4
♠ K Q J 4              N        ♠ 10 7 5 3 2
♥ 8 5                          ♥ 9 6
♦ K 10 5          W    E       ♦ A 9 8
♣ J 9 3 2             S        ♣ Q 10 5
              ♠ A 9
              ♥ Q J 10 3 2
              ♦ J 7 3 2
              ♣ K 7
```

What happened

West correctly led ♠K and declarer won ♠A, crossed
to ♥A, returned to ♥10, then led ♦2. Thinking that
declarer was likely to have ♦A, and unwilling to see
dummy's ♦Q win the trick, West rose with ♦K. He
eagerly cashed ♠Q and then switched to ♣2.

Declarer won ♣K and led ♦3 to ♦Q, forcing out
East's ♦A. He won East's club return with dummy's
♣A, crossed to ♦J and now held only trumps and the
master ♦7. 10 tricks and game made.

What should have happened

The motto for the defender playing second when a low
card is led is : 'Second Plays Low'. If, at Trick Four, West
had played his ♦5 on declarer's ♦2, the defenders would
have done rather better. East would beat dummy's ♦Q
with ♦A and lead to West's ♠J. West would exit safely
with ♣2, and declarer would win dummy's ♣A to lead
towards ♦J. West would beat ♦J with ♦K and cash ♦10
to defeat the contract. By playing low on the first round
of diamonds, ensuring that ♦A and ♦K beat honours,
West earns his side a third trick in the suit.

Did declarer have to rely on West's error?

Answer: No. The correct order of play is: win ♠A,
cash ♥Q, cash ♣K, cross to ♣A, trump ♣6, cross to ♥K
(noting the even split), trump ♣8, then exit with ♠9.
Whichever defender wins is forced to lead a diamond
or a spade. A diamond lead ensures only two defensive
winners in the suit; a spade lead allows declarer to
trump in hand and discard dummy's third diamond.
Either way, game made.

S	W	N	E
1♥(1)	Pass	4♥	End

(1) South opens using Rule
of 20: Open the bidding
when high-card points added
to number of cards in two
longest suits gets to at
least 20.

Contract: 4♥
Opening Lead: ♠K

Tip 150 Second hand plays low – on a low card.

Deal 151

We have learned that the motto for a defender playing second to a trick when a low card is led is: 'Second Plays Low'. Do not worry that the declarer, playing third, will win a cheap trick. Your partner is playing last to the trick and can usually prevent this. Is it the same story for the defender playing second when an *honour*, as opposed to a low card, is led?

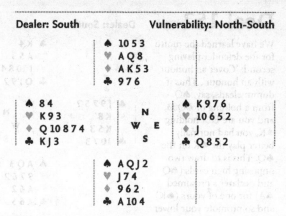

```
              ♠ 10 5 3
              ♥ A Q 8
              ♦ A K 5 3
              ♣ 9 7 6
  ♠ 8 4                      ♠ K 9 7 6
  ♥ K 9 3          N         ♥ 10 6 5 2
  ♦ Q 10 8 7 4   W   E       ♦ J
  ♣ K J 3          S         ♣ Q 8 5 2
              ♠ A Q J 2
              ♥ J 7 4
              ♦ 9 6 2
              ♣ A 10 4
```

What happened

West led ♦7 against the 3NT contract. Declarer won dummy's ♦K, East following with ♦J, and at Trick Two led ♠10. East played ♠6, declarer played ♠2 and West played ♠4. With ♠10 winning, declarer next led ♠3 to ♠7, ♠J and ♠9. He needed to lead a third spade from the dummy in order to continue finessing East for ♠K. To this end he tried another finesse, hearts, by leading ♥J. West played ♥3, dummy ♥8 and East ♥2. He followed by leading ♥4 to dummy's ♥Q, and then led ♠5 to ♠9 and ♠Q.

Declarer had six tricks in the bag and earned style points by playing aces to each of the next four tricks. First ♠A, then across to ♥A, then ♦A, then back to ♣A. 10 tricks and game made plus one.

S	W	N	E
1NT	Pass	3NT	End

Contract: 3NT
Opening Lead: ♦7

What should have happened

There is a motto for a defender playing second: 'Cover an Honour with an honour'.

When declarer leads ♠10 at Trick Two (remember: the ten is an honour) East must cover it with ♠K (key play). Declarer wins ♠A and ♠QJ, but never scores a fourth trick in the suit with dummy's ♠10. And when declarer leads ♥J at Trick Three, West must cover it with ♥K (key play). Declarer wins dummy's ♥A and ♥Q, but never scores a third trick in the suit with his ♥J.

Taking two of the opposing honours for just one of yours is a good trade. Declarer scores one fewer spade trick and one fewer heart trick. So instead of making an overtrick in his 3NT contract, he goes down one.

Tip 151 It is normally right to cover an honour with an honour.

Deal 152

Dealer: South **Vulnerability: East-West**

We have learned the motto for the defender playing second: 'Cover an honour with an honour'. Thus if dummy leads, say, ♠Q from a holding of ♠Q53, and you are East holding ♠K, you had normally better play the ♠K on the ♠Q. This is to draw two opposing high cards (♠Q and declarer's presumed ♠A) for one of yours (♠K) and so promote your lower

```
                    ♠ K 4
                    ♥ A 5 3
                    ♦ J 10 8 4
                    ♣ Q J 9 2
     ♠ J 9 7 5 2            ♠ 10 8 6
     ♥ K 8          N       ♥ Q J 10 4
     ♦ K 5 3      W   E     ♦ Q 9 7
     ♣ 10 7 3        S      ♣ K 8 4
                    ♠ A Q 3
                    ♥ 9 7 6 2
                    ♦ A 6 2
                    ♣ A 6 5
```

cards in the suit into tricks. But when dummy has *two* adjacent honours, and you as East hold one higher honour, should you cover the first honour?

What happened

West led ♠5 (fourth highest of his longest suit) against the 3NT contract. Declarer won dummy's ♠K and immediately led ♣Q. East covered with ♣K and declarer won ♣A. At Trick Three declarer successfully finessed against ♣10, leading to dummy's ♣9. He cashed ♣J, noting the even split, then followed with ♣2, a length winner (throwing ♥2 from hand).

Next he turned his attention to diamonds, leading dummy's ♦J. East again covered the first honour. His ♦Q was taken by ♦A and ♦2 led towards ♦10. West chose to rise with ♦K and lead ♠2. Declarer won ♠Q, cashed ♠A (discarding ♥3), then led ♦6 to ♦10. He completed the rout by cashing the master ♦8 and ♥A. 11 tricks and game made plus two.

What should have happened

When dummy has two touching honours, the defender should NOT cover the first honour, rather waiting for the second honour.

When declarer leads ♣Q at Trick Two, East plays ♣4 (key play). But if declarer then follows with ♣J, East covers with ♣K. This promotes West's ♣10 into a third round master.

Say instead of following with ♣J at Trick Three, declarer switches to diamonds, leading dummy's ♦J. East must play ♦7 not ♦Q (key play). West wins ♦K but East holds ♦Q9 over ♦108 and must make a second trick in the suit.

S	W	N	E
1NT	Pass	2NT	Pass
3NT	End		

Contract: 3NT
Opening Lead: ♠5

Tip 152 Cover the second of two touching honours.

Deal 153

Dealer: South **Vulnerability: Both**

The basic plays by the
defender playing second to
the trick can be
summarized: When a low
card is led: Play low.
When an honour is led:
Cover it (NB: cover the
second of two touching
honours).

We now move onto plays
by the defender playing
third. And there is a radical
difference. When you are
playing second, your

```
              ♠ 7 6 4
              ♥ A 10 8 6
              ♦ Q J 4
              ♣ J 4 2
♠ Q 9 5 2              ♠ K 10 8
♥ 9         N         ♥ 7 4
♦ 9 7 5 3 2  W   E    ♦ A 10 8 6
♣ A 9 6        S      ♣ 10 8 7 5
              ♠ A J 3
              ♥ K Q J 5 3 2
              ♦ K
              ♣ K Q 3
```

partner hasn't yet played a card to the trick. When you are playing third, partner has already
played a card (he was the first to play). So if he led a low card and declarer/dummy played a
low card, you had better play a high one, or dummy/declarer will win the trick cheaply.

What happened

West led ♠2 to the 4♥ contract, and dummy played ♠4.
It was East's turn to play. Sometimes a little knowledge
is a dangerous thing and East knew that it was wrong to
lead from a suit in which you have an ace at Trick One
in a suit contract. With West having therefore denied
♠A, he knew that declarer held ♠A. Does that fact
mean he should refrain from playing his ♠K?

At the table East was unwilling for ♠K to get its head
chopped off by ♠A, so he played ♠10. Declarer won ♠J,
drew trumps in two rounds, then led ♦K. East won ♦A
and switched to ♣8 to declarer's ♣Q. West won ♣A and
returned ♣9. Declarer won dummy's ♣J, discarded his
losing ♠3 on dummy's established ♦Q, and claimed.
11 tricks and game made plus one.

What should have happened

The motto for the defender playing third is 'Third Hand
High'. Knowing declarer has ♠A is no reason for East
to withhold his ♠K at Trick One. Quite the reverse:
he must play ♠K (key play) to force ♠A out, thereby
promoting the other high defensive spades.

Declarer wins ♠K with ♠A, draws trumps, then leads
♦K (as before). This time East wins ♦A and fires back
♠10. Declarer covers with ♠J (if he plays ♠3 then ♠10
wins the trick) and West wins ♠Q, cashes the master
♠9, and finally tables ♣A, the setting trick. Down one.

S	W	N	E
1♥	Pass	2♥	Pass
4♥	End		

Contract: 4♥
Opening Lead: ♠2

Tip 153 Third hand high.

Deal 154

Dealer: South **Vulnerability: Both**

The motto for a defender playing third to a trick is 'Third Hand High'. Such that if partner leads ♦3 and dummy holds only low cards, say ♦754, you should play ♦K from ♦KJ6; ♦Q from ♦Q102, ♦A from ♦AQ6, and ♦J from ♦J98. What about when you as third player hold two (or more) equally high honours, say ♦KQ2 or ♦QJ10? Though it does not matter to

```
              ♠ 10 5 4
              ♥ K 4 2
              ♦ Q 9 7
              ♣ A K J 4
  ♠ J 9 8 3 2            ♠ K Q 7
  ♥ J 10 8       N       ♥ Q 9 7 6
  ♦ A 4      W     E     ♦ 6 5 2
  ♣ 9 7 6        S       ♣ Q 10 8
              ♠ A 6
              ♥ A 5 3
              ♦ K J 10 8 3
              ♣ 5 3 2
```

you – the honours are equivalent as they are next in sequence – it can matter hugely to partner. The rule is to play the cheapest (the lowest) of those touching highest cards. Thus you would play ♦Q from ♦KQ2 and ♦10 from ♦QJ10. Let's see why this can be so important.

What happened

West led ♠3 against the 3NT contract and dummy played ♠4. It did not appear to matter which of his two equally high cards East played, and in fact he chose ♠K. Declarer won ♠A and set about establishing his diamonds.

At Trick Two he led ♦3 to dummy's ♦Q (West ducking) and then he led back to his ♦10. West won ♦A and did some thinking. He 'knew' that declarer held ♠Q (with both ♠K and ♠Q, East would play the lower, i.e. ♠Q, at Trick One). Worried (reasonably) that if he led a second spade, dummy's ♠10 would win the trick, West looked at his sequential holding in hearts.

Hoping that his partner held ♥AQ, West switched at Trick Four to ♥J. Declarer won ♥A and cashed his three remaining diamonds. ♥K and ♣AK brought his total to nine. Game made.

What should have happened

East should have played ♠Q at Trick One (key play). Declarer wins ♠A (ducking achieves nothing and advertizes his weakness in the suit) and leads diamonds. When West wins ♦A, he does not know who holds ♠K. But faced with a choice of playing his partner for one specific card, ♠K, or two specific cards, ♥AQ (plus length in the suit), it is clearly better to play him for ♠K.

West continues with ♠2 to East's ♠K. East's ♠7 return to West's ♠J98 defeats the contract.

S	W	N	E
1NT	Pass	3NT	End

Contract: 3NT
Opening Lead: ♠3

Tip 154 Third hand should play the lowest of touching highest cards.

Deal 155

Dealer: South **Vulnerability: East-West**

We have learned that the motto for the defender playing third to a trick is: 'Third hand plays high; but the lowest of touching highest cards'. Provided you are playing with a reliable partner who is going to remember to play the lower of the touching cards (the J from QJx, the 9 from J109x etc.), you can draw invaluable inferences from the card he plays when in third seat.

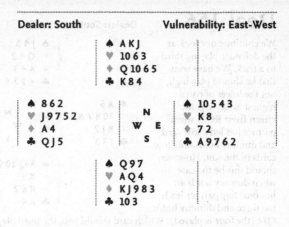

```
                    ♠ A K J
                    ♥ 10 6 3
                    ♦ Q 10 6 5
                    ♣ K 8 4
  ♠ 8 6 2                        ♠ 10 5 4 3
  ♥ J 9 7 5 2         N          ♥ K 8
  ♦ A 4          W         E     ♦ 7 2
  ♣ Q J 5            S          ♣ A 9 7 6 2
                    ♠ Q 9 7
                    ♥ A Q 4
                    ♦ K J 9 8 3
                    ♣ 10 3
```

What happened

West led ♥5 to dummy's ♥3, East's ♥K and declarer's ♥A. West should have paused to reflect upon this trick – he can work out who holds ♥Q.

At Trick Two declarer led ♦3 to ♦4, ♦Q and ♦2. He continued with ♦10, ♦7 ♦8 and West won ♦A. At Trick Four West continued with ♥2, presumably hoping his partner held ♥Q. Disaster! Declarer rose with dummy's ♥10, which won the trick, and was now able to cash his top winners. Three spades, three hearts and four diamonds gave him ten tricks. Game made with an overtrick.

What should have happened

When East played ♥K to the first trick, he denied ♥Q. With ♥K and ♥Q he would play the lower: ♥Q. So, with declarer marked with ♥Q, West should not have led a second heart when in with ♦A. Looking at dummy's strength in spades, West can realize that the only place for the defence to take tricks is clubs. In fact West can work out that declarer has at least nine tricks if he holds ♣A (♠AK, ♥AQ, ♦KQJ and ♣AK). West's only hope is that East holds ♣A.

After winning ♦A, West should switch to ♣Q (key play), leading top of his sequence. Say declarer ducks from dummy, playing ♣4. East naturally withholds his ♣A so ♣Q wins the trick. West continues with ♣J and now declarer is sunk. He covers with dummy's ♣K, but East wins ♣A and, noting declarer's ♣10, cashes ♣962. Down two.

S	W	N	E
1NT	Pass	3NT	End

Contract: 3NT
Opening Lead: ♥5

Tip 155

Knowing that partner is playing the cheaper of touching highest cards as the third player can give you huge inferences about the location of the missing high cards in the suit.

Deal 156

Dealer: South **Vulnerability: Both**

We continue our look at the defender playing third to a trick. We have seen that he should play high, but the lower of equal highest cards (e.g. the queen from KQ2) when partner has led a low card and dummy holds only low cards in the suit. However, should this be the case when dummy holds an honour? Say partner leads the three and dummy holds Q74 (the four is played). Which card should you, the third player, play from:

```
                  ♠ J 4 3
                  ♥ Q 4 2
                  ♦ A 4 3
                  ♣ K 9 7 6
   ♠ A 6                        ♠ 5 2
   ♥ 10 8 7 6 5       N         ♥ A J 9
   ♦ K J 7        W     E       ♦ Q 10 9 5
   ♣ J 8 3            S         ♣ Q 10 5 2
                  ♠ K Q 10 9 8 7
                  ♥ K 3
                  ♦ 8 6 2
                  ♣ A 4
```

(i) K105 or (ii) AJ5?

The basic principle is to keep your high card to beat dummy's honour.

(i) Play the ten. Assuming this is a suit contract, it is most unlikely that partner holds the ace (he would not tend to lead from an ace). Therefore, declarer holds the ace and you should play the ten, retaining the king to beat the queen.

(ii) Play the jack. If partner holds the king, the jack will win the trick and prevent dummy's queen from winning a later trick. If declarer holds the king, he will win the first round of the suit with that card, but you will prevent dummy's queen from scoring. If you erroneously play the ace on dummy's four, declarer will score both his king and dummy's queen separately on the second and third rounds of the suit.

What happened

West led ♥6 (although ♥8 – leading high for hate – would have been clearer) and dummy played ♥2. Eager to win the trick, East won ♥A. He then switched to ♦10. Declarer won dummy's ♦A, crossed to ♥K, returned to ♣K, cashed ♥Q discarding ♦2, then led ♠K. West won ♠A and cashed ♦K, but that was it. Declarer trumped ♦J, drew trumps and claimed. 10 tricks and game made.

What should have happened

East should keep back ♥A to beat dummy's ♥Q, so restricting declarer's heart tricks to one. He plays ♥J at Trick One (key play).

Declarer wins ♥K and leads ♠K. West wins and leads ♥10 to ♥Q and ♥A. East continues with ♥9, trumped by declarer. Declarer draws trumps, but has no way to avoid two diamond losers. Down one. That extra heart trick with dummy's ♥Q made all the difference!

S	W	N	E
1♠	Pass	2♣	Pass
2♠	Pass	3♠	Pass
4♠(1)	End		

(1) Rather optimistic acceptance of the invite.

Contract: 4♠
Opening Lead: ♥6

Tip 156 As third player, keep a higher card to beat an unplayed picture card in dummy.

Deal 157

Dealer: South **Vulnerability: Neither**

When partner leads a low
card and dummy holds only
low cards, the motto for the
defender playing third is:
'Third Hand High'. But
when dummy has an
honour in the suit (that is
not played), the third player
should keep a higher card
back to beat that honour.
Thus if partner leads the
three and dummy has J74,
you as the third player
should play the ten from

```
                    ♠ K 10 3 2
                    ♥ Q J 10 9 8
                    ♦ Q J
                    ♣ 7 3
        ♠ 9 7 5              N         ♠ 6
        ♥ 2                            ♥ K 6 5 3
        ♦ A 10 5 3 2    W       E     ♦ K 8 7
        ♣ A Q 9 4              S      ♣ 10 8 6 5 2
                    ♠ A Q J 8 4
                    ♥ A 7 4
                    ♦ 9 6 4
                    ♣ K J
```

K102 and the nine from Q92. So far so good – but what if the honour is actually played from
dummy? In that case the third hand should generally cover the honour with his higher
honour. This is simply an extension of the 'cover an honour with an honour' principle which
applies to the defender playing second. But, and this is a big but, there is no point in covering
an honour (in any position) unless there is some hope of promoting a lower card as a result.

What happened

West led ♥2 and declarer played dummy's ♥Q. Happy
to cover a queen with a king, East did not give the
matter much thought. Declarer grabbed his ♥K with
♥A. He drew the trumps in three rounds, then ran
dummy's hearts. Five trump tricks and five hearts made
ten. Game made without any heavy breathing.

S	W	N	E
1♠	Pass	3♠	Pass
4♠	End		

Contract: 4♠
Opening Lead: ♥2

What should have happened

East should realize that there is no point in covering
dummy's ♥Q at Trick One. West would not lead
away from ♥A at the first trick in a trump contract, so
declarer is marked with that card. There are no lower
cards in the suit to promote, so East is giving away his
♥K with no hope of achieving anything by so doing. He
should play low instead (key play).

After winning dummy's ♥Q, declarer crosses to his
♠AQ, leads back to ♠10 (drawing the last remaining
trump), and then leads ♥J. Again East plays low.
Declarer leads a third heart to ♥A, then can do no
better than cut loose with ♦4. East beats ♦J with ♦K
and switches to ♣5. West must score both his ♣AQ,
beating declarer's ♣J (if he chooses it) with ♣Q, or his
♣K with ♣A. He cashes the other club honour and ♦A
and the game is down one.

Tip 157 Do not cover an honour with an honour if there is no hope of promoting a
lower card in the suit.

Deal 158

The motto for defenders, 'Lead High for Hate, Lead Low for Like' is for use on the first round of each suit. At Trick One (when you do not know the extent of liking) the reality is that you lead low when you have an honour (or at least a picture card – jack and above), and high when you do not. Later on in the play, when you know far more, the motto effectively becomes, 'Lead Low if you want the suit returned, Lead High if you do not want the suit returned'.

```
                 ♠ 763
                 ♥ AKJ962
                 ♦ –
                 ♣ 10983
  ♠ J952                      ♠ A1084
  ♥ Q843          N           ♥ 1075
  ♦ Q864       W     E        ♦ 9
  ♣ 4             S           ♣ Q7652
                 ♠ KQ
                 ♥ –
                 ♦ AKJ107532
                 ♣ AKJ
```

What happened

West led ♣4 against the 5♦ contract, East's ♣Q(?) losing to the ♣A. Declarer cashed ♦AK, East discarding on the second round, and followed with ♦J. West won ♦Q and clearly needed to put his partner on lead in order to score his ♦8 via a club ruff. He switched to ♠2 to East's ♠A and declarer's ♠Q, but East returned ♠4. Declarer won ♠K, cashed ♦10 drawing West's ♦8, and claimed the remainder in top tricks. 11 tricks and game made.

What should have happened

After winning ♦Q at Trick Four, West had two goals.

(a) Putting East on lead (via the hoped-for ♠A).
(b) Getting East to return a club (for him to trump), rather than a spade.

West should have led ♠9 at Trick Five (key play). Being high, this card would have asked partner not to return a spade. Because the only other logical alternative (looking at dummy's hearts) is a club, West would soon have been smiling. East would have returned a club and West would have ruffed. Down one.

S	W	N	E
2♣(1)	Pass	2♥(2)	Pass
3♦	Pass	3♥	Pass
5♦(3)	End		

(1) 23+ points or any game-forcing hand.
(2) Positive: 8+ points and a 5+ card suit.
(3) An apparent misfit, South gives up on slam.

Contract: 5♦
Opening Lead: ♣4

Tip 158   If you lead a high spot card when play is underway, you do not want the suit returned. Leading a low card in a suit, on the other hand, is a virtual command for partner to return that suit.

Deal 159

Dealer: South **Vulnerability: Neither**

When *leading*, the motto
is 'Lead High for Hate,
Lead Low for Like'. When
throwing, however, either
on partner's lead or
when discarding (i.e. not
following to the suit led),
a high card in a suit is an
encouraging signal, and
a low card discouraging.
'Throw High means
Aye, Throw Low means
No.' Effective signalling
is essential for winning

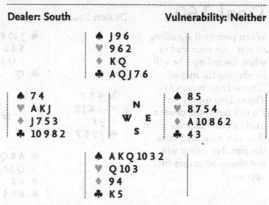

defence. If partner makes the appropriate signal and you interpret it correctly, you have
a vastly increased chance of finding the right subsequent defence.

On our featured deal you are West. Cover up the East and South hands and answer the
following question. You lead ♥A at Trick One versus 4♠. The trick goes ♥A, ♥2, ♥4, ♥3.
What would you play at Trick Two? (a) ♥K? (b) ♣10? (c) ♦7?

What happened

West correctly interpreted partner's ♥4 as discouraging
(it was known to be his lowest as ♥2 and ♥3 appeared
on the trick). Continue with ♥K and he realised
declarer's ♥Q would be promoted. But at Trick Two
West switched to ♣10. Oops.

Declarer won ♣K, drew trumps in three rounds,
then ran dummy's clubs, discarding ♥Q10. He merely
conceded to ♦A and so scored 11 tricks. Game made.

What should have happened

Interpreting the signal correctly was only half the
battle. West should not have led through dummy's
long strong clubs. Clubs could wait: if East held ♣K, he
would always make it (assuming declarer held at least a
doubleton). But if East held ♦A (and not ♣K), it would
be vital for West to switch to diamonds before declarer
threw his hearts on dummy's clubs.

West's diamond switch, the seven as a 'lead high for
hate' would be won by East's ♦A and a heart return
through ♥Q10 would see West winning cheaply and
cashing his other heart. Down one.

S	W	N	E
1♠	Pass	2♣	Pass
2♠	Pass	4♠	End

Contract: 4♠
Opening Lead: ♥A

Tip 159 'Throw High means Aye, Throw Low means No.'

Deal 160

Dealer: South

Vulnerability: Neither

When partner is signalling
to you – on your lead or
when discarding – he will
be obeying the motto:
'Throw High means Aye,
Throw Low means No'.
He will throw the clearest
card he can, but, even given
that, you must scrutinize
the pips. For things will
not always be as they first
appear.

```
                ♠ J 10 8 6
                ♥ 5 4 2
                ♦ K Q 10 5 4
                ♣ Q
   ♠ 9 3 2                      ♠ 7 5
   ♥ A K J 3         N          ♥ 9 8 7
   ♦ J 7         W       E      ♦ 9 8 6 3
   ♣ J 9 8 7         S          ♣ A 10 5 3
                ♠ A K Q 4
                ♥ Q 10 6
                ♦ A 2
                ♣ K 6 4 2
```

What happened

West led ♥A and the first trick went ♥2, ♥7, ♥6.
Partner's ♥7 looked high, so West continued with ♥K
and a third heart. Disappointed to see declarer win ♥Q,
he watched trumps being drawn and diamonds run. His
partner scored ♣A at the end, but declarer had made 10
tricks. Game made.

What should have happened

West did not scrutinize the heart pips. Had he done
so, he would have realized that East's ♥7 was his
lowest – all the lower heart spots were visible to him.
East was discouraging a heart continuation – meaning
that declarer held ♥Q. West needed to switch suits, to
enable a heart lead to come from his partner, crucially
through declarer's ♥Q. But which minor to lead?

As a general principle, it is a mistake to lead dummy's
long, strong suit – declarer will have to broach that
suit for himself. To switch to diamonds would only be
necessary if partner held ♦A and declarer held both ♣A
and ♣K. Switching to clubs would be necessary in the
doubly likely scenario that declarer held ♦A and partner
♣A (with or without ♣K).

A club switch at Trick Two would see East win
♣A and return ♥9. West would cover declarer's card
cheaply and cash his other heart. Down one.

S	W	N	E
1♠	Pass	3♠(1)	Pass
4♠	End		

(1) Upgrading his 8-point
hand because of the singleton
club. Using the Losing Trick
Count he has 8 Losing Tricks
(♠AKQ, ♥AKQ, ♦A, ♣A);
he is thus correct to bid 3♠
(adding his Losing Tricks to
opener's presumed seven
and subtracting the total (15)
from 18).

Contract: 4♠
Opening Lead: ♥A

Tip 160 Scrutinise the pips before deciding whether or not partner is making an
encouraging signal.

Deal 161

Dealer: South

Vulnerability: Both

Remember the motto for signalling – 'Throw High means Aye, Throw Low means No'. Say partner has led an ace (the assumption being that he also holds the king) and you have a doubleton. Would you automatically play the higher of the two cards? The answer is No. Here are some scenarios where you should play a discouraging lower card of the doubleton:

```
                 ♠ 7 5 4
                 ♥ Q J 10
                 ♦ K 10
                 ♣ A K J 5 2
♠ 10 8 6 3                      ♠ –
♥ A K 8 6 4         N           ♥ 9 3
♦ J 7 6         W     E         ♦ A Q 8 4 3
♣ 8                S           ♣ 10 9 7 6 4 3
                 ♠ A K Q J 9 2
                 ♥ 7 5 2
                 ♦ 9 5 2
                 ♣ Q
```

(i) It is notrumps. The ability to trump the third round is irrelevant.
(ii) You have no trumps.
(iii) You have Qx and cannot afford to spare the queen. NB: you can afford to drop the jack from Jx however.
(iv) You do not want to trump the third round because it will cost you a trump trick (say you have QJ10 of trumps).
(v) You can work out (from dummy's length) that declarer will overtrump you on the third round.
(vi) You want partner to switch to something else more than give you the ruff.
In other situations, you should throw top from your doubleton. But you do this because you positively want a continuation (in order to trump the third round), not simply because you have a doubleton.

What happened

West led ♥A against 4♠ (better than ♣8 – see Deal 140) and East signalled with ♥9. West duly continued with ♥K and ♥6, but East held no trumps. Winning dummy's ♥Q, declarer drew trumps in four rounds, then overtook ♣Q with ♣K and cashed ♣AJ discarding diamonds. He lost just one diamond at the end. 10 tricks and game made.

What should have happened

With a void trump, East does not want more hearts. He must signal with a discouraging ♥3 under ♥A. West switches to ♦6 at Trick Two (dummy's weakness) and East scores ♦AQ and leads back to ♥K. Down one.

S	W	N	E
1♠	Pass	2♣	Pass
2♠	Pass	4♠	End

Contract: 4♠
Opening Lead: ♥A

Tip 161 Don't automatically signal top from a doubleton. First ask yourself whether you want partner to continue the suit.

Deal 162

Dealer: South　　　　　　**Vulnerability: Neither**

By far the most important – and common – type of defensive signal is the 'attitude' signal: 'Throw High means Aye, Throw Low means No'. This is used when partner is leading (or when discarding). But when declarer is leading, it is inappropriate to use the attitude signal. Who do you think will be more interested, and use the

```
              ♠ 9 7 2
              ♥ 6 3 2
              ♦ 8 5 3
              ♣ K Q J 5
  ♠ Q 10 8 4 3         ♠ J 5
  ♥ J 9 7 4       N     ♥ Q 10 8
  ♦ 9 4       W     E   ♦ Q J 10 7
  ♣ 9 4           S     ♣ A 8 3 2
              ♠ A K 6
              ♥ A K 5
              ♦ A K 6 2
              ♣ 10 7 6
```

information to best use: partner or declarer? Right: declarer. However, there is one situation where your choice of spot card on declarer's lead should convey a specific message. Say dummy has a good suit missing the ace (which declarer is trying to flush out), but has nothing of worth outside (i.e. no entry). The defence is best winning their ace on declarer's last card, to prevent him from reaching dummy's remaining card(s) in the suit. To tell partner how many cards declarer holds (so that he knows when to win his ace), you must tell him how many cards you hold. You should give him a 'Count Signal'. The motto in such situations is: 'High = Even (i.e. two, four or six cards); Low = Odd (i.e. three or five cards)'. Mnemonic: 'HELO'. Thus play the underlined card from the following: 9̲3, 97̲42, 85̲2, J6̲52.

What happened

West led ♠4 to East's ♠J and declarer's ♠K. At Trick Two declarer led ♣10, which went ♣4, ♣5, ♣2. Trick Three went ♣6, ♣9 ♣J, ♣A. Declarer won ♠5 return with ♠A, led ♣7 over to ♣KQ, and took ♥AK and ♦AK. Nine tricks and game made.

What should have happened

West should have played ♣9 on the first round, to indicate an even number (HELO). When he next follows with ♣4, East knows his partner begun with two clubs, so declarer begun with three. He therefore holds up his ♣A until the third round. Declarer now has no way to reach dummy's last club and ends up down one.

S	W	N	E
2NT	Pass	3NT	End

Contract: 3NT
Opening Lead: ♠4

Tip 162　Give partner a 'count signal' in a suit declarer leads, when he needs to know your length (and thus declarer's length).

Deal 163

Dealer: South　　　**Vulnerability: North-South**

When declarer is leading,
the only message that you
should give partner when
you are following suit with
small cards is a 'Count
Signal'. The mnemonic is
HELO: 'High = Even
(i.e. two, four or six cards);
Low = Odd (i.e. three or
five cards).' Assuming
that partner already knew
your length to within one
card, he can now work out
exactly how many cards

```
              ♠ 4 3
              ♥ 9 7 5
              ♦ 10 9 3
              ♣ K J 8 6 5

♠ K J 9 7              ♠ Q 10 6
♥ Q 10 4        N      ♥ J 8 3 2
♦ 8 4 2      W   E     ♦ 7 6 5
♣ 4 3 2         S      ♣ A 10 9

              ♠ A 8 5 2
              ♥ A K 6
              ♦ A K Q J
              ♣ Q 7
```

you – and therefore declarer – started with. Bear in mind that such information is of
use to declarer as well as partner, so you should reserve such a signal for those situations
where it is essential for partner to know declarer's count. Say dummy holds a long, strong
suit missing a high card (typically the ace), but no outside entry. The defence would like
to win their ace on declarer's last card, so the partner of the defender with that ace needs
to give an accurate signal of his length in the suit.

What happened

West led ♠7, declarer letting East's ♠Q win the
trick. He took ♠10 with ♠A (if the suit was splitting
dangerously – i.e. 5–2 – he had exhausted East of spades)
and at Trick Three he led ♣Q.

West held the three lowest clubs and could not
believe it mattered which one he played. The one
nearest his thumb was ♣3. East correctly let ♣Q win
the trick. When declarer next led ♣7, West followed
with ♣2. Believing West held just ♣32 doubleton for his
'high-low' (thus declarer held a third club), East ducked
dummy's ♣J. Now declarer could run for home. His
nine tricks were ♠A, ♥AK, ♦AKQJ and two clubs.

What should have happened

Had West followed with ♣2, then a higher club,
showing an odd number (HELO), East would have
known declarer started with just two. He would have
won ♣A on the second round. With no second club
trick, declarer would end up one short. Down one.

S	W	N	E
2♣(1)	Pass	2♦(2)	Pass
2NT(3)	Pass	3NT	End

(1) 23+ points or any game-
force. Unrelated to clubs.
(2) Negative: 0–7 points.
Unrelated to diamonds.
(3) 23–24 balanced.

Contract: 3NT
Opening Lead: ♠7

Tip 163　　When partner needs to know the count of a suit declarer is leading, use
HELO. High = Even; Low = Odd.

Deal 164

Dealer: South   **Vulnerability: East-West**

Apart from the 'Attitude' and 'Count' signals, there is just one other worthwhile signal for the defence: the 'Suit Preference Signal' (SPS). Experts use this signal in all sorts of situations, essentially when both the attitude (i.e. like/dislike) and count (i.e. number of cards held) are known in a suit. I recommend, at least initially, that you use

```
                  ♠ K Q J
                  ♥ K J 9 8 4
                  ♦ Q J 3
                  ♣ Q 4
     ♠ 4                          ♠ A 10 8 6 3 2
     ♥ 10 7          N            ♥ 5
     ♦ 9 8 6 5 4   W   E          ♦ A 7 2
     ♣ J 10 9 8 3    S            ♣ 7 6 5
                  ♠ 9 7 5
                  ♥ A Q 6 3 2
                  ♦ K 10
                  ♣ A K 2
```

the SPS sparingly: when you are leading a suit for your partner to trump. Here is how it works: The lead of a high card calls for the return of the higher-ranking other suit; the lead of the lowest card calls for the lower-ranking other suit. When I say a 'high' card, I mean relatively high, not absolutely high. Say you hold A432: you win the ace and want the higher-ranking suit; you must return the four – high relative to the three and two. Conversely holding A987 and wanting the lower-ranking suit, you have no choice after winning the ace but to return the seven. Also note that there are always just two 'other' suits. The trump suit and the suit you are leading are both eliminated.

What happened

West led ♠4 and East won ♠A. At Trick Two he thoughtlessly returned ♠2 and West ruffed. Reading ♠2 as a SPS, West dutifully returned the lower of the two other suits (here the minors). He led ♣J.

No good. Declarer won ♣Q, drew trumps, and conceded to ♦A. Game made.

What should have happened

After winning ♠A, East should have returned ♠10 as a SPS for the higher-ranking suit, diamonds (key play). West would ruff, return ♦9 to ♦A, and receive a second spade ruff. Down one.

S	W	N	E
1♥	Pass	4♥	End

Contract: 4♥
Opening Lead: ♠4

Tip 164

When leading a suit for partner to ruff, use the Suit Preference Signal. The lead of a low card asks for the return of the lower-ranking suit; the lead of a high card asks for the higher-ranking suit.

Deal 165

The Suit Preference Signal (SPS) was invented in 1934 by Hy Lavinthal, although it is known by many in Britain as McKenney (in fact the US player of yesteryear William E. McKenney did nothing other than adopt it and publicise it). The crux is this: The lead of a low card asks for the return of the lower-ranking suit; the lead of a high card asks for the

```
              ♠ A 10 8 2
              ♥ 7
              ♦ K J 8 5
              ♣ K Q J 10
♠ 9 7 4                        ♠ 5
♥ K Q J 10 9 5 4      N        ♥ A 6 2
♦ 3                 W   E      ♦ A 9 6 2
♣ 9 5                 S        ♣ 8 7 6 3 2
              ♠ K Q J 6 3
              ♥ 8 3
              ♦ Q 10 7 4
              ♣ A 4
```

higher-ranking suit. The uses for the SPS are potentially wide-ranging. It can be used as a discarding method, although this is not recommended. (What if you do not have the necessary spot card to convey your message? Even if you do, is your card a suggestion or a command?) Experienced players use it whenever playing an 'idle card' (i.e. not an attitude or count signal), when dummy has a singleton (useful), and the list goes on. I recommend restricting the usage of the SPS, at least initially, to leading a suit (in the hope) that partner will trump.

What happened

West led ♦3 which East correctly read as a singleton (it could not be a doubleton; West would have led top from two). East won ♦A and returned ♦9 as a SPS for hearts (high requesting the return of the higher suit; between hearts and clubs).

However, West forgot and instead returned ♣9 after ruffing. No good, declarer won ♣A, drew trumps and discarded ♥83 on dummy's clubs. 11 tricks and game made.

What should have happened

West should have returned a heart (if he leads ♥K, East must overtake with ♥A) after ruffing ♦9. East wins ♥A and gives West a second diamond ruff. Down one.

S	W	N	E
–	3♥(1)	Dble(2)	4♥(3)
4♠	Pass	Pass	Pass(4)

(1) 3–10 points with a good seven-card suit.
(2) Take-out: opening points with short hearts.
(3) Raising the barrage in the ten-card fit.
(4) Tempting to bid 5♥.

Contract: 4♠
Opening Lead: ♦3

Tip 165   Do not forget the Suit Preference Signal in trumping situations.

THE DEALS: DEFENCE   197

Deal 166

From signalling, we move on to discarding: what to get rid of when you cannot follow to the suit led. You have twin goals:

(1) Keeping the right cards. We have all thrown the wrong card away in a two-card ending and seen a surprised declarer score the last trick with some low card, us having just discarded a higher card in that suit at Trick 12.

```
              ♠ 7 6 5
              ♥ A K Q 5
              ♦ K J 2
              ♣ 4 3 2
♠ K Q J 10                    ♠ 9 8 3
♥ 6 4 3 2         N           ♥ J 10 9
♦ 6 5 4       W     E         ♦ 8 7 3
♣ K J            S            ♣ A 10 6 5
              ♠ A 4 2
              ♥ 8 7
              ♦ A Q 10 9
              ♣ Q 9 8 7
```

(2) Helping partner to defend correctly, by efficient signalling ('Throw Low Means No, Throw High Means Aye').

Focussing on (1), to prevent unnecessary length winners for declarer, you as a defender must keep equal length with dummy (provided your highest card is higher than dummy's lowest).

What happened

West led ♠K against 3NT. Declarer withheld his ♠A, but won ♠Q continuation with ♠A at Trick Two (fearing a club switch if he ducked a second time). He then led out four rounds of diamonds, forcing West to make a discard. What would you discard as West?

Unwilling to throw a winning spade, or a club from ♣KJ, West thought he had an easy decision. Away went ♥2 from the seemingly useless ♥6432. Curtains! Declarer could now lead over to dummy's ♥AKQ, felling all the remaining cards in the suit, and scored his ninth trick via dummy's ♥5. Nine tricks and game made.

What should have happened

West is looking at dummy's four-card heart holding and can see that his ♥6 can beat dummy's ♥5 on the fourth round, but only if he retains all his cards in the suit. He can afford to discard from either black suit on the fourth diamond and declarer is held to his eight top tricks. A heart, however, he cannot spare, even though his holding in the suit is so meagre. Did you resist the temptation to let go of one of those 'useless' hearts?

S	W	N	E
1NT	Pass	3NT(1)	End

(1) It could be right to bid 2♣ Stayman (a request for four-card majors): trying for a 4–4 heart fit. But the 4333 shape argues for 3NT.

Contract: 3NT
Opening Lead: ♠K

Tip 166   When discarding, keep equal length with dummy.

Deal 167

When discarding, it is important to keep equal length with dummy. It is equally important to keep equal length with declarer, although not as easy to do as you cannot see his hand.

```
                    ♠ 9
                    ♥ J 10 8 6
                    ♦ A 9 6 3 2
                    ♣ K J 5
    ♠ 7 5 4 3 2               ♠ 10 8
    ♥ 9 5          N          ♥ 7 3 2
    ♦ K J 7     W     E       ♦ Q 10 8
    ♣ A 9 7        S          ♣ Q 6 4 3 2
                    ♠ A K Q J 6
                    ♥ A K Q 4
                    ♦ 5 4
                    ♣ 10 8
```

What happened

West cashed ♣A against the 6♥ slam, although this proved to help declarer by resolving his king-jack guess in the suit. He continued with ♣9.

Declarer was hopeful of making his slam. On a 4–3 spade split, he would have five spade winners, five trump winners (including a ruff in one or other hand), ♦A and ♥K. So he rose with dummy's ♣K and ruffed ♣J with ♥Q. He then cashed ♥AK and led over to dummy's ♥10.

On the third trump, West had an easy ♦7 discard. But declarer then followed with dummy's ♥J, discarding ♦4 from hand. What should West discard now?

At the table West discarded from those lousy spades. No good. Declarer crossed to his ♠AKQJ, felling all West's four remaining cards in the suit, and tabled the promoted ♠6. Dummy's ♦A took the last trick. 12 tricks and slam made.

What should have happened

Your defence will improve in leaps and bounds if you try to work out declarer's distribution. Having opened spades and rebid hearts, he has shown (at least) five spades. It is imperative West keeps all his five spades, in the hope that his highest spade, ♠7, is higher than declarer's lowest spade. Provided West discards ♦J on the fourth trump, declarer is unable to score his ♠6 and finishes up a trick short.

S	W	N	E
1♠	Pass	2♦	Pass
3♥(1)	Pass	4♥	Pass
5♥(2)	Pass	6♥(3)	End

(1) Jumping to create a game-force.

(2) Raises to Five of the agreed Major invite slam and tend to show two losers in unbid suit(s).

(3) Holding first round diamond control (♦A) and second round club control (♣K).

Contract: 6♥
Opening Lead: ♣A

Tip 167 Try to work out declarer's distribution and keep equal length with him.

Deal 168

When discarding (i.e.
throwing away when
unable to follow suit), try
to keep equal length with
dummy in a suit unless:
(1) Your highest card
in the suit is lower than
dummy's lowest card. Say
dummy has AKQ6; keep all
four cards from 7432 but
discard freely from 5432.
(2) Partner can also guard
that suit. If there is another
suit that only you can
guard, then you should
keep that other suit and let
partner keep the suit that
both guard. Take our featured deal.

```
              ♠ A K 6
              ♥ A K Q 8
              ♦ 8 6 5 2
              ♣ 7 4
  ♠ Q 10 8              ♠ J 9 7 3
  ♥ 9 6 3 2      N      ♥ J 10
  ♦ 9 4       W   E     ♦ 7
  ♣ J 8 5 2      S      ♣ A Q 10 9 6 3
              ♠ 5 4 2
              ♥ 7 5 4
              ♦ A K Q J 10 3
              ♣ K
```

What happened

West led ♣2 to ♣A, and East continued with ♣Q,
ruffed. Declarer drew trumps in two rounds, then
crossed to ♠AK. He then led a trump back to hand and
ran his remaining trumps. As he led his last one, West
had to discard from ♠Q and ♥9632, dummy, still to
discard, holding ♠6 and ♥AKQ8. West elected to throw
♥2, but now, after dummy's ♠6 was thrown, declarer
could lead to ♥AKQ and table the promoted ♥8. Slam
made.

What should have happened

Unless declarer has just one heart (unlikely given that
he has just one club), West is the sole guarder of hearts.
Therefore West must hope his partner can guard spades
(holding ♠J). He must discard ♠Q on the last trump.
Declarer now has no twelfth trick; down one.

   Question: Could declarer have made his contract
against perfect defence?

   Answer: Yes. After two rounds of trumps, he crosses
to ♥AK, observing the fall of the ♥J10 from East.
He then returns to a trump in hand and finesses ♥8,
discarding his spade loser on ♥Q.

S	W	N	E
–	–	1♥	2♣
2♦	3♣(1)	5♦	Pass
6♦(2)	End		

(1) With disruption in mind.
(2) Optimistic in spite of the
excellent trumps – ♣K is
hardly pulling its weight.

Contract: 6♦
Opening Lead: ♣2

Tip 168   When two suits need to be guarded, each defender should guard a different one.

Deal 169

Dealer: South   **Vulnerability: East-West**

Discarding when declarer
is running a long suit is
one of the toughest parts of
the game. Here is the best
approach:

(a) Work out how many
cards declarer holds in his
long suit, and therefore
how many discards you
need to make.

(b) As far as possible,
plan those discards at the
beginning (to minimize
give-away pauses at critical

```
                    ♠ 6
                    ♥ 10 8 6 5 3 2
                    ♦ A 7 3
                    ♣ K 5 4
    ♠ 5                          ♠ 9 8 7 3 2
    ♥ K Q J 9 7          N       ♥ —
    ♦ Q 10 8 4 2    W       E    ♦ K J 9 5
    ♣ 7 2               S        ♣ Q 10 8 6
                    ♠ A K Q J 10 4
                    ♥ A 4
                    ♦ 6
                    ♣ A J 9 3
```

moments). Do not necessarily discard the easiest card first (again, making life tougher for
declarer). However, often you cannot know exactly what your discards will be; they may
well depend on partner's.

(c) If partner is throwing from one suit, you should tend to keep that suit. It is no good
both of you weakening the same suit.

(d) Try not to void a suit (assuming trumping a further round is not an option). One top
card from declarer will reveal your void and partner's holding will be known. Take our
featured deal.

What happened

West led ♥K and East, knowing declarer held ♥A,
surprised him by trumping. At Trick Two East led
a passive trump (tough to find the best defence of
returning a diamond). Declarer won and drew three
more rounds of trumps on which West discarded both
his clubs.

Bad idea. When at Trick Six declarer led ♣3 to
♣K, West discarded. Declarer could win ♣K, take the
marked finesse of ♣9, return to ♦A, then finesse ♣J.
Slam made.

What should have happened

West should discard red cards and keep ♣72. Not
knowing of the club position, declarer would now cross
to ♣K and finesse ♣J. This would leave him with a
fourth-round club loser (although in fact he can still
succeed via a double squeeze).

S	W	N	E
2♠(1)	Pass	3♥(2)	Pass
6♠(3)	End		

(1) Strong Two – showing
eight playing tricks (or around
20–22 with a fine suit).
(2) Positive response –
showing a five-card suit in a
hand with an ace and a king
or any eight points.
(3) The practical, give-
nothing-away approach.

Contract: 6♠
Opening Lead: ♥K

Tip 169 Try not to void yourself of a suit on the run of a long suit from declarer.

Deal 170

Dealer: South   **Vulnerability: Neither**

When discarding, you have twin goals. (1) is generally more important when declarer is on lead. (2) tends to be more critical when partner is on lead. (1) Holding on to the right cards. Though there is no substitute for counting each suit and trying to work out declarer's initial hand-pattern, accurate discarding is made easier by adhering to a few mottoes

```
                    ♠ Q 6 3
                    ♥ 6 3 2
                    ♦ 7 2
                    ♣ K 10 7 6 2
    ♠ 10 9                         ♠ 8 7 5 4 2
    ♥ 7 5 4            N           ♥ A K Q 9
    ♦ J 8 6 4 3    W     E         ♦ 10 5
    ♣ A 9 3           S            ♣ 8 4
                    ♠ A K J
                    ♥ J 10 8
                    ♦ A K Q 9
                    ♣ Q J 5
```

e.g. (a) keep equal length with dummy (and declarer); (b) retain four-card holdings; (c) if partner is throwing a suit, you keep that suit. We have focussed on (1) the past few deals. Now we move on to: (2) Helping partner to defend correctly, by efficient signalling with your discards. As with signals, 'Throw High means Aye, Throw Low means No'. You therefore have a choice of throwing high in a suit you wish partner to lead, or low in a suit you do not wish partner to lead. Although the 'throw high means aye' discard is clearer, frequently, especially in notrumps, you cannot spare the high card. As East found to his cost.

What happened

West led ♦4 (fourth from the top of the longest and strongest) to East's ♦10 and declarer's ♦Q. At Trick Two declarer led ♣Q, ducked by West. ♣J continuation was also ducked and ♣5 won by West's ♣A.

West's delay in winning ♣A was correct for two reasons: by winning ♣A on declarer's last club, it cut declarer's communication with dummy; it also allowed East to make an informative discard.

East chose ♥9 – 'throw high means aye'. West duly shifted to ♥7, but, although East could win ♥AKQ, he had discarded ♥9 which would have been the setting trick. Declarer won East's ♦5 return and soon claimed his game.

What should have happened

East needed to keep ♥9 and should have flagged his desire for a heart by negative means. He should have thrown ♠2 to reject the only other viable alternative for West (diamonds were out as East's third hand high diamond at Trick One was merely ♦10). West would have switched to ♥7 but East could now have scored ♥AKQ plus ♥9. Down one.

S	W	N	E
2NT(1)	Pass	3NT	End

(1) 20–22 balanced

Contract: 3NT
Opening Lead: ♦4

Tip 170 Particularly in notrumps, it is generally more sensible to throw low in a suit you do not want, as throwing high from a suit you do want often costs a trick.

Deal 171

Dealer: South   **Vulnerability: North-South**

When seeking to steer
partner in the right
direction with your discard,
it is usually more sensible
in notrumps to throw low
in a suit you do not want
led, rather than throwing
high in the suit you do
want (as the latter ploy
often costs a trick). But you
must select the right suit
to 'throw low means no'.
This East did not help his
partner, throwing low from
a suit that West was never going to lead.

```
                  ♠ Q 2
                  ♥ J 4
                  ♦ A Q 5 4
                  ♣ K J 10 9 8
   ♠ 7 5 4                      ♠ A K J 10
   ♥ 10 6 5 3        N          ♥ Q 8 2
   ♦ 9           W     E        ♦ J 10 6 3 2
   ♣ A 7 6 5 4      S           ♣ 2
                  ♠ 9 8 6 3
                  ♥ A K 9 7
                  ♦ K 8 7
                  ♣ Q 3
```

What happened

West led ♣5 (fourth from the top of the longest and
strongest) and declarer won ♣Q and correctly fired back
♣3 at Trick Two (he could not garner enough tricks in
the red suits). West won ♣A and awaited his partner's
discard, expecting it to resolve his dilemma of which
major to lead (diamonds were out as dummy was too
strong in the suit). East knew that he could not afford to
throw a high spade (he needed to keep all four cards).
Instead he threw ♦2.

West sighed – East's ♦2 discard had in no way
resolved the decision as to which major to lead.
Eventually West (reasonably) guessed to lead ♥3. No
good. East played ♥Q on dummy's ♥4 and declarer
won ♥K, crossed to promoted ♥J, cashed ♣KJ10,
returned to ♦K, cashed ♦A, then led to ♦AQ. Ten
tricks and game made plus one.

What should have happened

East should have realised that West, looking at dummy's
strength in the suit, was never going to lead a diamond;
rather he was choosing between the majors. East should
therefore have discarded ♥2 (key play). By saying 'no'
to hearts, he was in effect flagging spades. West would
have switched to ♠7 and East would have taken his four
winners in the suit. Down one.

S	W	N	E
1NT	Pass	3NT(1)	End

(1) Admittedly nervous about
majors, but where else will
game be made?

Contract: 3NT
Opening Lead: ♣5

Tip 171

When seeking to help partner with your discard, do not throw low in a suit
partner was never going to lead. Instead throw low from a suit partner might
be considering leading.

Deal 172

Dealer: South **Vulnerability: East-West**

In notrumps, you often cannot afford to throw high in the suit you want led (for fear of losing a trick by the extravagant discard). However, in a trump contract, the aim is typically to attract a particular lead in order to cash one or possibly two tricks in that suit; but rarely – unlike notrumps – more. A clear 'throw high means aye' discard is therefore less risky. West regretted his nebulous choice of discard on our featured deal.

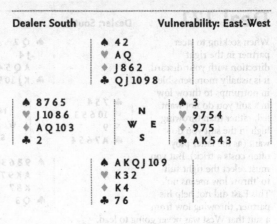

```
                ♠ 4 2
                ♥ A Q
                ♦ J 8 6 2
                ♣ Q J 10 9 8
  ♠ 8 7 6 5                    ♠ 3
  ♥ J 10 8 6        N          ♥ 9 7 5 4
  ♦ A Q 10 3     W     E       ♦ 9 7 5
  ♣ 2               S          ♣ A K 5 4 3
                ♠ A K Q J 10 9
                ♥ K 3 2
                ♦ K 4
                ♣ 7 6
```

What happened

West led ♣2 against the 4♠ contract – a clear singleton from East's perspective as West would lead top from a doubleton (and would hardly be likely to lead from a doubleton in dummy's bid suit). East therefore won ♣K and cashed ♣A. West threw ♥6.

This was an unhelpful discard: looking at dummy, East was never going to lead hearts. East now had to choose between switching to a diamond (around to dummy's weakness); or a third club (aiming for a trump promotion should partner's trumps be, for example, ♠10xxx). Perhaps he should have worked out to switch to a diamond anyway – arguing that West would have discarded a discouraging low diamond if he wanted a third club. But it was hardly clear cut and he instead led a third club.

No good: declarer ruffed the third club (high, perforce). He drew trumps, crossed to ♥AQ, and discarded ♦K4 on ♣QJ. He trumped a diamond and cashed ♥K. 11 tricks and game made plus one.

S	W	N	E
1♠	Pass	2♣	Pass
3♠	Pass	4♠(1)	End

(1) 3NT would have been easier to make, but North can hardly be criticized for raising partner's known good six-card suit.

Contract: 4♠
Opening Lead: ♣2

What should have happened

West was desperate for a diamond lead from partner and could have afforded to throw a clear ♦10 ('throw high means aye') to flag the suit. Even a dozy East would have been alerted and would have switched to a diamond. Whether or not declarer played ♦4 or ♦K, West would win his ♦AQ. Down one.

Tip 172 Discard the clearest card you can afford.

INDEX

This index directs the reader to the pages in the book where the key terms and concepts are explained. Places where the terms are mentioned as part of the commentary on the deals are not listed in the index.